The Middle Class in Emerging Societies

This volume examines the discursive construction of the meanings and lifestyle practices of the middle class in the rapidly transforming economies of Asia, Latin America, Africa and the Middle East, focusing on the social, political and cultural implications at local and global levels. While drawing a comparative analysis of what it means to be middle class in these different locations, the essays offer a connective understanding of the middle class phenomenon in emerging market economies and lay the groundwork for future research on emerging, transitional societies. The book addresses three key dimensions: the discursive creation of the middle class; the construction of the cultural identity through consumption practices and lifestyle choices; and the social, political and cultural consequences related to globalization and neoliberalism.

Leslie L. Marsh is Associate Professor in the department of world languages and cultures at Georgia State University, USA.

Hongmei Li is Associate Professor of strategic communication in the department of media, journalism and film at Miami University, Ohio, USA.

Routledge Research in Cultural and Media Studies

For a full list of titles in this series, please visit www.routledge.com.

48 **Performing Memory in Art and Popular Culture**
Edited by *Liedeke Plate and Anneke Smelik*

49 **Reading Beyond the Book**
The Social Practices of Contemporary Literary Culture
Danielle Fuller and DeNel Rehberg Sedo

50 **A Social History of Contemporary Democratic Media**
Jesse Drew

51 **Digital Media Sport**
Technology, Power and Culture in the Network Society
Edited by Brett Hutchins and David Rowe

52 **Barthes' *Mythologies* Today**
Readings of Contemporary Culture
Edited by Pete Bennett and Julian McDougall

53 **Beauty, Violence, Representation**
Edited by Lisa A. Dickson and Maryna Romanets

54 **Public Media Management for the Twenty-First Century**
Creativity, Innovation, and Interaction
Edited by Michał Głowacki and Lizzie Jackson

55 **Transnational Horror Across Visual Media**
Fragmented Bodies
Edited by Dana Och and Kirsten Strayer

56 **International Perspectives on Chicana/o Studies**
"This World is My Place"
Edited by Catherine Leen and Niamh Thornton

57 **Comics and the Senses**
A Multisensory Approach to Comics and Graphic Novels
Ian Hague

58 **Popular Culture in Africa**
The Episteme of the Everyday
Edited by Stephanie Newell and Onookome Okome

59 **Transgender Experience**
Place, Ethnicity, and Visibility
Edited by Chantal Zabus and David Coad

60 **Radio's Digital Dilemma**
Broadcasting in the Twenty-First Century
John Nathan Anderson

61 **Documentary's Awkward Turn**
Cringe Comedy and Media Spectatorship
Jason Middleton

62 **Serialization in Popular Culture**
Edited by Rob Allen and Thijs van den Berg

63 **Gender and Humor**
Interdisciplinary and International Perspectives
Edited by Delia Chiaro and Raffaella Baccolini

64 **Studies of Video Practices**
Video at Work
Edited by Mathias Broth, Eric Laurier, and Lorenza Mondada

65 **The Memory of Sound**
Preserving the Sonic Past
Seán Street

66 **American Representations of Post-Communism**
Television, Travel Sites, and Post-Cold War Narratives
Andaluna Borcila

67 **Media and the Ecological Crisis**
Edited by Richard Maxwell, Jon Raundalen, and Nina Lager Vestberg

68 **Representing Multiculturalism in Comics and Graphic Novels**
Edited by Carolene Ayaka and Ian Hague

69 **Media Independence**
Working with Freedom or Working for Free?
Edited by James Bennett and Niki Strange

70 **Neuroscience and Media**
New Understandings and Representations
Edited by Michael Grabowski

71 **American Media and the Memory of World War II**
Debra Ramsay

72 **International Perspectives on Shojo and Shojo Manga**
The Influence of Girl Culture
Edited by Masami Toku

73 **The Borders of Subculture**
Resistance and the Mainstream
Edited by Alexander Dhoest, Steven Malliet, Barbara Segaert, and Jacques Haers

74 **Media Education for a Digital Generation**
Edited by Julie Frechette and Rob Williams

75 **Spanish-Language Television in the United States**
Fifty Years of Development
Kenton T. Wilkinson

76 **Embodied Metaphors in Film, Television, and Video Games**
Cognitive Approaches
Edited by Kathrin Fahlenbrach

77 **Critical Animal and Media Studies**
Communication for Nonhuman Animal Advocacy
Edited by Núria Almiron, Matthew Cole, and Carrie P. Freeman

78 **The Middle Class in Emerging Societies**
Consumers, Lifestyles and Markets
Edited by Leslie L. Marsh and Hongmei Li

The Middle Class in Emerging Societies

Consumers, Lifestyles and Markets

Edited by Leslie L. Marsh and Hongmei Li

NEW YORK AND LONDON

First published 2016
by Routledge
605 Third Avenue, New York, NY 10017

and by Routledge
4 Park Square, Milton Park, Abingdon, Oxon OX14 4RN

First issued in paperback 2017

Routledge is an imprint of the Taylor & Francis Group, an informa business

Library of Congress Cataloging in Publication Data

The middle class in emerging societies: consumers, lifestyles and markets / edited by Leslie L. Marsh and Hongmei Li.
pages cm. — (Routledge research in cultural and media studies; 87)
Includes bibliographical references and index.
1. Middle class—Developing countries. 2. Consumers—Developing countries.
3. Lifestyles—Developing countries. I. Marsh, Leslie L. II. Li, Hongmei, 1974-
HT690.D44M53 2015
305.5'5091724—dc23 2015023181

Typeset in Sabon
by codeMantra

ISBN 13: 978-0-8153-8645-2 (pbk)
ISBN 13: 978-1-138-85882-4 (hbk)

Contents

Acknowledgments

The editors wish to thank:

S. Tamer Cavusgil for his kind support of our interest in studying the middle class from an interdisciplinary perspective. As the director of the GSU-CIBER, we also wish to thank him for hosting the conference "The Middle Class Phenomenon in Emerging Markets 2013: Multi-disciplinary and Multi-country Perspectives" held September 26–28, 2013 at Georgia State University.

Ilke Kardeş for her contributions to the organizing of the Middle Class Conference.

Dawn Foster, for her indefatigable spirit, humor, remarkable patience, and organizational brilliance.

Penny Prime, for her support for the Middle Class Conference.

The Georgia State University (GSU) Center for International Business and Education Research (GSU-CIBER), GSU-University Research Services Administration and the China Research Center.

We especially extend our thanks to all of the scholars who shared their research at the Middle Class Conference held at Georgia State University, September 26–28, 2013.

Hongmei wishes to thank her children Sam and Joseph, her parents and siblings, and her husband for their support and love. She specially wants to thank her co-editor Leslie for her resolution, humor, and unyielding support and comradeship.

Leslie wishes to thank her parents for their enduring love and support. She also extends heartfelt thanks to her co-editor Hongmei for her perseverance, optimism and dedication to seeing this project to fruition. What was a chance encounter has become a rich, interdisciplinary collaboration and unique friendship.

Introduction

The Global Middle Classes: Towards the Study of Emergent Citizenship

Leslie L. Marsh and Hongmei Li

The Middle-Class Phenomenon

The rise of the middle class in rapidly transforming economies of East Asia, Latin America, Africa and the Middle East is one of the most remarkable phenomena of recent decades. A number of countries (including, Brazil, Russia, India, China, South Africa, South Korea, Turkey, among others) have witnessed marked economic growth, subsequently earning them the denomination as "emerging nations." Within these countries, vast numbers of people have benefited from economic improvements and entered the ranks of the middle class. The rapid growth of the middle class outside Europe and North America also means a shift of economic and political powers. For example, while Asia now makes up less than a quarter of the world's middle class, it is estimated that by 2020 middle class consumers in Asian countries could constitute more than half of the global middle class and their consumption could represent 40 percent of global middle-class consumption (Kharas). Nearly one sixth of the world's population has moved from poverty to the middle class in the last two decades. According to a 2009 report published in *The Economist*, the growth seen in emerging nations means that for the first time in history over half of the world's population can now be defined as belonging to the middle class (Parker). Notably, the middle classes in emerging nations have come into being quickly on the heels of neoliberal economic reforms. In a number of nations, where one had found few members belonging to the middle class – or, officially none in the case of China – one now finds significant populations who have experienced improvements in their economic status. In a number of emerging nations one finds sizable new social groups living, acting and thinking in new ways. This economic shift leads to broader social, political and cultural transformations.

Given the magnitude of the transformations in locations across the globe, as well as the importance the issue holds in the realms of society, politics, business, economics and culture, examining the middle classes in emerging nations has become a topic of investigation in multiple areas of academic inquiry. Yet, appealing numbers and persuasive statistics make it easy to become overly sanguine about the rise of the new middle classes in a number of formerly labeled "third world" nations. Thus, discussion of the middle class in emerging nations needs to be studied with critical awareness that distinguishes between rhetorical fervor (or even propaganda) from lived realities. It is in this spirit that this volume aims to complement existing scholarship and intervene in understanding this phenomenon for future discussions.

Before proceeding further, it is imperative to address briefly what we mean when we talk about class, the middle class and how the middle class comes to be defined by scholars in different disciplines. Similarly, we must define what we mean by emerging nations. First, class itself is a complex concept. Karl Marx defined one's class in terms of one's relationship to the means of production: those who own the means of production comprise the bourgeoisie, those who do not are the proletariat with no group that presumably exists between these two polarized classes.[1] The economic base produces one's class consciousness and, in turn, reproduces class distinctions. With a rising number of professional and managerial workers, the Marxist idea of class has given way to a more sophisticated understanding that also illustrates the essential role of everyday practices in defining class, thus broadening the discussion of class politics into social and cultural arenas (Thompson). As a social marker and construct, class joins race, ethnicity and gender as an axis of social differentiation and global inequality.

From a perspective that emphasizes economic indicators, the middle class generally refers to a growing number of households in emerging markets who have access to disposable income that enables consumers to direct money toward discretionary purchases and consumption (e.g., cars, home appliances, better housing and educational opportunities, leisure time and so forth). Economic shifts may have prompted greater interest in the world's growing middle-class population, which has been largely defined according to household income with subdivisions within this category (e.g., lower-, middle- and upper-middle income), but this is certainly not the only or most important way to define who belongs and how people belong to a broader category called the middle class. While there is no clear consensus among the authors included in this volume about precisely how the middle class should be defined, a general understanding is that the definition should go beyond economic indicators and include a broad range of factors concerning, for example, how culture is produced and reproduced, educational and professional achievement, political attitudes and participation, consumption practices, or simply self-identification. Indeed, the rise of middle-class consumers in emerging nations is a multifaceted phenomenon signifying changes beyond discretionary consumption. The evolution of the middle class is also correlated with rapid urbanization along with its consequences (e.g., housing and real estate pressures, environmental degradation, unequal access to infrastructure, and so forth).

In fact, the rise of the middle class in locations across the globe heralds profound changes in societal, political and cultural values. For these reasons we encourage thinking more in terms of middle *classness* or, that is to say, in terms of the multiple factors (of which income level is just one) that contribute to defining how people are grouped by others into this category of "the middle class" and the ways that individuals understand who they are and how they belong to this group in the neoliberal context of local and global transformations. On the one hand, we note the importance of historically and culturally contextualized studies of the middle class in emerging nations. Yet, we also acknowledge that the definition of what defines middle classness is dynamic; for example, in the case of Russia, what has defined the middle class in the past differs from the present. As Patico observes, the emerging middle class needs to be seen as a set of evolving "circumstances, values, and projects that stretch across a broad swath of both relatively affluent and more marginally affluent individuals and households" (Patico, chapter 1 in this volume). In particular circumstances and driven by certain values, what is considered appropriate and what is not thus becomes a crucial part of how middle classness is performed through consumption and an idealized way of living. Further, middle class, as a marker of respectability, is not a self-contained category, but rather is a shifting process that constantly defines exclusion and inclusion. Indeed, for the middle class in emerging nations, the desire to become a member of the middle class is one of various defining characteristics.

In terms of undertaking interdisciplinary research on the middle class in emerging nations, definitions of the middle class must be seen with nuance. There are certain *a priori* assumptions made by scholars in different fields regarding their definition of class and middle-class status that lead to discipline- and study-specific *emphases*. A survey may demand identifying specific household income levels according to established methodologies while an ethnographic approach may seek nuances concerning how individuals understand themselves as belonging to the middle class and various practices that constitute middle-class identity (Heiman, Freeman and Liechty). Still, a critical studies approach may unravel the discursive formation of middle-class identity. None of these are mutually exclusive approaches. Rather, scholars are encouraged to acknowledge their specific departure point. Whereas some scholars in this volume are more definitive in their definition of the middle class in terms of income levels (especially those undertaking quantitative studies as well as those in business and economics), they do acknowledge the inherent vagaries of defining the boundary points for their study of the middle class. By contrast, others acknowledge income levels as an important factor but emphasize in their definitions that the middle class is a mindset, outlook or subjective identity. Although these definitions of "the middle class" from scholars in different disciplines differ, we believe they not only overlap but they mutually inform one another.

Just as important as defining what we mean by class and middle classness, we must establish what we mean by emerging nations. The authors in this volume focus on Brazil, China, India, Mexico, Russia, and countries in the Middle East and North African (MENA) region (looking at Tunisia and Kuwait specifically). These countries are among the most important emerging nations in terms of their growing economic power and geopolitical significance to shape shifting global power dynamics. For all these countries, neoliberalism is a key ideology that structures market reforms and broader social, political and cultural transformations. In broad strokes, Brazil transitioned from a military regime (1964–1985) to a democracy which coincided with an economic transition from import-substitution industrialization (1930–80) to neoliberal policies which were very notably put into place by the Collor administration (1990–1992). China began market reforms starting in 1978 when the Chinese Communist Party made a historical shift from class struggle to economic development; neoliberal influence has intensified since the early 1990s. India initiated economic liberalization in 1991 to move the country into a market-driven economy and become more competitive globally. For Mexico, the 1982 debt crisis is often viewed as the beginning of neoliberalism in the nation and President Carlos Salinas de Gortari (1988–1994) adopted a wide range of neoliberal reforms supported by the United States. After the collapse of the Soviet Union in 1991, Russia adopted various neoliberal reforms to adjust its economic and political structures. Tunisia implemented neoliberal policies under President Ben Ali (1987–2011) and the nation was celebrated in the West as a successful model until 2011 when public demonstrations and protests (or, the Arab Spring) spread quickly throughout the MENA region. Meanwhile, Kuwait has begun adopting neoliberal economic policies more recently. Although these countries implement different versions of neoliberalism because of their particular histories, their policies share key neoliberal principles such as deregulation, privatization, attracting foreign investment, the reduction of taxes and the exit of the state in daily economic management. Neoliberal policies have produced a rising middle class but they have also simultaneously polarized society, leading to increasing inequality in wealth distribution in these countries. For example, these countries' Gini index, a measure of the equality of wealth distribution, has dramatically increased in the last few decades, with many emerging countries' Gini index having surpassed the global warning line of .40 in 2010–2012.[2] As many of the essays in this volume suggest, the middle class experiences conflicting feelings of hope, aspiration, empowerment, as well vulnerability and anxiety.

The middle classes in these countries have very different experiences in comparison with developed (or, industrialized) nations. While rapidly growing economies in these emerging nations often mean that citizens tend to feel more optimistic about the future, the middle classes in the United States and in some nations of Europe since the 2007/2008 global financial recession has been shrinking, and many feel anxious about losing their status and uncertain about the future. Also, these emerging nations have different histories that shape the present and future of the middle class: India, Russia, and China share the legacy of socialism, but China is the only country of the three controlled by one political party. While most of the emerging nations implement political democracy, China is an authoritarian country and Kuwait is still a constitutional monarchy. Therefore, the middle class in each country encounters very different localized experiences because of varying local and global conditions. The trajectories of the middle classes in these nations should not be expected to demonstrate the same patterns of progress, standards or expectations relative to those of already industrialized nations in North America and Europe. The essays of this volume reveal that one may find similarities between "old" (European, North American) and "new" middle classes but it is unwise to assume that the middle classes in emerging nations replicate the patterns of middle classness found previously in other locations.

Why the Middle Class? Why Now?

The significant and ongoing transformations described above underscore the importance of examining the middle class in emerging nations. Numerous precedents exist for putting the middle class at the center of analysis of a comparative study. In the introduction to the edited volume *The Making of the Middle Class: Toward a Transnational History*, authors López and Weinstein assert that across the globe for the past two hundred years, the middle class has been "one of the major transnational political projects of modernity through which historical actors have struggled to define themselves as belonging to a social collectivity" (21–22). Similarly, the edited volume *The Global Middle Classes: Theorizing through Ethnography* by Heiman, Freeman, and Leichty claims the crucial significance of the middle class in local and global identity politics.

The middle class has played a central role in defining new patterns of political, economic, and social relations. Considering recent decades, placing the middle class at the center of analysis also serves to gauge globalization and the impact of neoliberalism. Whether configured as consumer group or social affiliation, the middle class is seen as the backbone of market economies and political stability. Recent transformations are uneven and wrought with tensions. For instance, India's professional classes have shed their indifference to politics and become politically engaged on social-networking sites. For its part, the new middle class in Brazil, under increasing strains in recent years, demands greater accountability from regional and federal governments. In China, the new middle class has simultaneously demonstrated a willingness to support the current social political order and a desire for more political participatory power. Yet, given the Chinese government's control over civic participation, the middle class often engages in affairs that are likely to benefit them personally rather than those that have broader social and political consequences. While historically the middle classes in the U.S. and the U.K. took the lead in consolidating democracy, the same cannot be said in Russia where recent laws have been passed to crack down on political protestors. In fact, increasing nationalism has caused concerns regarding Russia's future. Even though the absolute number of the middle class in Mexico is still quite small, the Mexican government has demonstrated increasingly efforts to incorporate this group in its policy making and political and cultural campaigns (see Hind, chapter 2).

As the worst economic slump since the Great Depression constrained developed economies in North America and Europe in 2007/2008, the consumption potential of the middle classes in emerging markets has been relied on increasingly as the engine for global economic growth. Investors and corporations eagerly seeking capital gains wish for emerging nations to follow a consistent trajectory of upward growth. What is more, the highly interdependent nature of contemporary middle classes cannot be denied. For instance, Brazilian and Chinese citizens have been pushed to consume goods to sustain GDP growth at home. Meanwhile, the very growth and stability of the Brazilian middle class depends, in part, on the economic performance of China. Traditionally one has found predominantly an exchange between periphery or semi-periphery nations and developed (or, industrialized) nations, but now emerging nations increasingly exchange goods and ideas between themselves and form their own strategic alliances and multilateral organizations such as the New Development Bank (NDB) – formerly known as the BRICS Development Bank – and the Beijing-based Asian Infrastructure Investment Bank (AIIB). These organizations challenge European and U.S. dominance in controlling the global political, financial, economic, and cultural order.

As the ranks of the middle classes grow, traditional values and past hierarchies confront new demands to reconfigure social relationships. Different social groups in emerging nations undergoing economic change and under the weight of modernizing forces face the challenge to negotiate which values and beliefs should be preserved as cornerstones of their cultural existence and which practices should be adopted or left behind. New members of the middle classes begin to occupy new social spaces and participate in formerly inaccessible activities but they do not necessarily engage with those spaces and activities on the same terms as previous members of the middle classes in given locations. Thus, it is unwise to assume that a change in socioeconomic status results in a seamless entry into modern, democratic, capitalist existence. Rather, one finds a range of negotiations in a process of re-signifying meanings. New members of the middle class impact the significance of established symbolic goods and practices as much as they themselves become impacted by these goods and practices. The massive growth of wealth, rising consumer culture as well as the polarizing of society has gradually marginalized policies and values for equality and social justice. In a way, the rising middle class has reconfigured the dynamics between tradition and modernity, local and global, and developed and developing economies.

The essays in this volume and the broad transformations they reflect upon prompt a series of questions: What does it mean to be middle class in these different international contexts? As economies improve and large numbers of people enter the ranks of the middle classes, will they develop new political subjectivities? If so, how will political agency be manifested? What are the prospects for transnational cooperation? In more abstract terms, to what degree do middle-class identities transcend regional particularities? To what degree is a global middle class possible? Would a global middle class counter or promote globalization? As previously excluded members of the emerging nations gain economic power, will Nestor García Canclini's thesis that consumption may contribute to "the integrative and communicative rationality of a society" bear fruit? (10). How do the new middle classes influence the discourses of citizenship and the development of civil and human rights practices both locally and globally?

***

This volume complements existing research on the middle classes but it differs from existing literature on the subject in several key ways. First, we focus on emerging nations and the rise of the middle classes following the implementation of neoliberal economic reforms in recent decades. Despite the significance of the changes seen in the world's population in recent years, there is a scarcity of research on this phenomenon. While specific cultural and political contexts vary as do the specific trajectories these nations exhibit in forming their middle classes, the rise of the middle classes on the heels of neoliberal economic reform is a process these nations share in common. Second, this volume brings together different disciplines to analyze recent sociopolitical, cultural and economic transformations. Thus, we aim to stimulate further interdisciplinary discussion of the global middle classes. Because the concept of the middle class is nuanced and dynamic, we do not believe that one field nor is one research methodology sufficient to discuss the middle classes in emerging nations. Thus, the essays in this volume from different theoretical and academic perspectives aim to expand our knowledge of the middle-class phenomenon in emerging societies.

Numerous academic fields are engaged in the study of the middle class. Scholars from such disciplines as economics, business, film, media, communication, sociology, anthropology, political science, literature, education, history, art, urban studies, geography, and architecture actively examine this topic. A special interest of some scholars is to contrast the contemporary developments in emerging markets with those already experienced by mature, post-industrial economies. Some also approach the middle class as a phenomenon that derives meaning from social and cultural practices, while others treat it as a political power with the capacity to shape a country's social, political, economic, and cultural landscape. We argue that it is important to study the middle-class phenomenon from a multidisciplinary and multicountry perspective given the global nature of the phenomenon. Therefore, a comparative and multidisciplinary perspective can lead to some common understandings of this remarkable phenomenon. In an effort to create connections (rather than sustain categories), we organize the discussion around three interrelated areas: media and society, economics and consumer practices, and politics and ideology. We encourage readers to compare and contrast the observations offered by the interdisciplinary team of contributors to this volume.

Toward the Study of Emergent Citizenship

Talking about the middle class is a frequent departure point for engaging in broader debates. In addition to an interest in examining the middle class in specific emerging nations, an issue that becomes salient in the essays by the authors in this volume is the question of citizenship. Many authors in this volume reflect on how new notions of citizenship have evolved in recent years. If we consider the transformations that have taken place in emerging nations as defining a new economic, political and social moment, then we propose thinking about the new middle classes in terms of emergent citizenship. If we follow Marx's basic assertion that classes emerge out of a differentiated relationship to capitalist modes of production, then new phases or changes in a given group's relationship to those modes leads to the development of new economic, social, and political subjectivities. In other words, the emerging middle class also calls forth new modalities of citizenship.

In recent years, academic discussion of citizenship, like class, has become more complex. Citizenship is understood as extending beyond a matter of rights and responsibilities to encompass cultural, political, social and economic aspects in an ongoing relational process. In 1950, T. H. Marshall laid the groundwork (in the West) for a more multifaceted understanding of citizenship, which he proposed as being composed of civil, political, and social phases. Notwithstanding critiques regarding the proposed evolution of these phases, Marshall's understanding of citizenship leads to an appreciation of how one's economic status is a key factor that shapes citizenship. Indeed, Marshall asserted that the lessening of income gaps is one of the most significant factors involved in developing social citizenship (or, "full" citizenship).[3] Thus, we call for an examination of how placing the middle class at the center of analysis serves not just as a way to gauge globalization and the impact of neoliberalism more generally but leads specifically toward thinking about emergent citizenship or, how large groups of people take on new sociopolitical roles and identities. Consider the frequent conflation of middle-class status with national identity. Being in the middle becomes synonymous with sociopolitical belonging.

Thus, we propose the idea of emergent citizenship as a framework and direction for theorizing middle classness in emerging nations. We believe this framework to be productive for scholars in different disciplines studying the middle classes in emerging nations. The authors in this volume refer to the middle classes they study and its new members in terms of coming-into-being. The emergent citizen is one whose transformed economic status leads to new modalities of sociopolitical participation and new pressure points for belonging. The emergent citizen develops new expectations, makes new demands, performs new identities, and feels the stress and disappointment when that performance is challenged. New behaviors, ideas, and attitudes hold the potential to have broad impact at both the local and global levels. Drawing on the discussions put forth by the authors of this volume and also by way of introduction to their essays, we outline below five parameters for thinking about emergent citizenship: consumption; occupying new spaces – both imagined and physical; tensions that arise between class groups; pathways taken to performing middle classness; and state-civil society relations in shaping the middle class.

Consumption

Having greater disposable income is a key factor used by some scholars to define the middle classes. Whether or not it is fostered by the state as a way to develop a nation's GDP and reposition a country in a global landscape, consumption (writ large) is an important marker of identity, can reflect the mobilization of personal aspirations and become converted into a modality of citizenship. Consumption not only reflects one's economic capital, but also reinforces and reproduces one's class status and habitus (Bourdieu). What to consume and how to consume it symbolizes one's cultural capital, which can further advance one's economic capital. Consumption classifies people through taste and moral values demonstrated in the consumption process. As Bourdieu remarked, "[t]aste classifies, and it classifies the classifier. Social subjects, classified by their classifications, distinguish themselves by the distinctions they make, between the beautiful and the ugly, the distinguished and the vulgar, in which their position in the objective classifications is expressed or betrayed" (6). Despite the fact that cultural capital is related to economic capital, they are not the same: there are always aspirational consumers who purchase products beyond their means; and consumers with higher-level purchasing power may not treat consumption as an important identity marker. Both producers and consumers actively develop new meanings in reference to signifiers in the local and global context. Producers are consumers and consumers are producers.

Besides clearly contributing to capitalist profits, how can we understand consumption as a facet of emergent citizenship? One area of exploration concerns whether or not increased materialistic consumption leads to greater openness to foreign cultures and contributes to shaping a global cultural identity. This is one of the central questions asked by Javalgi and Grossman (chapter 7). In their essay, they observe that concomitant to the growth of India's middle class and increasing consumerism one finds Indian consumers becoming more open to foreign cultures. While government policies in these nations have certainly supported increasing consumerism to transform their national economies, consumption practices do not automatically conform to capitalist drives. Patico (chapter 1) asserts that consumption in Russia is regulated by a cultural past wherein "culturedness" and modest versus more conspicuous consumption are conditioned by one's educational capital and one's own position in the social cultural hierarchy. Both Xin Wang (chapter 3) and Rocha and da Rocha (chapter 4) reflect on consumption practices in China and Brazil, respectively. Xin Wang (chapter 3) analyzes how Chinese media portrays the middle class and argues that consumption and material success have become important identity markers for middle-class consumers. Also, consumption takes on specific symbolic meanings where consumption begets consumption: being able to consume leads to future access to resources. Rocha and da Rocha (chapter 4) examine the consumption of leisure products (or, cruises in the specific case of their research) by the new middle classes in Brazil. Their research shows how this new consumer group creates meaning from leisure activities. Notable among their findings is that being able to purchase a cruise is a sign of achievement and social integration.

Occupying New Spaces

Where one is located in physical and imagined space is linked to one's citizenship status. The word "citizen" in English refers to an inhabitant of a physical place (i.e., a city) who holds membership to a state. With transformations to economic status, where people are located and how they are positioned in those spaces also changes. People who may not have once entered into certain territories (metaphorically or literally) begin to appear and take on new roles. Since space can be understood in physical as well as virtual terms, we assert the importance of thinking about how members of the new middle class occupy spaces in terms of their new or renewed physical presence as well as in terms of how they are imagined in media. In terms of occupying both imagined and physical space, Xin Wang (chapter 3) illustrates how the image of the middle class has become more frequent in contemporary Chinese media, which serves to shape middle-class identity as well as capitalize on increasing numbers of middle-class audiences. Members of the Chinese middle class are portrayed as an upward and westward class that consumes new urban spaces (such as glistening glass skyscrapers, Western coffee houses, trendy stores and shopping malls) as well as foreign travel destinations. Wang also notes that occupying and enjoying these new spaces functions as a way to assert middle-class status. In this, Wang's research reveals how the new Chinese middle class is encouraged to take on a new presence in physical space as consumers and new actors in the urban sphere.

As individuals move into higher income brackets and subsequently venture into new spaces of leisure (i.e., shopping malls, restaurants, airplanes, tourist destinations and so forth), one finds new sets of cross-class relationships in terms of labor. Increased income and expanded educational opportunities mean that some who had been members of the working class (or, in the service sector) find themselves receiving the benefits of working class labor rather than being on the giving end. We suggest that future research may consider examining whether or not these individuals take with them a more critical perspective on labor relations.

Citizenship is often understood as being geographically rooted. But, what if the spaces of consumption, activism and identity construction take place in spaces that are geopolitically unbounded? Montoya's essay (chapter 5) makes a strategic move from understanding the middle class in a nationalized context to a global and virtual context. Using the video game *Diablo 3* as a departure point, he draws on Anderson's idea of "imagined communities" to explore theoretically how virtual, parallel economies condition the emergence of a global middle class and how that class is imagined. He argues that virtual economies are meaning-making spaces and are by extension sites of resistance and exploitation. His research shows that "discretionary income evident in virtual economic activity is already producing a social class system – a middle class derived from a small but fast-evolving technocracy," thus linking the local, national and global. Javalgi and Grossman (chapter 7) also explore global connectivity as an aspect of contemporary middle classness in India, noting that access to the Internet is becoming more common for those in the middle and upper classes. Similar trends can be found in other emerging nations. For instance, of the top ten countries with the highest number of Internet users, five are "emerging nations" (including China, India, Brazil, Russia, and Nigeria), thus making technology an essential aspect of global middle classness.

Tensions Between Classes

If classes are understood as emerging fundamentally from social relationships and economic interactions, then we must examine tensions between classes as an aspect of emergent citizenship. Exploring these tensions takes two key directions. First, it is necessary to explore social friction among classes in geopolitically defined spaces. Second, it is important to examine oppositions between classes in terms of the processes taking place in emerging nations that differ from Western (or Eurocentric) models, thereby avoiding the simplification that the formation of classes in emerging nations simply repeats or closely follows past paradigms. The authors in this volume reflect on the ways in which tensions between classes frequently emerge when examining lifestyle practices such as leisure activities and education.

Hind (chapter 2) cogently observes in the context of Mexico how middle-class status is mobilized by governments to erase class tensions and political divisions. Serendipitously, everyone ends up belonging to the middle class. Yet, class conflicts and divisions do exist and develop. As people begin to move into new spaces and take on new sociopolitical roles, clashes between "old" and "new" members of the middle classes can emerge. Not just a confrontation between past and present, we argue that one finds a renegotiation of identity markers and lifestyle practices that come to define what it means to belong to the middle class. In doing so, we end up recognizing the importance of income but look to other factors that define class status. Coinciding with Bourdieu (1984) and his observations that economic and cultural capital underpin class differences, both Patico (Chapter 1) as well as Rocha and da Rocha (chapter 4) observe that cultural capital (i.e., educational level, manners, values, etc.) are key elements to understand consumption behaviors. As individuals who had previously occupied lower income groups move into higher income brackets, they do not necessarily cross over seamlessly nor do they fully embrace those lifestyle practices and values established by existing members of the middle class. For instance, in the essay by Rocha and da Rocha we see that people going on their first cruise critique the wastefulness and conspicuous consumption of the "leisure class" (as theorized by Veblen, 2000). What is more, Rocha and da Rocha show that novice cruisers (or, new members of the middle class) do not necessarily even know the "right scripts" that should guide their behavior. Thus, it is important to consider how the emergent citizen may experience feeling awkward or out-of-place but also reject some established middle-class norms.

Processes of Becoming: Pathways Toward Middle Classness

Before new lifestyle practices are engaged in, a shift in perspective about oneself may precede or coincide with becoming a member of the middle class in emerging nations. Contemporary states depend greatly on the middle class for political and economic stability. They are particularly dependent on middle-class subjectivities that privilege consumerism, self-improvement, and individual responsibility and subsequently shift attention away from collectivist action and demands for social transformation. Thus, it is important to consider the pressures placed on individuals and the ways that people embody these neoliberal economic ideas.

One area for investigation is the question of self-help or self-improvement to become a better neoliberal subject. Whereas Xin Wang (chapter 3) points out the rhetoric of self-improvement present in the works he examines and Emily Hind (chapter 2) refers to the regimented, self-improvement aspects in recent government-sponsored reading campaigns in Mexico, Patico (chapter 1) examines contemporary programs in Russia that encourage personal responsibility and emotional self-awareness as keys to success in a marketized society. More generally, one finds the development of new disciplinary regimes as vehicles of middle classness and the cultivation of new mindsets for members of the new middle classes.

Education is frequently seen as a primary way of achieving social mobility. In the case of Hind (chapter 2) and her discussion of reading campaigns in Mexico, we find an ambivalent cultivation of more traditional middle-class lifestyle practices such as reading literature in tension with the cultivation of a new middle-class neoliberal sensibility toward reading – seen at once as educational endeavor and aspirational activity. It merits noting that leisure activities (such as travel and entertainment) require disposable income and free time, which are generally limited for the working classes and lower income groups. In fact, the ability to engage in leisure activities is often considered a hallmark of middle-class status. Both Xin Wang (chapter 3) and Rocha and da Rocha (chapter 4) discuss how leisure activities like travel are a sign of accomplishment and status marker. By contrast, Hind (chapter 2) shows how some activities like reading literature are being redefined and conform to utilitarian, neoliberal expectations. In this, we can see how an activity formerly seen as simultaneously educational and entertaining is transformed to conform to economic demands with the goal of forming middle-class Mexican citizens in possession of practical, marketable skills.

For some citizens of emerging nations, education is closely linked to the histories of these nations as former sites of European colonialism. Dakhli and Ketata (chapter 9) address the former colonial status of nations of the MENA region (Middle East and North Africa) and further investigate middle-class perceptions of higher education beyond its role in securing higher paying jobs and social mobility. While education can be seen as a way to attain membership in the global middle class, Dakhli and Ketata note that education in the MENA region is a space where conflicts between modernity and conservatism are seen. They also foresee a continuing evolution in the educational systems of the MENA region where regional cultural values and norms will drive the adaptation of Western-style educational models.

Closely related to the question of education, occupation also contributes to the formation of middle-class status. Although the the middle classes of mid-twentieth century Europe and the United States could aspire to a relatively comfortable middle-class status with unionized, "blue-collar" jobs – institutionalized racism and sexism aside, labor becomes an important marker and determinant of class status in emerging nations. One of the key effects of the global neoliberal shift has been the increased pressures on individuals to develop greater personal responsibility as states have retreated. As a consequence of neoliberal policies, individuals are required to be more proactive in their individual affairs and show independent entrepreneurship, which are traits assumed to lead individuals into safe, comfortable and prosperous middle-class existence. It may then not be entirely surprising to note how political discourses in emerging nations promote various modalities of entrepreneurialism ranging from support of a creative economy in Brazil to direct participation of the Chinese state in promoting entrepreneurialism. Whether or not these discourses have had any direct impact, Javalgi and Grossman (chapter 7) observe that India's entrepreneurial spirit is growing with nearly half of the work-force being self-employed. In his analysis of contemporary audiovisual representation of the middle class in China, Xin Wang (chapter 3) notes that the construction of class consciousness and identity underscore how members of the new middle class in China are portrayed as aspirational and entrepreneurial. Similarly, Patico (chapter 1) reveals how personal success appears central to new middle-class identities in post-Soviet Russia.

State and Civil Society Relationships

Owing to its position somewhere between the proletariat and the bourgeoisie and assumptions that the political affiliations of the middle class would align either with a professional, managerial class or with the working class, the middle class itself has been seen as holding limited political agency. If the middle class is in a contradictory or even ambivalent position, then what is the nature of their political agency? To what degree do the middle classes enact change? To what degree do the middle classes serve the purposes of the elite and provide stability to those in power? If this division is a specious one, then in what more complicated ways do the middle classes navigate differing class interests? Whereas the above section considered tensions between classes as a modality of habitus, we consider in related fashion multiple ideological leanings and tensions.

Governments are not monolithic in their actions. Returning to the point above concerning the links between economic status and occupying new spaces, the authors in this collection suggest that we examine the links and evolution of class status and how people take on roles in civil society to assert their various demands that at times may conflict with official policies. Although states may change their official orientations and redirect economies from more socialist towards neoliberal policies, moral frameworks do not disappear as quickly. Traditional values and teachings remain and coexist with new value systems. For instance, Merchant, Rose and Gour (chapter 8) examine how urbanization, economic development, and aspirational lifestyles are interpreted through the lens of traditional collectivist Hindu beliefs, which influence consumer attitudes regarding the role and use of money in India. In their reflections on the meaning of money, they reveal that money provides a means of performing one's *dharmic* duty. Prosperity is seen as fickle and motivates saving over unchecked consumerism.

During the past thirty years, the Chinese government has focused on economic development to the detriment of social and environmental problems. The middle class that has emerged out of China's economic boom has influenced policy-making, consumption patterns and the behavior of society more generally. Zhao and Cavusgil (chapter 6) show that a significant percentage of the Chinese middle-class consumers are concerned with environmental protections and support sustainable development even if it may negatively impact the economy. Their research suggests that the Chinese middle class is not a passive stakeholder in economic development supported by the Chinese government; rather, the Chinese middle class has developed a political and environmental consciousness that questions the ethical and environmental limits of consumption as the driver of economic development.

The assumption that the middle classes generally support democracy and progressive political initiatives must also be interrogated. After a series of incremental reforms put in place by the Chinese government in the 1980s, a sizable middle class emerged in the later 1990s. With this, conventional wisdom dictated that a sizable middle class would eventually exert pressure on authoritarian rulers to allow for increased democratic participation. In other words, the prevailing logic has been that a large middle class signals a subsequent transition to democracy. Wedeman (chapter 10) explores these assumptions regarding the direction and evolution of political activism and its link to rising incomes. He explains how one does find an increase in the propensity of the Chinese middle class to take to the streets to defend its rights in what would be defined in the West as not-in-my-back-yard (or, NIMBY) protests to local nuisances (e.g., construction projects, housing developments, power plants, etc.). These protests are largely reactive, conservative, and localized. The individualized nature of protests is related not only to neoliberalism, but, more importantly, to the severe control and violent suppression that activists have encountered. Yet, Wedeman argues that even these reactive protests may have broader social and political implications in the future.

Concluding Remarks

The essays included in this volume originate from a conference held in Atlanta in September of 2013 that was sponsored by the Center for International Business and Education Research (CIBER) and the University Research Service Administration at Georgia State University in collaboration with the China Research Center. The conference brought together scholars from Brazil, China, Germany, India, Israel, Mexico, the Middle East, Russia, South Africa, Spain, and Turkey. Researchers from the humanities dialogued with experts in the social sciences and business. Critical theories blended with quantitative research methodologies.

Notwithstanding the push in recent decades in academia for interdisciplinary research, academics by and large work in specific departments, publish in defined journals and with certain presses, and teach classes in established degree programs. Yet, no one field functions like a Rosetta stone to decipher an understanding of the middle class in emerging nations. It is with this spirit of questioning established paradigms as well as academic hierarchies and boundaries that we proceed with this volume. Like the muscles of the body, intellectual enquiry should be stretched and tested regularly. Given that class formation is not a permanent outcome, but rather a continual process, we anticipate numerous opportunities in the future to examine the global middle classes from multidisciplinary and multicountry perspectives.

Notes

1. Of the writings by Marx see, for example: *Theories of Surplus Value* (Amherst: Prometheus, [1863] 2000); *Economic and Philosophical Manuscripts of 1844* (New York: International Publishers, [1844] 1964); and *Capital: Critique of Political Economy* (New York: International Publishers [1867] 1967.
2. See recent Gini data reported here: http://data.worldbank.org/indicator/SI.POV.GINI. Accessed May 26, 2015.
3. See his text *Citizenship and Social Class* (Cambridge: Cambridge University Press, 1950).

Works Cited

Bourdieu, Pierre. *Distinction: A social critique of the judgement of taste*. Trans. by Richard Nice. Cambridge, Mass: Harvard University Press, 1984. Print.

García Canclini, Néstor. *Consumers and Citizens: Globalization and Multicultural Conflicts*. Minneapolis: University of Minnesota Press, 2001. Print.

Heiman, Rachel, Carla Freeman, and Mark Liechty, eds. *The Global Middle Classes: Theorizing Through Ethnography*. Santa Fe: School of American Research Press, 2012. Print.

Kharas, Homi. "The Emerging Middle Class in Emerging Countries." OECD Development Centre. Working Paper no. 285. Web. January, 2010.

López, A. Ricardo, and Barbara Weinstein, eds. *The Making of the Middle Class: Toward a Transnational History*. Durham: Duke University Press, 2012. Print.

Marshall, T. H. *Citizenship and Social Class: And Other Essays*. Cambridge: Cambridge University Press, 1950. Print.

Thompson, E. P. *The Making of the English Working Class*. Vintage, 1963. Print.

Parker, John, "Burgeoning Bourgeoisie." *The Economist*. 12 February 2009. Available at http://www.economist.com/node/13063298. Last accessed May 25, 2015.

Schielke, Samuli. "Living in the Future Tense." *The Global Middle Classes: Theorizing Through Ethnography*. Eds. Heiman, Rachel, Carla Freeman, and Mark Liechty. Santa Fe: School of American Research Press, 2012. 33–56. Print.

Veblen, Thorstein. *The Theory of the Leisure Class*. New York: A. M. Kelley Booksellers, 1965. Print.

Section I

Media and Society

1 Culturedness, Responsibility and Self-Help

Middle-Class Contexts in Post-Socialist Russia

Jennifer Patico

Introduction

In the past decade, there has been increasing scholarly interest in the development of middle classes in emerging markets, including post-socialist contexts. In a recent edited volume on the global middle classes, anthropologists Rachel Heiman, Mark Liechty, and Carla Freeman observe that around the world, "neoliberal state ideologies that privilege entrepreneurial labor ... make possible new middle-class subject positions, new forms of immaterial and affective labor, and new patterns of class mobility, consumption, and capital accumulation" (25). A key challenge has been to theorize the common experiences that appear to characterize middle classes cross-culturally without falling into the trap of positing some essential and inevitable middle class that exists outside of specific historical and local context. As Heiman, Liechty, and Freeman ask, "how can we theorize the differences and similarities among middle-class formations through time and across space in a way that does not fall into a teleological understanding of the history of class?" (5).

Avoiding such teleology necessitates grounded attention to the patterning of social relationships and texture of social life in each setting. More specifically, it requires an understanding of people's changing work lives and consumer engagements – classic concerns in the study of class – but also of how these are entangled with shifting experiences of morality, selfhood, and kinship. Indeed, recent anthropological scholarship has approached emergent middle classes not as discrete groups easily defined by income levels or consumer indicators (though labor relations are treated as central to these class identities), but rather in terms of the ideologies, material environments, and institutional and interpersonal scenarios through which middle classness becomes a lived experience and an articulated self-positioning (e.g., Liechty; Patico, *Consumption*; Fehervary; Zhang; "In Search of"; see also Heiman et al. 8–9).

In those veins, this chapter reviews recent anthropological and sociological scholarship on the middle class in contemporary Russia. Specifically, I draw from my own ethnographic fieldwork in St. Petersburg in the late 1990s and early 2000s as well as more recent studies by American, Russian, and Finnish researchers working in the same city. As I shall discuss, current ethnographic and sociological research points to the emergence of arguably neoliberalized ways of thinking of about personal success in post-Soviet St. Petersburg that appear central to new middle-class identities. While these discourses parallel middle-class and entrepreneurial orientations that have been described by anthropologists working in the United States and elsewhere in the world (see, for example, Martin, Cahn, Dunn), one source of specificity lies in how Russian class perspectives continue to reflect Soviet framings of material culture, respectability, and the social meanings of inequality. Moreover, research in St. Petersburg highlights how neoliberal-leaning middle-class discourses, which emphasize individual responsibility for personal success and the need for self-training and self-transformation to navigate changing labor markets, also are linked inevitably with shifting and local forms of sociality.

Thus, I synthesize social scientific approaches to the Russian middle class not with an eye toward demonstrating or refuting its fulfillment of any classic, generic, or international model of middle-classness, but rather with the goal of identifying a few important social arenas in which perceptions and meanings of class are being negotiated in post-Soviet life. Accordingly, while criteria such as income and educational attainment can be used to demarcate middle classness and will be mentioned later in this chapter, this essay treats the middle class of today's Russia not as a distinct, bounded stratum but rather as a set of (still emergent and contested) circumstances, values, and projects that stretch across a broad swath of both relatively affluent and more marginally affluent individuals and households.

"Middle Class" in the Soviet and Early Post-Soviet Eras: Consumerism and Moral Discourse

Officially a "classless" society established in the name of the working masses, the Union of Soviet Socialist Republics (USSR) distributed resources more equally than did most countries of North America and Europe in the twentieth century. Job security, universal health care, and free childcare were among the privileges enjoyed by Soviet citizens, even if persistent consumer shortages and a lack of political freedoms made their quality of life somewhat debatable (particularly from the perspective of those accustomed to the freedoms afforded and insecurities accepted in market-driven economies). Income and lifestyle gaps certainly existed, but they were narrower than in, for example, the United States during the same period (Patico, *Consumption* 43). Still, the differences that did exist were socially and politically meaningful; if the evils of class were supposed to have been abolished, this is not to say that social differences marked by income, professional standing, and, importantly, *access* to scarce consumer goods were not highly salient. As I have discussed elsewhere, "a hierarchical structure [was] institutionalized and naturalized, organized according to individuals' educational backgrounds, professional identities, and statuses in the Communist Party, and it was maintained through the differential distribution of not only monetary compensation but also more direct consumer privileges and allotments" (ibid.). For example, special baskets of desirable foodstuffs were distributed through workplaces and only elites were provided entry to certain well-stocked and hard-currency stores. In this sense, "people were encouraged to interpret the relative worth of their contributions to society in terms of the material privileges to which they were granted access" (44; see also Dunham).

Though "middle class" was not an emic (that is, locally used) category in Soviet society, historians and sociologists define a Soviet middle class made up primarily of educated specialists (known as the "intelligentsia") as well as relatively well-off workers (Gladarev and Tsinman, Gurova 152, Patico, *Consumption*). Counter to the image many Americans hold of an utterly drab Soviet existence, that middle-class sensibility certainly included consumerist values and aspirations. Soviet middle classness was indicated by "financial security and an apartment of one's own as well as fashion, luxury, cosiness and pleasure," especially from the 1960s, even as the official aesthetic emphasized moderation and simplicity (Gurova 153; see also Dunham, Patico, *Consumption*). The contrasts between the Soviet case and North American/west European industrialized settings are clear, but the USSR's "old" middle-class parallels the "traditional" middle classes elsewhere in the world inasmuch as they "emerged from the populist, modernist, bureaucratic, state-driven economic policies of mid-twentieth century states" (Heiman et al. 14, following David Harvey). The Soviet state can certainly be included among the twentieth century's modernist, bureaucratic, state-driven economies; indeed, it would seem to exemplify these tendencies far better than most of its European or North American counterparts.[1] As we shall see, in the twenty-first century the parallels continue, though mitigated by important local specificities.

My research in St. Petersburg involved twelve months (1998–99) of semi-structured interviewing with approximately two dozen public school teachers, participant observation in informal social settings, classroom volunteering, and other research activities such as accompanying teachers on routine shopping trips. (Follow-up research was conducted in St. Petersburg in summer 2003). The project centered on consumer practices and daily experiences of social and economic upheaval in the wake of post-Soviet marketization, with particular attention given to the teachers' conceptualizations of class identity, the moral meanings they attached to capitalism, and the re-positioning of Russian consumers in global "civilizational" hierarchies (Patico, *Consumption*).

In the Soviet Union, teachers were not particularly well paid, but they were considered to be part of the intelligentsia and in this regard enjoyed a relatively high social position. My interlocutors were mostly women (as women dominated the teaching profession); some were career teachers with academic qualifications in education, while others had trained in different fields (for example, engineering) but had joined the ranks of teachers when the enterprises that had employed them collapsed along with the Soviet state economy. Either way, while their work had not been highly compensated nor prestigious in the recent Soviet past, professionally speaking they had come of age accustomed to a modicum of respectability, security, and the sense that they were making recognized and valued contributions to society. For all of these reasons, teachers could be considered part of the "old" Soviet middle class.

In the 1990s, post-Soviet marketization allowed for a proliferation of more varied aesthetic discourses and images, while most consumers simultaneously suffered the effects of rapid inflation, growing unemployment, and shrinking social welfare supports. At the time of my initial fieldwork in 1998 and 1999, in the midst of an acute financial crisis that had led to new waves of inflation, teachers were reeling – scrambling for additional income as tutors and tightening their families' belts. Meanwhile, many of their students as well as their private tutoring clients came from families who had fared better financially: they were those who had been able to make a go of it by starting lucrative commercial enterprises, and who were in some cases suspected by the teachers of criminal activity and criticized for their lack of education, tact, and proper deference to teachers' professional expertise. These socially immediate critiques mirrored more impersonal and widely circulating jokes and stereotypes about the post-Soviet *nouveaux riches*. The so-called "New Russians" were roundly ridiculed and resented, caricatured as crass and immoral. Though the archetypical New Russian was male, New Russian wives were depicted similarly as empty-headed, bored, and socially useless people engaged only in superficial, self-absorbed activities such as shopping and getting facials.

What did such discourses say about the teachers' senses of their own class positioning at that historical moment, and about their attitudes toward marketization more broadly? In many ways teachers' critiques fit easily into archetypically Russian notions of morality and social justice. It has been argued widely – in scholarly literature and in everyday Russian talk – that Russians, influenced by peasant collectivism, Orthodox Christianity, and Soviet rhetoric concerning the evils of capitalism, tend to valorize the spiritual over the material and the collective over the individual, casting extreme individual wealth as a sign of moral degradation (see Patico, *Consumption,* "Spinning the Market").[2] In the late 1990s, I found that many people in St. Petersburg, including the teachers, were indeed engaging in this kind of talk in which money was seen as a corrupting influence and the poor represented Russia's good and true *narod* (people, as in "the Russian people"). Thus while some of them tentatively defined themselves as middle class – essentially, differentiating themselves from the poor by acknowledging that they had small amounts of disposable income and a degree of security, as well as marking their continuing identification with the intelligentsia – they did not embrace the new marketplace as a viable medium for meaningful class mobility. Rather, bitterly aware of having been left behind by a rising consumer class, they derided what they perceived as the social emptiness and moral transgressions of the newly affluent: that is, those most visibly involved in and benefiting from commercial transactions in the new economy.[3] Further, they recalled the ways in which people had leveraged social networks and friendly relationships in order to combat shortages in Soviet days, making consumer strategies socially rich (see Ledeneva, Pesmen, Patico, *Consumption*); teachers noted that such strategies were no longer as effective since cash had become the most necessary capital for acquiring desirable goods and as, indeed, it seemed that in pursuit of income, no one had as much time for soulful socializing as they had had before.

On the other hand, in our more concrete conversations about various kinds of commodities and strategies for decision-making in consumption, people engaged in a different kind of moral discourse. In this context, the notion that respectable consumption was the sign of a socially competent and valued person was often more in the foreground. Indeed, that association had been promoted in the twentieth century by the Soviet state, notably through its articulation of the concept of "culturedness" (*kul'turnost'*), which linked modest and tasteful consumer practice within urbane sophistication, cultural development, and narratives of Soviet progress (Patico "To Be Happy", *Consumption*); and these sensibilities were taking on new significance in the context of marketization and economic crisis. For if the teachers were wary of remarkable wealth, they also understood *modest* consumer respectability to be a reflection of one's personal value and consumer *access* as an expression of the recognition of that value by society at large. This meant that their constrained consumer possibilities were loci not only for social critique and outrage – anger that the New Russians were the ones reaping the rewards of the new economy – but also for self-questioning and uncertainty about their own actual or rightful place in the social fabric. If their consumer access was so limited, what did this say about their value in and recognition by a transforming Russia? Given that their own contributions seemed so little rewarded by material affluence, the teachers struggled to gauge and define their own social worth and class positioning.

Identifying a New Middle Class

By the time I conducted follow-up field research in St. Petersburg in 2003, however, I found that the same teachers were no longer deriding New Russians in the same biting tones; they seemed to be more open to the idea that in Russia's market economy, admirable personal effort and hard work might result in material prosperity. I interpreted this as a sign not only that people were feeling more hopeful about the direction of the Russian economy, but also that the disparities of wealth that had been so polarizing and unsettling in the 1990s were becoming increasingly normalized – that is, legitimated and expected (Patico, *Consumption*). At the same time, structures of wealth were shifting: while late-1990s observers of Russian society had doubted whether any middle class existed amidst startling new polarizations of rich and poor, Gladarev and Tsinman (191) note that by the turn of the 2000s post-collapse polarization of wealth had slowed and a new middle class – somewhat distinct from the "old" Soviet middle class – appeared to be emerging.

The nature of this middle class is still debated among scholars; while most agree that a middle class does exist in today's Russia, "the key debates," as Melin and Salmenniemi observe, "have dealt with the nature of the social structure, the criteria and size of the middle class, and whether social classes actually exist in Russia due to the weakness of the entrepreneurial sector and professional and class-based social organizations (30)." Some scholars define Russia's middle class as "an ideal or a normative model" rather than an actual group (Melin and Salmenniemi 35). Income level is sometimes used as a means of measuring the middle class, though it is a difficult measure to use because subjects are hesitant to report their incomes (Gladarev and Tsinman 191). Occupational or professional status and education (secondary specialized education or higher) also are used frequently to qualify middle-class membership (Melin and Salmenniemi 35). Russian studies published between 2006 and 2008 suggest that around 20 percent of the population qualifies as middle class according to their educational level and professional position whereas larger numbers (about 40–60 percent) self-identified as middle class (ibid. 36–37), which speaks to the new power of "middle class" as a broad aspirational and subjective category.

Such quantitative measures provide a general sense of scale using conventional socioeconomic measures, but more important to the current discussion are the qualitative affinities researchers have linked with middle-class identification or striving. Understanding these depends on deeply qualitative, particularly ethnographic, research. Middle classness may depend upon relative affluence in the Russian context, but anthropologists and sociologists also have examined it more directly in terms of the values, desires, and strategies that are meaningful to those who would call themselves "middle class." For example, certain areas of consumption have been flagged as definitive of Russian middle classness. Gurova (155–158) describes clothing as a key medium of middle-class identity, focusing on how her St. Petersburg interviewees treated fashion quite seriously as a means of socially positioning themselves – proper clothing helped provide a sense of social order and belonging – even as they also took pains to distance themselves from what could be perceived as a snobbish or materialistic investment in clothing and shopping. To Gurova, these equivocations demonstrated their ongoing commitment to culturedness and other "values embraced by the [old] Soviet middle class" (ibid. 157, 158).

Other expenditures and investments are less obviously commodifiable, yet figure importantly in performances and perceptions of class.

For example, Gladarev and Tsinman (200) suggest that the Russian middle-class values "time for oneself," treating leisure time (*dosug*) as a means of building identity. They are people who care about education, real estate, and health care and are willing to devote resources to these (ibid.).[4] Health care, in particular, has been identified as a realm with special symbolic relevance relevant to imaginations of class: Rytkonen and Pietila, drawing on interview data collected in St. Petersburg in 2004, found that for their highly educated informants, "the visibly healthy body [is] not only a signifier of a healthy way of life but [also] of a wealthy social position" (194). Interviewees discussed the body as a resource and a healthy lifestyle as a sort of luxury good; moreover, they understood their concern about health to signify "their commitment to being a responsible person" who understands why health is meaningful (ibid. 199). Similarly, Rivkin-Fish argues that spending money on health services holds great significance for Russians who present themselves as members of a long-suffering Russian intelligentsia; they understand their own ability and inclination to devote resources to health as setting them apart both from the poor and from those whose displays of wealth they perceive as crass and superficial. Here is an example of how people define the "lower" and "upper" boundaries of middle-class identity not only through assessments of relative affluence (or even professional and educational status), but also by judging tastes and behaviors deemed to be appropriately moderate and responsible (or not).

New middle-class sensibilities involve not only attention to the physical body but also work on the self. Finnish sociologist Suvi Salmenniemi has analyzed the growing field of self-help literatures in Russia, arguing that lack of affordable health care and distrust of the official system of health services are among the reasons why self-help approaches have become so appealing. "The structural distrust characteristic of Russian society, coupled with a sense of political powerlessness ... encourages people to work on what they feel can be influenced and transformed: their own feelings, thoughts and behavior" ("Post-Soviet" 68). Salmenniemi finds that Russian approaches to self-help differ (for example, some are explicitly westernizing and others more slavophilic), but what they share is that they tend to treat failure as individual pathology and to connect class identity with assessments of personal responsibility (ibid. 73, 81).[5] This also suggests how "middle-class" strategies for dealing with daily problems vary along with subjects' relative affluence, since some may display responsibility for health through the purchase of health services while others seek to do the same through more self-administered (and less expensive) efforts such as purchasing a book or attending a workshop. In short, projects of respectability and self-care may define middle classness in a broad fashion, but the distinct ways in which such projects are pursued and their success judged undoubtedly index economic and social differentiation among those who might call themselves "middle class."

Self-Help, Self-Reliance and New Social Encounters

Recent ethnographies illustrate more vividly how new genres of self-help offer class-inflected models for working on the self. Anthropologist Andrea Mazzarino worked among business women in the late 2000s in St. Petersburg and observed how self-help discourses were presented in the context of various training seminars. These increasingly popular events included opportunities for women to learn "emotional independence" in order "to forge more satisfying relationships" as well as trainings geared toward identifying one's professional calling or learning how to communicate effectively with business contacts (Mazzarino 1). Trainings included activities such as walking on hot coals and chanting mantras designed to build self-esteem.[6] They coached participants in interpersonal skills and provided contexts for mutual support and cultivation of "new forms of interpersonal communication than what they experienced in their families and their workplaces, based on a willingness to listen to one another's ideas without criticism, openness to new friendships and business partnerships, and mutual affirmation of one another's aspirations" (ibid. 2). In short, the seminars were oriented toward teaching affective and interactive styles that exemplified the kind of charisma and flexibility understood to be required of successful leaders and businesspeople. In contrast to the institutional constraints, clearer hierarchies, and predictable career trajectories to which Soviet women (and men) had been accustomed, these new programs encouraged them to envision new futures for themselves and, perhaps, to be more open to risk-taking in their professional and personal lives. In post-Soviet Russia, as elsewhere, "traditional middle classes struggle to maintain their living standard" while a new middle class, the "product of the ... global neoliberal turn," is "charged with the responsibility of being independent entrepreneurs and consumers, especially in the realm of services" (Heiman et al. 14).

Tomas Matza ("Moscow's Echo", "The Little Army," "Good Individualism") goes further to consider how self-help and the popularization of psychotherapeutic techniques specifically contribute to class formation in St. Petersburg. He examines self-help in the context of the television talk show, which he describes as one venue of a new Russian market in psychotherapy; this trend is related, again, to current imaginations of what it takes to achieve success in a market society. As Matza puts it, "therapeutic idioms like self-esteem, self-realization, self-knowledge, self-management, independence, personal potential, and responsibility have articulated with consumer desire, capitalist self-fashioning, and careerism" (Matza "Moscow's Echo" 492). Whereas Soviet pedagogies of self-examination were oriented toward self-control and self-sacrifice, the new approach encourages Russians "to ignore social judgment in forming a view of themselves and the world, thus revising the sources of authority from the *kollektiv* to the ideology of the autonomous subject" (500–501). Meanwhile, in state psychological assistance centers, Matza ("The Little Army") finds, psychology is used to pathologize and individualize the struggles of children from lower income families. By contrast, the children of the wealthy elite attend camps that are devoted to self-discovery and development of psychological fitness. These elite programs, which Matza observed in the late 2000s, offer psychological education that is designed to provide students with forms of self-awareness and polish expected to translate into competitive advantage – that is, future success in business is understood to depend upon management of one's emotions (Matza "Good Individualism" 807).[7]

Ultimately, Matza suggests, applications of psychology contribute directly to processes of class formation inasmuch as they help to create new subjectivities that are directed toward market success while, simultaneously, being used to describe and "correct" youth and families who are seen as more problematic and less resourceful (Matza "The Little Army", "Good Individualism"). Stated otherwise, psychotherapy becomes for urban Russians both a means of *interpreting* the nature of class difference and a means of actually *producing* different modes of being and interaction that become meaningful as class.Thus while in the USSR consumerism and the accomplishment of all kinds of daily tasks depended upon extensive informal exchange practices and ideologies of mutual help, in the early twenty-first century individual self-reliance and self-investment have emerged as explicit markers of Russian middle-class aspiration and belonging.

However, if self-help programs home in on the individual as the seat of success or failure and as the locus for reform, it is important to highlight that social relationships and networks are far from irrelevant or obsolete in these processes; rather, they are necessarily subject to change or slated for transformation as individual selves are recalibrated and reoriented (see also Cohen). This is particularly well illustrated by recent research on the organization of childrearing and domestic work in St. Petersburg.

Rotkirch, Tkach, and Zdravomyslova argue that one way to mark oneself as middle class in urban Russia today is to be willing and able to hire domestic workers, particularly nannies. A number of factors come together to encourage families to employ nannies from outside the family, a situation that was far more unusual in the past. In Soviet Russia, standard practice was for grandmothers to take their retirement pensions and stay home to raise grandchildren while their own daughters returned to the work force. More recently, as Zdravomyslova ("Working Mothers") explains, change is happening from two sides: with state-provided social supports no longer providing adequate income for retirees, grandmothers are now compelled to work past retirement age. In this context, "working grandmother" becomes a more legitimized and expected life stage, replacing the late-Soviet model of "grandmother bringing up her grandchild" (Zdravomyslova, "Working Mothers," 204–5). At the same time, young mothers, facing intensified labor market pressures and time crunches, nonetheless prefer now to organize their own home lives and not to acknowledge the authority of grandmothers as caretakers (ibid. 204) – reflecting, again, the growing emphasis on self-reliance and self-governing discussed above. The result is that there is a new demand for paid nannies. Childcare becomes commercialized, middle-class families become increasingly nuclearized, and "the gender structuring of childcare as a whole changes" (ibid. 204–5).

Ultimately, Zdravomyslova, Rotkirch, and Tkach (Rotkirch et al., Zdravomyslova, "Niani," "Working Mothers") portray this arrangement as reinforcing social inequalities among differently class-positioned women: continuing career mobility for middle-class women becomes possible through new and reinforced forms of class inequality (see especially Zdravomyslova, "Working Mothers" 222). This is true not only because nannies' pay tends to be relatively exploitative, but also in that people are enacting class difference and distance in the very relationship between domestic employers and employees. From day to day and week to week, the parties negotiate not only salaries but interpersonal encounters that produce relations of relative hierarchy or egalitarianism, familial closeness or professional formality.

Conclusion

In summary, recent scholarship paints middle classness in Russia as a means of defining social identity that is dependent upon a degree of affluence, to be sure, but also upon values of culturedness and respectability that in some ways are consistent with longer-term (Soviet) ways of thinking about inequality, propriety, and deservedness. Thus responsibility, moderation, and self-discipline are among the moral cadences that accompany middle classness in contemporary St. Petersburg; middle-class identity gains meaning from its contrast with those cast as less "responsible" and less respectable, whether poor or wealthy. Indeed, post-Soviet opportunities for entrepreneurism, adaptation to new labor market pressures, and acclimation to greater income disparities have led to growing emphasis on transformation of the self and the notion that one's success is determined ultimately by one's own physical, psychological, and social fitness. While exhortations toward self-examination and individual development may strike many readers as simply healthy and even empowering, the inspirational language of self-realization is the flip side of many Russians' struggle to come to terms with the new uncertainties and anxieties that are presented by a transformed economy and by shifting regimes of social and cultural value.

More broadly, the studies discussed here make clear that individualizing or self-help programs by definition have implications for people's ongoing social relationships; each project shapes the other as social boundaries are explored and re-drawn. Ethnographers and other qualitative researchers are attending to the ways in which frameworks such as self-help and psychotherapy come along with face-to-face scenarios in which class takes on shifted – but not entirely new – meanings and possibilities, and where class is an uncertain and emergent aspect of local social interactions. Thus, for example, urban Russians likely to think of themselves as middle class may be involved in active efforts to transform their relationships and interactive styles for possible success in a neoliberal marketplace; they are also likely to be weathering logistically and perhaps emotionally stressful changes to kinship structures, as variously positioned working women (and men) contribute to the increasing nuclearization and commercialization of households. People's sense that a middle class now exists develops in tandem not only with norms that help guide the behavior and recognition of its (potential) members, but also with these new dilemmas and contexts for the interpersonal negotiation and performance of class difference. In these day-to-day episodes, people remake, repackage, and relearn their own social identities.

Categorizing all these classed orientations, ideologies, and interactions as "neoliberal" phenomena, as do Salmenniemi, Mazzarino, and Matza, points helpfully to some of the ways they are connected with political economic shifts – such as heightened labor insecurity and lost social support resources – that are not unique to the former Soviet Union but nested within broader capitalist processes. The moral cadences mentioned above, though continuous in specific ways with Soviet ideologies and lifestyles, also resonate with the "individuated, 'self-made,' entrepreneurial" images of middle classness salient in many other neoliberal contexts (Heiman et al. 18). As research on the emergent middle classes continues, comparative analysis can shed brighter light on how recurrent themes such as the popularity of self-help, the moral significance of good health, and global entrepreneurial trends express the pressures, motivations, and dilemmas those positioned as "middle class" in various locales loosely share.[8]

Still, we must maintain a critical awareness of the potentially divergent grounding details and the complex political effects of these middle class ways of being. These are areas ripe for further research, though a few ethnographers have already begun such work. For example, Matza ("Moscow's Echo", "Good Individualism") asks us to consider how self-help discourses and psychological trainings work both to create new ethical subjects and to discipline them in Putin's Russia, constituting new forms of governmentality that seem to be particularly effective in what Matza describes as "a context in which neoliberal economy has been divorced from liberal politics, [where] one is left with a 'neoliberalism without liberals'" (Matza, "Moscow's Echo" 493–4). Individuals are encouraged to engage with economic challenges not, for example, by critiquing state policies nor (as teachers did in the late 1990s) by decrying the moral degradation of the newly affluent, but rather through changing themselves to fit current demands. Salmenniemi makes a similar point, arguing that the ideology of personal responsibility advanced by self-help texts "propos[es] an individual-centred cure to a range of problems originating from social-structural relationships of power" ("Post-Soviet" 81). In short, Matza and Salmenniemi bring into focus how the self-development strategies so important to middle-class identification in today's Russia can also be understood as means to excuse, distract attention from, and shift responsibility for the effects of state policies and the hardships of Russia's market economy.

Though ideologies such as self-help are appealing far beyond Russia – and Matza suggests that "neoliberalism without liberals" may characterize neoliberalism more generally ("Moscow's Echo" 494) – future research should continue to explore how the satisfactions and disciplines associated with middle-classness in Putin's Russia work to help sustain and legitimize its highly constrained forms of democratic governance (see ibid. 512–3). The same developments can, of course, be interpreted and framed in other ways. Case in point: Mazzarino, viewing these developments in a more redemptive light, argues that while self-help strategies are not "politically confrontational," they can be thought of as empowering to participants in the sense that they provide "a social setting in which language from neo-liberal capitalist programs is appropriated by people to imagine and sometimes, realize more expansive futures" (9).

These divergent analyses undeniably result from divergent analytical lenses: lenses that foreground the insidious strictures of new disciplinary regimes or, alternatively, that highlight how individuals adapt to new circumstances through creative, agentive use of available cultural tools. As research on the global middle classes continues, scholars will need to be as explicit as possible about the ways in which their own intellectual commitments emphasize certain aspects of middle-class phenomena at the expense of others. Yet such contrasting views, taken together, also draw to our attention that vehicles of middle classness such as self-help most likely have effects that are *simultaneously* liberatory and oppressive, both enabling new forms of self-realization and channeling and constraining which forms it can take. Moreover, while they may transcend national borders, they have more specific histories and, accordingly, effects on the ground. The ideologies and practices that define emergent middle classes around the world must, then, be deeply contextualized in order that we may grasp their complex political ramifications and resonance.

Notes

1. For a general discussion of Soviet and post-Soviet class formations, see Salmenniemi, "Introduction."
2. On morality in post-Soviet everyday life more generally, see Zigon.
3. Though "New Russians" were not thought of as "middle class," their new affluence and teachers' critiques of it parallel Heiman, Liechty, and Freeman's observation about conflicts among old and new middle classes: "Ethnographically, around the world we see the tensions between these middle-class formations playing out in a fascinating array of moral politics ... these dual (dueling) middle classes represent different visions of the state, different modes of capitalist (re)production, and ... different forms of subjectivity" (14).
4. Such long-term and future-oriented investments have been identified as middle class attributes elsewhere in the world as well; see, for example, Heiman et al. 19.
5. Zhang ("Refashioning") discusses parallel discourses of responsibility and individual personality in neoliberalizing China.

6. For parallel ethnographic examples of how physically and psychologically challenging trainings are mobilized to fashion and discipline individual subjectivities and to make them economically useful (in Japan and the United States, respectively), see Kondo and Martin.
7. For a comparative case of how youth psychologies are targeted for critique and reform in a neoliberalizing setting (Kerala, India), see Chua.
8. For a recent discussion of how therapeutic and self-help approaches to mental health have become salient for the contemporary Chinese middle class, for example, see Zhang, "Refashioning."

Works Cited

Cahn, Peter. "Building Down and Dreaming Up." *American Ethnologist* 33.1 (2006): 126–142. Print.

Chua, Jocelyn Lim. "Making Time for the Children: Self-Temporalization and the Cultivation of the Antisuicidal Subject in South India." *Cultural Anthropology* 26.1(2011): 112–137. Print.

Cohen, Susanne. "Image of a Secretary: A Metapragmatic Morality for Post-Soviet Capitalism." *Anthropological Quarterly* 86.3 (2013): 725–758. Print.

Dunham, Vera. *In Stalin's Time: Middleclass Values in Soviet Fiction*. Cambridge University Press, 1979. Print.

Dunn, Elizabeth. *Privatizing Poland: Baby Food, Big Business, and the Remaking of Labor*. Ithaca: Cornell University Press, 2004. Print.

Fehervary, Krisztina. "The Materiality of the New Family House: Postsocialist Fad or Middle-class Ideal?" *City and Society* 23.1 (2011): 18–41. Print.

Gladarev, Boris, and Zhanna Tsinman. "Dom, shkola, vrachi i muzei: potrebitel'skie praktiki srednego klassa." *Novyi Byt v Sovremennoi Rossii: Gendernye Issledovaniia Posvednevnosti*. Eds. Elena Zdravomyslova, Anna Rotkirch, and Anna Temkina. Saint Petersburg: European University Press, 2009. 189–221. Print.

Gurova, Olga. "'We are Not Rich Enough to Buy Cheap Things': Clothing Consumption of the St. Petersburg Middle Class." *Rethinking Class in Russia*. Ed. Suvi Salmenniemi. Burlington, VT and Farnham, England: Ashgate Publishing, 2012. 149–166. Print.

Heiman, Rachel, Carla Freeman, and Mark Liechty. Introduction: Charting an Anthropology of the Middle Classes. *The Global Middle Classes: Theorizing Through Ethnography*. Santa Fe: School of American Research Press, 2012. 3–30. Print.

Kondo, Dorinne. *Crafting Selves: Power, Gender, and Discourses of Identity in a Japanese Workplace*. Chicago: University of Chicago Press, 1990. Print.

Ledeneva, Alena. *Russia's Economy of Favours: Blat, Networking and Informal Exchange*. Cambridge University Press, 1998. Print.

Liechty, Mark. *Suitably Modern: Making Middle Class Culture in a New Consumer Society*. Princeton, NJ: Princeton University Press, 2003. Print.

Martin, Emily. *Flexible Bodies*. Boston: Beacon Press, 1995. Print.

Matza, Tomas. "Moscow's Echo: Technologies of the Self, Publics, and Politics on the Russian Talk Show." *Cultural Anthropology* 24.3(2009): 489–522. Print.

"'The Little Army of Psychologists': Experts and the Post-Soviet State". Annual Meeting of the American Anthropological Association, Montreal. 16 November 2011.

"Good individualism"? Psychology, ethics, and neoliberalism in postsocialist Russia. *American Ethnologist* 39.4 (2012): 804–818. Print.

Mazzarino, Andrea. "'The Impossible is Possible': Cultivating Self-Certainty and Community among Muscovites." Annual Meeting of the American Anthropological Association, Montreal. 16 November 2011.

Melin, Harri, and Suvi Salemenniemi. "Class Analysis in the USSR and Contemporary Russia." *Rethinking Class in Russia*. Ed. Suvi Salmenniemi. Burlington, VT and Farnham, England: Ashgate Publishing, 2012. 23–41. Print.

Patico, Jennifer. "To be Happy in a Mercedes: Culture, Civilization and Transformations of Value in a Postsocialist City." *American Ethnologist* 32.3 (2005): 479–496. Print.

———. *Consumption and Social Change in a Post-Soviet Middle Class*. Stanford, CA and Washington, D.C.: Stanford University Press and Woodrow Wilson International Center Press, 2008. Print.

"Spinning the Market: The Moral Alchemy of Everyday Talk in Postsocialist Russia." *Critique of Anthropology* 29.2 (2009): 205–224. Print.

Pesmen, Dale. *Russia and Soul*. Ithaca: Cornell University Press, 2000. Print.

Salmenniemi, Suvi. "Introduction: Rethinking Class in Russia." *Rethinking Class in Russia*. Ed. Suvi Salmenniemi. Burlington, VT and Farnham, England: Ashgate Publishing, 2012. 1–22. Print.

"Post-Soviet *Khoziain*: Class, Self and Morality in Russian Self-Help Literature." *Rethinking Class in Russia*. Ed. Suvi Salmenniemi. Burlington, VT and Farnham, England: Ashgate Publishing, 2012. 67–84. Print.

Rivkin-Fish, Michele "Tracing Landscapes of the Past in Class Subjectivity: Practices of Memory and Distinction in Marketizing Russia" *American Ethnologist* 36.1 (2009): 79–95. Print.

Rotkirch, Anna, Olga Tkach, and Elena Zdravomyslova. "Making and Managing Class: Employment of Paid Domestic Workers in Russia." *Rethinking Class in Russia*. Ed. Suvi Salmenniemi. Burlington, VT and Farnham, England: Ashgate Publishing, 2012. 129–148. Print.

Rytkonen, Marja, and Ilkka Pietila. "Wealth Brings Health? Class, Body and Health in Russia." *Rethinking Class in Russia*. Ed. Suvi Salmenniemi. Burlington, VT and Farnham, England: Ashgate Publishing, 2012. 187–202. Print.

Zdravomyslova, Elena. "Niani: kommertsializatsiia zaboty." *Novyi Byt v Sovremennoi Rossii: Gendernye Issledovaniia Posvednevnosti*. Eds. Elena Zdravomyslova, Anna Rotkirch, and Anna Temkina. Saint Petersburg: European University Press, 2009. 94–136. Print.

"Working Mothers and Nannies: Commercialization of Childcare and Modifications in the Gender Contract." *Anthropology of East Europe Review* 28.2 (2010): 200–225. Print.

Zhang, Li. *In Search of Paradise: Middle-class Living in a Chinese Metropolis*. Ithaca: Cornell University Press, 2012. Print.

"Refashioning the Self through New Therapeutics in Urban China." Emory University, 24 October 2013.

Zigon, Jared. *Making the New Post-Soviet Person: Narratives of Moral Experience in Contemporary Moscow*. Boston: Brill, 2010. Print.

2 The Rise of Reading Campaigns in Post-NAFTA Mexico

Emily Hind

What do you do after having sold blankets, shirts, and sweaters? What do you do?

—Poet Jaime Sabines in an interview with Ana Cruz, cited in Bravo Varela[1]

Introduction to the Middle Class in Mexico

Until recently, Mexicanist scholars tended to ignore the middle class. This lack of academic interest is perhaps surprising given the group's "enormous faith in education," to borrow the wording from Lawrence James's history of the British middle class (James 593). It may not be a coincidence that praise for recent examination of the enrollment-swelling ranks of the Mexican middle class comes at a time of reduced rosters and resources for the Liberal Arts classroom. Respect for the middle class—the sort that prompts academic volumes on the "global middle classes"—may swing upward when that middle sector's crucial interest in the humanities seems to wane. Certainly, the Mexican middle class has been earning new respect among budget-strapped historians as a politically pushy collective, rather than a force of self-absorbed stagnation. In a "transnational" history collection on the middle class, Suzanne Eineigel and Michael Ervin, with separate articles, challenge the notion of the conservative middle and instead view the group as agents of change immediately following the Mexican Revolution. The Latin American Studies Association (LASA) likes this angle of the "edgy middle," and it gave the 2013 Humanities Book Award to Steven B. Bunker's *Creating Mexican Consumer Culture in the Age of Porfirio Díaz*. Bunker notes that during the Porfiriato, a nineteenth-and early twentieth-century dictatorship, Mexico hosted a bourgeois culture that "was as much a cultural as an economic category" (109). This message earned another award when the Mexico section of LASA bestowed the 2014 prize for the Best Book in the Social Sciences on Louise Walker's *Waking from the Dream: Mexico's Middle Classes After 1968*, which also broadens the definition of the middle class to encompass more than an income-determined classification. Walker writes always in the plural "middle classes" because the concept identifies both "a socioeconomic category and a state of mind" (76).

Still, this remains a touchy subject. The preface to the English-language translation of *Mexico: A Middle Class Society. Poor No More, Developed Not Yet* (2010, 2012) acknowledges the passionate disagreement among Mexicans that the first edition provoked:

> Even thinking about Mexico as a middle class seems odd, out of place and, of course, politically incorrect. Venturing to write that Mexico is now mostly a middle-class country has been deemed a provocation by some analysts and politicians accustomed to crafting their public discourse in terms of a an extended and impossible to overcome poverty.
> (De la Calle and Rubio no page)

Indeed, the contentious nature of the "*Poor No More*" thesis may explain the reluctance on the part of authors Luis de la Calle and Luis Rubio to specify the income needed to count as middle class. Instead, the meatiest discussions of the topic couch themselves in terms of deciles 1 through 10, and this rhetoric obscures the difference, for example, between the wealthiest man in Mexico, Carlos Slim Helú, whose fortune *Forbes* magazine estimates at US$77 billion, and the next-to-nothing (or flatly nothing?) sum that the lowest percentile in Mexico possesses. Rihan Yeh analyzes the reaction to De la Calle and Rubio's declaration that Mexico is now a middle-class country in terms of the "we" employed by Internet readers of an article summarizing the books' findings. Those who agree with the "*Poor No More*" optimism define themselves as members of this new identity, against naysayer web users' absence of a "collective subjectivity, whether of the middle class or the pueblo" (197). In line with the revisionist histories then, the contemporary Web users who support the middle class "we" demonstrate the implicit political power of this classification, regardless of its statistical accuracy.

Certainly, the numbers spark debate. A governmental research unit, the National Institute for Statistics and Geography (INEGI), argues that using data such as expenses per capita rather than income results in better information because informants have fewer incentives to "underdeclare" what they spend ("Cuantificando" 2). Spending power interests the relevant analysts, and for example De la Calle and Rubio cite the findings from the Mexican Association of Market Research to frame their argument in terms of consumer rankings. These categories range from the lowest groups of D/E to the highest of A/B; the largest sector of Mexico, 35.8 percent in 2008, falls in the D+ category, $6,800 to $11,599 (De la Calle and Rubio 9).

In his interview-girded study, Dennis Gilbert defines the Mexican middle class as households with incomes at least 50 percent higher than the median (12). Gilbert, to his surprise, discovers growth among this group at the turn of the twenty-first century: "The middle class has fared better in the Neoliberal Era than is commonly believed. By 2000, it was notably bigger, better educated, and more affluent than it was in the early 1980s—trends all the more remarkable given Mexico's uneven economic performance"

(100). INEGI backs Gilbert's early conclusion and in data gathered from 2000 to 2010 the governmental group finds that the national middle class rose by 4 percentage points ("Cuantificando" 5). The INEGI report avoids a definition of the middle class among strict salary numbers and contemplates seven strata; in 2010 the strata of the "middle class" include 42.4 percent of homes, with 39.2 percent of the total national population (3). Given governmental and other researchers' reluctance to settle on precise income levels among their definitions, and given the overwhelming attention paid to consumption habits, education, profession, and assorted household circumstances, it seems that even the mathematically inclined experts prefer a nuanced verbal approach. In the midst of the statistics, they seem mindful of the need to coach aspiration. The circumspect vocabulary may have to do with the possibility of conjuring a "we" into existence by force of suggestion, and it may take into account the moral force that literary critic Kathleen Woodward calls "statistical panic." As Woodward explains, "It is statistics, rather than economics, that should be known as the dismal science" (179). Woodward claims that statistics today inform decisions based on risk calculations of the sort that emerged from the field of epidemiology (199). Possibly, academics and governmental analysts handle statistics gingerly because of the latter's tendency to evoke a "dismal" mood. If a particular frame of mind denotes the middle class, proper management of the always emotionally tinged statistics may help to conjure precisely the sector these invested experts hope to see develop.

What is the Mexican middle-class mindset? One crucial trait is optimism, to judge from a 2011 poll that asked Mexicans to classify their social rank; while 1% labeled themselves as "rich" and 16 percent as "poor," an astonishing 82 percent ranked themselves in the middle class (Castañeda 61). Other countries evince similar statistics; the Latinobarómetro poll from 2007 revealed that nearly four of every five respondents in Chile, Argentina, and Panama considered him or herself part of middle class (Hopenhayn 11). Hard times do not necessarily cancel the majority claim. In the midst of the Great Depression, a 1939 Gallup Poll found that more than 75 percent of the U.S. public rated themselves as middle class, "even when they considered themselves poor" (Hornstein 201–202). The very amorphousness of the category constitutes part of its power (Hornstein 206). In fact, middle-classness may be so persistent because it confounds itself with national identity, an identification that challenges politicians and academics who stake "Mexicanness" in a rhetoric of discouraged financial struggle. That rhetoric may reflect an older tradition that may be giving way to a new national self-image, whether or not the "real" numbers justify the optimism. Aforementioned historian Louise Walker locates this shift toward a middle-class national identity earlier than some readers might expect. In 2013, she shook up the Mexicanist field by proposing that in the mid-twentieth-century, the ruling PRI (Party of the Institutional Revolution) achieved its remarkable stability by forging a pact with the middle classes, who in turn dominated the collective Mexican identity: "[T]he middle classes came to represent the modern, developed Mexico, symbolizing the goal toward which all Mexicans ought to strive" (9).

This change in the national imaginary supports the statistic that De la Calle and Rubio celebrate as happily outdated: "just a half-century ago, 80 percent of Mexicans were poor, and thus, so was the entire country" (31). In 2010, the INEGI-interpreted figures assessed 55.1 percent of homes and 59.1 percent of the population as the euphemistically termed "other side of the social spectrum" ("Cuantificando" 3–4). That report chooses its language so carefully because it makes a distinction between the "lower social class" and the "poor." That is, the report views the condition of poverty as statistically more probable, but not an automatically applicable condition among the lower 55.1 percent of homes due to the mitigating factors of government assistance (4). Despite the double-talk that this report engages on one level, on another the urge to separate poverty from the "lower social class" may serve as a place-marker for future improvement. Twenty-first-century Mexican governmental programs such as "Oportunidades" have expanded and provide meaningful assistance to families able to comply with education and health requirements. That type of conditional governmental aid may justify the government researchers' interest in the distinction between poverty and the experience of the "lower" class. Public benefits that hinge on children's school attendance and health checkups seem aimed, however minimally, at paving the way for those children to fare better than their parents in terms of educational achievement and life expectancy.

Nuance is key in the interpretation of the Mexican middle class. When academic and former Secretary of Foreign Affairs (2000–2003) Jorge Castañeda announces triumphantly in his book from 2011, "Mexico today has become finally a middle-class society," he immediately issues a near retraction, perhaps a wise move in view of the storm of opinions that De la Calle and Rubio weathered. According to Castañeda's hedging, the country is not "definitively nor categorically" a middle-class society because Mexico has "barely passed the bar where paradise begins," and the economy is "still highly vulnerable to relapse" (35). Persistent vulnerability appears reflected in more global discussions of the middle class and its mindset. For example, an otherwise cheery book published by the World Bank admits that two thirds of the population in Latin America and the Caribbean concentrate in the "poor and vulnerable classes," even though in 2009, for the first time in history, one in three people in these same regions lived with a per capita income greater than $10 per day, which "integrates" them into the ranks of the middle class (Ferreira et al 146). Here, it seems evident why strict salary divisions do not supply the favored rhetorical strategy. A per capita income of $11 a day is not enough to become middle class in many contexts, and yet conceivably such a minimal fortune could represent a stronger financial foothold for some situations. Regardless of the intricacies of context, it seems precarious in the twenty-first century to claim middle-class status on $11 per day. With good reason, then, scholars often describe the middle-class mood as teetering between the "enthusiasm of joining in and the fear of falling out" (Franco and Hopenhayn 26).

The following analysis contemplates attempts to manage that mercurial collective mood through pro-reading publicity in Mexico. Twenty-first-century Mexican emphasis on the value of reading has funded traveling book fairs, free books passed out in the metro, expanded school libraries, new public reading rooms, reforms for book markets and education, and intensified interest in organizing the supply of reading materials for elementary school students. The privately and publicly funded publicity surrounding the promotion of reading has met with doubtful educational results. The publicity trades on the middle-class faith in education and likely manages aspirations and anxieties more than it wants to procure sweeping change.

The Underlying Binary: Literacy Skills over Literary Appreciation

In his world history of debt, David Graeber notes the paradox of the best functioning capitalism as a wildly optimistic gamble balanced by predictions of apocalypse. At the same time that healthy capitalism fears dips and dives in the market, it also "enshrines the gambler as an essential part of its operation" (Graeber 357). Evidently, the middle-class optimism regarding education enables pro-reading campaigns to benefit from the pessimistic manipulation of statistics, as per Woodward's notion of "statistical panic," in ways that manage anxiety in a crash-prone system. For instance, note the moral force in statistics employed in iconic advertising for the Mexican bookstore Gandhi. The bright yellow ads featuring black or purple lettering aim to appeal to people who can already read and, especially, to middle-class readers because that group has the disposable income to spend on Mexico's relatively expensive new books. The Gandhi website keeps a marketing archive organized by year of such goading catchphrases as: "Schools should teach reading" (2003), "Break a record: read a book" (2004), "Four hours daily of television and half a book a year. Way to go, Mexico!" (2003), "Come and form part of the 5%" (2004), "Nine of ten Mexicans read. In their dreams" (2008), "Accepting that you don't read is the first step" (2012), "The reader: Endangered species" (2013), and "Like this, but 20 minutes minimum" (2013). That last command alludes to the reading campaigns sponsored by the business association known as the Council of Communication (Consejo de la Comunicación), the self-anointed "Voice of Businesses" (Voz de las Empresas), which advocates a twenty-minute-daily reading habit (Martínez). Following the Council, some governmental messages urge Mexicans to read for twenty minutes each day (Aguilar Sosa). The "twenty minute" standard revises the original promotion of "Just 5 minutes a day" (2009) on a Gandhi billboard that promises, "Immediate results!" (Gandhi). It would seem that the Council of Communication and the governmental campaigns affected the Gandhi bookstore slogans, and in turn it is a safe bet that the cheeky Gandhi advertising style influenced these other efforts. All sides apparently want to manage the middle-class belief in education as a counterbalancing force to that group's dread of instability, which limits the gambles that this class might otherwise take. In fact, in framing the notion of "statistical panic," Woodward refers to Ulrich Beck's claim that the industrial society has evolved into a risk society, defined as a society that fears risk itself (Woodward 180). This risk society, haplessly subject to unsteady markets, has everything to do with a middle-class mindset because precisely that group has so much to lose, unlike the bottom ranks, and contradictorily, so little wealth to help them recover from major losses, unlike the topmost layers.

Although the words "middle class" never appear in the Mexican pro-reading ads, a slick and almost ineffable image of this status saturates the campaigns. The trick of analyzing this publicity hinges on contemplating, as if from a distance, the middle-class ideal, which is of course never significantly distanced from professional scholarship. Oddly perhaps, given the power of numerically couched forecasts, current middle-class thought on the value of reading retains a nineteenth-century paradigm that happily proposes a difference between disciplined literacy skills and dreamy literary appreciation. In other words, the middle-class mindset suffers significant ambivalence when it comes to the idea of funding "progress-oriented" education that ignores the artistic and aesthetic categories of human achievement. The pro-reading campaigns prove insensitive to that ambivalence in the same way that much presidential discourse fails to acknowledge the benefits of what might be termed imaginative and "inefficient" art appreciation. Of course, to make the argument that art matters for non-statistical reasons is simply to champion middle-class ideals, rather than to analyze them.

A clever historical articulation of middle-class support for the two reading levels—both literacy and literary abilities—appears in Thomas Pfau's analysis of *Wordsworth's Profession*. According to Pfau, the British poet's shrewd marketing of texts helped to transform an amorphous public into a "cohesive middle-class community that believed it had distinguished itself through its seemingly unlimited imaginative mobility" (Pfau 9). That is, Wordsworth framed the reading of literature in both transcendent and pragmatic terms by encouraging the middle class to treat poetry on the one hand as an aesthetic object destined for consumption, indicative of the greatness of the consumer's spirit, and on the other hand, as a material to be experienced in "an essential *productive* manner" (7). This bifurcation eventually leads to the Neoliberal Era education discourse that, to judge from the germane publicity, prefers practical skills over less efficient matters of emotional quests, empathetic experiments, canonical mastery, and the creative pause that hunts for deeper meaning. By contrast to that restricted focus, the traditions of the middle class encompass a multicity of approaches. Just like middle-class professionalism that views work as both a spiritual "calling" and a pragmatic means of social contribution, middle-class reading practices confuse leisure and labor, perhaps as an anxiety-reducing technique and not just as preparation to face the next day better armed with more information. Peter Gay's Eurocentric examination of *The Making of Middle-Class Culture, 1815–1914* notes that in the face of "intractable uncertainties in the public arena," the middle-class Victorians' ideal home life privileged the notion of a "close-knit, harmonious family intent on absorbing high culture in its leisure hours" (285). Gay believes that industrial innovations brought about seemingly unpredictable waves of change, and thus the middle class wished to duck for cover in a counterbalancing realm of free-time study that invested art with both practical and transcendent value. Such an idealized and placid domestic withdrawal, familiar to the middle-class mindset since the nineteenth century then, may have something to do with the current official support in Mexico for literacy skills, especially to the degree that literary imagination can be postulated as divisible from the disciplined act of reading.

At the very least, the split value between practical literacy ability and high-flying literary imagination explains how Peña Nieto won the presidential election in 2012 after proving himself a grossly inept reader of literature, but still a literate man. The presidential candidate's lack of familiarity with a personal library emerged at the International Book Fair in Guadalajara (FIL) with a journalist's "easier" question that asked for books that had influenced Peña Nieto's life. The presidential candidate never lost his reassuring tone of authority, but floundered as he attempted to list authors and titles, eventually confusing fiction writer Carlos Fuentes with historian Enrique Krauze (Guevara Ramos 222). A report on this mistake in *The Economist* couches Peña Nieto's gaffe in terms of the middle class, perhaps because this group is expected to manage both levels, that of intimate personal artistic appreciation and that of school-coached, skills-based experience: "Some middle-class adults set a poor example: book lovers cringed when Enrique Peña Nieto [...] seemed stumped when asked at Guadalajara to name three books that had made a mark on him" ("Publishing"). The event is preserved on YouTube with a video that has attracted in almost four years more than three million views ("Libros"). That scandal notwithstanding, Mexican tradition disdains literary learning, as distinguished from basic literacy skills. One historian notes that military figure and sometime president of nineteenth-century Mexico, José Antonio López de Santa Anna, "boasted that he had never read a big book and delegated the writing of letters, the composition of speeches, and the fashioning of public manifestos to underlings" (Ruiz 66). A visit to Chapultepec Castle, a museum in Mexico City where dictator Porfirio Diaz's study is preserved, reveals a plaque on the end-of-the-nineteenth- and beginning-of-the-twentieth-century president's consistent spelling mistakes, which he never bothered to correct. Battle-honed leaders tended to gain power from gutsy, law-breaking moves, and once in power they may have worried that their image as fearsome men of action would decline if others suspected any submission to the rule of spelling and grammar.

Gabriel Zaid observes that only in the mid-twentieth century did Mexican self-understanding begin to modify the archetypical assumption that "men of books" lack common sense, and it suddenly became important for politicians to hold university degrees (*De los libros* 11). Still, as Zaid points out, a university degree does not guarantee an affinity for books, which explains how the educational rates can rise without handily rescuing the publishing industry. Percentages have grown from 1950—when "barely" one in one hundred young Mexicans pursued the BA degree—to much larger numbers, now with twenty-seven out of every one hundred "university-aged" Mexicans studying this degree (De la Calle and Rubio 83). University education does not necessarily produce bibliophiles as Peña Nieto and former President Vicente Fox prove. Fox's visit to the FIL in Guadalajara elicited a journalist's snide comment that the president shook attending young people's hands and advised them to read, but only hypocritically: "Fox arrived without books and he left the same way. He did not apply the advice he gave the youngsters to himself" (González). The same report adds that the previous president, Ernesto Zedillo, did not visit the book fair at all during his six years in office. As middle-class values help to infuse the FIL with more prestige than ever, the longstanding irrelevance of literary knowledge survives, perhaps because transcendent literary appreciation connotes impractical dreaminess. Reading, if undertaken freely, can serve as much more than a pragmatic encounter with content, and thus the public-service attempt to frame the encounter with the text as purely efficient trips certain inconsistencies in the message.

Reading in Context: Privatization Fears

Perhaps the point of some of the ultimately disjointed reasoning advocated in the pro-literacy advertisements is not to inspire the audience to read—and therefore to turn away from the publicity—but to keep the audience *thinking* about reading and turned toward the ads. In support of this suspicion, the publicity bids for attention by constantly renewing itself. President Vicente Fox's "Toward a Country of Readers" (Hacia un país de lectores) in effect from 2003 to 2007, President Felipe Calderón's "Mexico Reads" (México Lee) from 2008 to 2013, and President Enrique Peña Nieto's general call for "Quality Education" find increasingly faithful counterparts in privately funded campaigns. For instance, since 2010 the previously mentioned Council of Communication has released the successive slogans "Read to Learn" (Leer para aprender), "Have Fun Reading" (Diviértete Leyendo), "Read more" (Leer más), and "What Matters Is in Your Head" (Lo que importa está en tu cabeza). The materials from the Council of Communication sometimes flirt with championing change for the sake of change. Under the slogan "Read + More Is Extraordinary," available on its rangy and at times ill-connected web pages, some of which use the main address "www.divierteteleyendo.com" (havefunreading.com), the Council publicizes a blankly activist message with an improperly punctuated sentence: "This movement is not a dream, it is a reality. Change begins by reading." Another version of this ad shows the neck-down image a man opening his button-down shirt to reveal a tee that reads: "For you and for me ... Change begins by reading. Join the movement." The nature of the change set to occur remains vague. Perhaps in order to keep the social shifts moderate enough to ensure that the Mexican leaders behind the presidency and the Council of Communication will remain in power, publicity for the pro-reading "movement" sometimes flirts with nonsensical praise of the image of reading.

For instance, a recent poster available on the Council of Communication's website shows a drawing of a storybook queen laid out in a would-be enticing book next to the caption, "Princess, witch, sorceress, fairy godmother. Let's promote equality. Change begins by reading. 20 minutes a day." The notion of reading twenty minutes a day defies the imaginative release that reading can offer from the measured work world and insinuates a reinsertion of that regulation. Furthermore, equality among princesses, witches, and fairy godmothers disregards the exceptional role that each of these archetypical literary characters plays. In the same advertising series, a pseudo-human rights discourse imparts scrambled logic in poster that asks, "Oz, Narnia, Wonderland, Crypton. What worlds will you leave your children? Change begins by reading. 20 minutes a day." The insinuation that middle-class parents leave a fictional world to offspring perhaps ignores the need for human rights discourse in the here and now. The almost parodic social justice discourse may elicit less wariness from a cynical public when it simply repeats the official message. In the explanation of the "What Matters Is in Your Head" phase of the campaign, slated to run from October 2104 through March 2015, the Council of Communication claims that reading habits support the goal of achieving a "quality education" in Mexico (Nuñez Siller). In the same way, the watchdog force Mexicanos Primero (Mexicans First) has declared on its website that "Only Quality Education Changes Mexico" (Sólo la Educación de calidad cambia a México). This same non-profit group researched the information presented in the muckraking documentary on Mexican public education, *¡De Panzazo!* (Barely Passing) (2012). Like the government, Mexicans First trusts in standardized test scores, and on the ten guiding principles stated on the group's website, belief number six reasons in painful hyperbole, "What isn't evaluated can't be improved."

The principle of statistical panic warns that the test scores used to inform public opinion may facilitate a negative assessment, and certainly the tests as they are crunched into easily publicized statistics can be slanted to whip up panic among parents that their children are not learning the skills needed to survive and rise in a complex economy. Standardized test scores in Mexico have been falling even as the pro-reading publicity has intensified, which means that the pro-reading publicity has it both ways when it bemoans the test scores and thereby bolsters the urgency of the moral message, which instead of conveniently solving the "problem" defends the continuing campaigns ("Read MORE"). In example of the declining test results, the Mexican national ENLACE study found in 2008 that 47.7 percent of tested students failed to read at an adequate level; four years later, the number of poor readers expanded to reach the 50 percent mark. That is, in 2013 of more than one million students tested, 50 percent could not understand what they read in Spanish—or to put this finding another way, about half the students tested in Mexico scored at "insufficient and elemental" reading levels (Enlace). Another study, this one from the Mexican Foundation for the Promotion of Reading (Fundación Mexicana para el Fomento de la Lectura), claimed in 2012 that national reading habits have declined from the year 2006. The 2012 numbers calculate that total book readers fell 10 percent from 2006 to 2012, and that more than half the national population "does not read books anymore" (Fundación 21). Even an online article sponsored by a television channel spreads the intended-as-dismal news that according to UNESCO findings, only 2 percent of Mexicans have a "real habit of reading" (Ortiz). Perhaps the most-often cited incendiary statistic repeats the governmental finding that per capita for those over twelve years of age the national average of books read per year stands at 2.9 (CONACULTA 36). Fortunately for the national mental health, not all onlookers succumb to the numerically based anxiety.

Susan Meyers, for one, doubts these "rhetorics of literacy crisis" (31). The non-readers blamed for the national "problem" are not illiterate, in Meyers's view, "but rather strategic in the ways in which they invest their energies in literate skills that serve their specific needs" (32). The sheer quantity of text-based materials about the alleged Mexican illiteracy crisis certainly ought to give pause to the panicked. This abundance of written text, which by definition requires a literate public, anticipates the existence of some positive literacy findings, which include a UNESCO report from 2011 that pegged literacy rates in Mexico at 93.4 percent of persons over age fifteen, and 98.5 percent of people aged fifteen to twenty-four (UNESCO). Turn-of-the-previous-century cultural critics would have rejoiced over those numbers. From 1895 to 1910 only a small percentage of Mexicans could read; during that period national literacy rates slowly grew from 14.4 percent to 19.7 percent (Gonzales citing Vaughan 526). After the Mexican Revolution, the newly created Department of Public Education (SEP) saw illiteracy as a threat to patriotic spirit and aimed to teach people who resided in the countryside "not only to read and write but also to embrace their place in the new nation" (Joseph and Buchenau 109). Secretary of Education José Vasconcelos spearheaded the effort to alphabetize post-Revolutionary Mexico, and this longtime book lover made cheap editions of "classics" available to those would-be readers aspiring to the middle classes. By 1960, the newly nationalist population scored a record high literacy rate of 62.2 percent (Greer

467). Nevertheless, contemporary public discussion in Mexico laments the fact that the country's test scores do not compare favorably with those of Sweden, Finland, Japan, Canada, or the U.K. Instead of post-Revolutionary patriotism and an appreciation of the literary canon, the contemporary terms of the crisis turn on productivity, that is, literacy skills defined in isolation from less "efficient" elements of literary appreciation.

In evidence of this pro-productivity angle, Peña Nieto's National Plan for Development, 2013–2018, released on May 20, 2013, sets the third of five national goals as creating a "Mexico with Quality Education," ahead of improving the economy at number four. This ambitioned national education seems more attuned to the "Mechanical" than "Liberal" Arts in the presidential wording:

> Lack of education is a barrier to the country's productive development as it limits people's ability to communicate efficiently, work in teams, solve problems, effectively use informational technology to adopt high-level processes and technologies, as well as to understand the environment in which we live and innovate.
>
> (Plan Nacional de Desarrollo)

In order to persuade the audience attuned to middle-class ideals regarding this would-be non-transcendent, grittily pragmatic education, the administration employs the fearsome lash of statistical panic. On September 8, 2013, the first year of President Enrique Peña Nieto's term, Secretary of the Treasury Luis Videgaray emphasized gloomy percentages in nine of the ten financially oriented points, beginning with the idea that in the last thirty years the national economy grew, on average, "a mediocre 2%," thanks to the lack of growth in productivity, which contracted yearly since 1990 by –0.4 percent (Córdova). Treasury Secretary Videgaray continued to spin a dreadful statistical narrative: 45.5 percent of the Mexican population lives in poverty, the same percentage as thirty years ago; 61.2 percent of Mexicans lack access to social security; 60 percent of the population works in the informal economy, where business productivity is 45 percent less than the formal sector; public spending as a percentage of GDP is only 19.5 percent, against 27.1 percent in the rest of Latin America and 46.5 percent in the other OCDE countries (Córdova). By the time Videgaray arrived at point eight out of ten, anxiety had been primed as the interpretative key for the news that 30 percent of the adult population in Mexico is obese.

The moral authority drawn from epidemiology that Woodward traces to statistical panic seems tailor-made for fat panic. The statistic was meant to justify Peña Nieto's proposed and ultimately approved value-added (IVA) tax on soft drinks and junk food. Books once again escaped the IVA tax, perhaps because on a metaphorical level reading is seen to combat "fat." The class status associated with books seems key here: reading is not a physically laborious activity; it does not actually "burn fat," and yet the reading campaigns feature almost no overweight models, with the exception of the occasional portly (and older) celebrity. Not one photograph of a noticeably fat child or teen appears in the pro-reading campaigns, in a country with something like one-third of children rated as overweight by the number-crunchers. This insinuated healthy quality attributed to books begs the question of whether Mexico is prepared for the consequences if more citizens begin to "get in shape" and read.

To judge from the numbers, Mexico cannot reliably uphold the literacy contract, which Meyers defines as "an implicit agreement in which schools require student compliance and promise economic reward in return" (63). Mexico is the only country in an OECD report from 2012 with an unemployment rate among tertiary-educated individuals that is higher (at 5 percent) than the rate for those who attained an upper secondary education (at 4.6 percent) and for those without an upper secondary education (who are unemployed at a 4 percent rate) (OECD 5).The OECD notes that this employment pattern in Mexico has remained stable for more than a decade (5). Data gathered by researchers Moreno-Brid and Ros notes that for the groups with a relatively high educational level—at least a decade of school—the percentage of young people employed in the low-productivity occupations of the informal sector in Mexico increased from 1989 to 2002; among those young people with thirteen and more years of formal schooling, their numbers in the informal sector rose a whopping 40 percent (Moreno-Brid and Ros 237). In fact, the authors note, because these groups are the only ones for which the unemployment rate expanded, it seems that "the best trained young people are not finding jobs appropriate to their qualifications" (237). Escobar Latapí and Pedraza Espinoza use the word "cerrazón" (impasse) to describe the contemporary constriction in Mexico of employment opportunities in the private sector for students who are not already economically privileged (369). They cite statistics that suggest that university degrees are increasingly necessary but less "sufficient" in themselves to predict continued membership in highest levels of the middle class (377).

Interestingly, the very categories of the Council of Communication's Reading Olympics (Olimpiada de la lectura)—the fourth of which concluded on November 24, 2014—divide public and private schools and set up certain connotations through the distinct categories of competition that distribute teams of readers from third through sixth grades, in groups of eight students and one teacher, among the ranks of "urban public school, rural public school, private school, and indigenous school." The arrangement hints that these classifications respect qualitatively different levels of education that would compete unfairly without initially separate ranks. It is possible that the prevailing contemporary context encourages the assumption that "private schools" mean the best ones. The tight overlap between government and business messages suggests a problem here: business leaders may not have public welfare in mind as they pose their advertising as a public service. After all, what better faction than private interests to suggest the superiority of the private? A conflation of public and private roles repeatedly figures in the Council of Communication press releases. The Council celebrates its educational campaigns with events that host marquee political guests, and on April 15, 2013, Peña Nieto opened the official Mexican residence, Los Pinos, to host the ceremony marking the change of leadership for the Council of Communication ("Propone"). Peña Nieto convened his cabinet secretaries of the Interior, Finance, Education, and Labor to witness the change of power in the Council from Pablo González Guajardo of Kimberly Clark Mexico to Ángel Alverde Losada of Office Depot. The confusion thickens in light of the Council's website, which sometimes insinuates responsibility for publicly funded events: note the post of an advertisement for a Mexico City Book Fair slated for October, 2014, organized by Mexico City's local Secretary of Culture.

A similar blurring of public and private resources emerges with the Council's website publicity for the "Read MORE" challenge of 2014; the Council lists 117 participating businesses, among which appear the public Department of Transportation for the State of Puebla, and corporations such as American Express, the television conglomerates Azteca and Televisa, cement maker Cemex, the grocery chains Comercial Mexicana, Grupo Chedraui, and Walmart, technology companies Dell, Hewlett-Packard, IBM, Microsoft, GE, and Google, and many other capitalist enterprises ("Reto 'Leer MAS' 2013"). These brands surely seek to promote more than just reading habits as they reiterate the governmental message; they inevitably promote the very concept of brands, and their brands in particular, as solutions to an implied problem.

Some articulate observers of Peña Nieto's plan for "Moving Mexico" fear that the president means to throw support toward the privatization of the school system (Martin). The middle-class opinion may fall either way on this issue. By the 1980s degrees from public institutions had already undergone a cultural devaluation in Mexico, which coincided with a rise in private school enrollments: "Enrollment in private postsecondary institutions increased 92 percent between 1980 and 1990; in comparison, enrollment in public institutions increased 40 percent" (Walker 167). Another statistic shows that from 1984 to 2000, the portion of elementary school students in private institutions grew nationally "by more than half" (Gilbert 99). In the last few decades, the average number of years of formal education among Mexicans has doubled, reaching 8.3 years in 2006, and overall educational coverage has tripled, when measured from 1980 to 2009 (De la Calle and Rubio 47). Private education has helped to fill the gap, although at a hefty price tag. This costly education helps to explain why, among the "university aged" group of young people in Mexico, only 8 percent of the enrolled university body issues from the 40 percent of the poorest Mexicans, while 32 percent of the university enrollment stems from 40 percent of medium income families (De la Calle and Rubio 83). It takes money to study, and yet not all expensive education is worth the investment.

An editorial from 2013 Printed in the leftist newspaper *La Jornada* points out that private schools do not necessarily outperform public ones. A comparison of the standardized ENLACE test results reveals that between 15 percent and 35 percent of the private schools elicit good evaluations, while 65 percent of them score below the average for public schools (Calderón Alzati). The editorial fears that if 17 percent more students enroll in private school, and thus end up comprising 33 percent of the total eligible population in private schools, the resulting "supermillionaire" education business would spell trouble: its "total economic and social cost to the country would certainly be disastrous" (Calderón Alzati). Exactly why that shift toward privatization would be calamitous remains unspecified, but others share the concern. Joining the chorus of worriers, Escobar Latapí and Pedraza Espinoza's heavily researched study of the Mexican middle class cautions that private education is not necessarily better than public. They note that some private universities have opened multiple campuses, as many as ten and thirty branches in two instances, which dilutes these costly institutions' "promises of privilege" (Escobar Latapí and Pedraza Espinoza 372). The holdout private universities that remain more exclusive and, therefore, difficult to enter for applicants who do not already come from a privileged background only aggravate the education divide. The researchers summarize the dilemma as follows: "for the lower middle class, sending children to a second-rank private institution has become a forced option" (Escobar Latapí and Pedraza Espinoza 390). These same academics warn that it would be of serious consequence for the middle class's "constitution, reproduction, and cost of living" if the Mexican government were to withdraw support from higher public education (378). The pro-reading publicity may manage this diffuse anxiety regarding increased education costs by conflating the "Voice of Businesses" with that of the government and declaring a relatively empty but highly self-serving call for change.

Steady-State Activist Advertising: Heated Desire and Cool Imagination

The propagandistic recommendation to read twenty minutes a day, as if reading were a chore or duty in the first instance, promotes disciplined literacy skills over meandering literary ones. The need to restrain "inefficient" or "unproductive" reading pleasure seems to influence a trio of posters produced by the Council of Communication for elementary school students in the "Have Fun Reading" campaign. These posters impart reading tips that fall under a central subheading, which at first glance reinforces the literary and not literacy angle: "You have a magical power: to turn letters into stories!" The notion of magic would seem to lend support to dreamily indulgent "literary" pursuits. However, another underlying message curbs this would-be freedom in fantasy. The poster for students in fifth and sixth grades advertises the limitations of this "magic" power as hemmed in by conformist consumption: "If you don't know what to read, go to a bookstore and ask for the most popular book. For sure it's the one in style." The idea that reading is fun if a would-be reader buys *the* fashionable book—and thus reads not necessarily what s/he wants to read, but what everyone else is *capable* of reading due to high prices, monopolistic markets, and the strong influence of television and cinema over book sales—seems to touch on routine matters of consumption rather than creative literary experiments with imagination. Reading as cast by advertising in the role of "trendy activity" provides an impossible escape from capitalism, an only hypothetically "magical" release that actually responds to financially entangled consumer styles.

The literacy argument that poses reading as productive labor, which dutifully restrains the literary imagination, finds support in the mathematical accounts kept by the campaign. The Council's publicity uses famous athletes to promote reading, including professional soccer and football players, cheerleaders, and more, and under this sporty approach, books seem to point the way to winning "scores." Logically then, in view of the "training" that sports demand, the "Read MORE!" (Leer MÁS) posters that the Council produced for the 2013 campaign allege productivity in the surpassed goal of "5,377,009.5" hours spent reading and more than 90 books recommended. In February 2014, the Read MORE website announced that the 2013 goal had ultimately been exceeded by one million hours: the total reading time added up to "8 million 994 thousand 346 hours" and in two years reached the grand total of "15 million 669 thousand 278 hours of reading, impacting more than 380 collaborators and families" ("Reto 'Leer MAS' 2013"). The new goal, established for 2014, aimed for nine million hours, which would add up to a three-year total of "twenty-three million hours of reading" ("Reto 'LEER MAS' 2013"). Because these hours are probably not all coming from the work day, but borrowed from leisure time, the publicity must convince people to invest free time into the newly defined "discipline" or even "competition" of reading. Not surprisingly, the dominant angle for this efficiency-minded and pleasure-oppressing argument favors elements drawn from visual media. For example, the Council of Communication's advertising often features a backwards "E" in the capitalized variations of the word "READ." Many of the videos place the word "READ" (LEER or LEE) near the bottom of the screen and allow the letter "E" to rotate and finally end up in reverse, with cartoon-inspired spunk. The posters also harness graffiti-like energy by flipping the "E" backwards. Visual media further informs the selection of celebrities from the big and small screens featured in many of the ads. Perhaps the most bizarre example of movie stardom appears in the latest round of publicity, released in October 2014, with a poster that pairs a photo of a Star Wars storm trooper with the slogan "What Matters Is In Your Head" (as usual, the command "READ" reverses the "E"). Fans of Star Wars will know that storm troopers do not have much of anything in their robotic heads, except for Darth Vader's orders.[2]

Lest it seem that only private initiative engages in such nonsensical ploys, an example from the State of Mexico's "Read to learN" ("Leer para creceR") program riffs on the Council's design and capitalizes the first and last letters of the slogan, which make little sense in literary terms because no resulting pun emerges. Possibly, the last letter means to illustrate growth, but such clumsy capitalization falls short of an easily legible literary trope. Under this unliterary pro-reading title, the state government program requires students to fill out online book reports. A search on YouTube for official campaign materials turns up as the top result a homemade video narrated by an adult male, Irving Hernández, who explains to parents—and obviously to students as well—how to cheat on the book reports by cutting and pasting from already-completed texts available on the web ("YouTube Leer para Crecer o Crecer para Leer Edo mex."). As of March 9, 2015, this website had attracted 41,582 visits, 9 thumbs down, and 15 thumbs up. Would-be cheaters must have access to an Internet connection in order to complete their online homework, which suggests middle-class status. It may be that parents and students from the middle classes are interested in learning how to cheat because the family's literacy skills already strike them as satisfactory, or at least that is the suspicion that Meyers's analysis coaches.

Incidentally, the matter of whether a tutorial on cheating attracts hits mostly from parents or mostly from students brings up the confusing issue of the target audience for these various messages. Does the Star Wars storm trooper speak to the middle-aged generation that received the film when it first appeared or to the younger demographic that watches the prequels? Historically speaking, the answer is a double "yes." When it comes to reading, the Mexican middle class does not necessarily require age-specific publicity, at least according to the history lesson from cultural critic Carlos Monsiváis, who reviews a one-size-fits-all approach prevalent in the comic book industry of mid-twentieth-century Mexico; comic book censors practiced a paradoxical tolerance for texts "Suitable for children aged eight to eighty" (589). In the same style, much of the contemporary pro-literacy advertisements simply appeal to the ability to read, and anyone with that skill is welcome to admire the literacy cause. After all, until the 1990s Mexican publishers did not bother to cultivate much in the way of reading materials for children and bookstores did not offer much space for these materials.

Exceptions exist to the "age eight to eighty" rule of thumb. The latest round of publicity, for the first time, has the Council of Communication framing young people as the target "agents of change" who can spread the pleasure of reading to "children and society" ("'Lo que importa'"). Interestingly, the publicity report stresses the idea of young people's engagement or ability to "commit" (comprometerse), a verb perhaps closely associated in mid-twentieth-century Mexico with political radicalism (Nuñez Stiller). According to the sloppily drafted copy, the pro-reading materials mean to attract young people by imitating their values, and applauding "individuality," as well as teens' "freedom" to "express themselves, dress, and be young;" for critics, it will be obvious that these lauded qualities advance a consumption value, expressed as respect for stylistic diversity and a fashionably "retro" nostalgia for mid-century ideals of committed activism. This confusion of hot political activism and cool consumption standards recalls the twenty-first-century $500 peso bill, which today features communist party members and sexual adventurers Frida Kahlo (on one face of the bill) and Diego Rivera (on the flip side). It seems that Rivera and Kahlo are supposed to convey an idealized middle-class willingness to take creative risks that turn out to be massively profitable. Sarah Brouillette's ideas help to signal the problems inherent in posing Kahlo and Rivera as model "creative" types. Brouillette notes that the mystique of the nineteenth-century bohemian artist serves the Neoliberal ideal of flexibility; although the iconoclast artist appears at odds with the capitalist system that turns artwork into money, the artist's very precariousness and vulnerability as an informally employed but driven worker postulates the reputed "psychology of creativity" as best stimulated under conditions of insecurity and overload; the artist fails to distinguish labor from leisure and forges a feverish career of alleged self-sufficiency that demands careful distance from collective politics and social responsibility (52, 56). Such an image fails to account for Kahlo's and Rivera's interest in Communism, but the Mexican government apparently overlooks that allegiance in the first place. Despite the post-NAFTA placement of artists on the $500-peso bill, it would be incorrect to assume that the middle-class values art only for its ability to generate monetary profit from uncertain labor conditions.

The relative inarticulateness of many press releases about the Council of Communication elicits criticism from Juan Domingo Argüelles, who grouses, "Reading's biggest problem is that people who don't read recommend it" ("Al compás"). Domingo Argüelles recognizes the incompatibility of imaginative literary reading with much of the pro-reading approach when he notes that the literacy push aims for a superficial "culture *express*: memorized, quantitative, and epidermal"—perhaps a perfect summary of the "rushed culture" that shrugs at the incongruent presence of Kahlo and Rivera on capitalist currency ("Educación y lectura"). Further evidence of "epidermal" literacy programs appears with a spot from 2010 sponsored by Council of Communication that depicts an anonymous father reading a fairy tale to his son and daughter on a picnic blanket. The acted-out picture book that the father shares takes reading to the level of theater. Computer graphics complete the conversion of the father into the antagonist hairy beast mentioned in the narrative, and thereby the home audience is meant to understand how this banal reading could be gripping. Even more interesting than the all-in-good fun, no-thanks-to-Freud wolf-father, is the remarkably redundant "magic" that the computer animation attributes to the power of reading. The graphics for the spot draw over the natural setting and impose an assortment of animated birds, flowers, bunnies, and red apples. While it may be true that some parks in Mexico lack birds, flowers, rabbits, and fruit, for the purposes of pro-reading publicity it seems unimaginative to add these elements to already manicured outdoor scenery.

The implicitly applied restrictions on the literary imagination find a different articulation with a representative spot from the third phase of the Council of Communication's "Have Fun Reading" series. Soap opera and movie actor Ana Claudia Talancón, who laughs for the camera with nary a book in sight, smiles winsomely through the declamation of the first two lines of "Hombres necios" (Stubborn men), the famous feminist poem by colonial writer Sor Juana Inés de la Cruz. For its levity and brevity, the spot hints that Talancón may not be able to recite more than the first two lines of the text. Perhaps only similarly curtailed portraits of the power of imagination would select an actor as an ideal spokesperson for reading. The technique of intermittently allowing Talancón to voice over her own seductive presence makes for a relatively inarticulate image of someone at times overcome with the giggles. Because the spot begins with a clapperboard and Talancón claims that she reads often due to her work, the aesthetics emphasize the role of performer over that of reader. This implicit issue of personal finances, nonetheless, turns reading into the perfect plug for a movie star. In the public eye, a celebrity *is* his or her job, and this lucrative personification of work can be envied as a spectacular achievement, which explains how, in the would-be pragmatic context of the campaign, the call to invest twenty minutes of leisure time in disciplined "work" can come to seem reasonable.

This star power of personifying professionalism that may explain why the "Have Fun Reading" series produces another video with the famous *lucha libre* wrestler "Místico" (Mystic), who stars in an exaggerated version of Talancón's spot. Due to Místico's fragmented testimonial voice-over, and because the celebrity speaks through a mask that obscures entirely his mouth and facial expression, the spectator must take it on faith that Místico is, in fact, articulating his love of reading rather than gesticulating erratically in front of the camera. Near the end of the spot, without fully tensing his muscles, Místico raises both fists in a friendly boxing stance; this gesture baffles. The "fun" of reading is never described explicitly as a fight, and the narrative never specifies the connection. To counter the nonsensical qualities, Místico employs redundancy and so verbally, at least, stays on message. The wrestler lists the repetitive reasons that he likes to read: "It is a way of learning, cultivating myself, bettering myself." Místico concludes the spot with another rhetorical trio by recommending that parents share with children twenty minutes a day of reading so that the kids can "learn, imagine, and have fun." Místico's script seems to aim for a presentation of the act of reading—suitable for ages eight to eighty—as both magically imaginative and a substance tightly controlled by redundant phrasing and the twenty-minute-a-day habit.

Some lines from Místico's dialogue reoccur with a "Have Fun Reading" spot anchored by married actors Ingrid Coronado and Fernando del Solar. The latter adds to Místico's message that reading to children, "is a very cool [muy padre] way to stimulate their imagination." The middle-class's consumerist, fashionable longing to be cool *and* hot, that is, both coolly consuming and hotly fashionable, is—in a word—hallucinatory. The very point of imagination, as opposed to other forms of thought, is that it roams freely, not coolly or fashionably. Although the Council of Communication and even the Mexican government may want to restrain the "unproductive" and fantasizing impulse of reading—of reading just to read—sooner or later more than literacy goals end up implicated. That indulgence is what addictive leisure habits, rather than disciplined work practices, trigger. With only a little exaggeration, it can be said that enjoyable reading activity cultivates a certain kind of madness, captured in the excessive fantasies of the protagonists of *Don Quijote* and *Madame Bovary*, who see giants where there are windmills or romantic heroes where there are only regular joes. It wouldn't do to have the middle-class mindset latch on to such wildly creative escapism, for one thing because such excess might relax the group and weaken the panic at the statistics needed to curb the gambling impulse. In other words, self-motivated love of literature risks more than the pragmatic skills of the Council's campaign that simply want to imagine extra birds in a park. The "Have Fun Reading" campaign unconvincingly, for book lovers, points to a limited "literacy" ability rather than "literary" imagination; such a limited literacy is perhaps meant to provide a tame kind of aspiration to social mobility, the mildly fantastic sort of aspiration imagined as separate from quantifiable material improvement in the way that imagining flowers in a park harmlessly decorates the tangible urban environment. What the propaganda may fear is that pleasurable, undisciplined engagement with literature can spark more than fantasies of change. Of course literature, being what it is, refuses efficient proof of such a claim. As Zaid puts this dilemma for the literary critic who would errantly wish to borrow scientific discourse, "Believing or not in books as a means of action is above all just that: to believe or not to believe" (*Los demasiados libros* 51).

Conclusion: On Vitamins, Small Business Owners, and the Movies

Apropos of the benefits to the status quo of controlled imagination, my analysis only appears to switch topics when it turns to Peter Cahn's cynical article on "multilevel marketing" by Mexican companies such as the vitamin supplier Omnilife. Jorge Vergara's notorious company, as demonstrated by Cahn's article, convinces desperately hopeful would-be salespeople to invest money in Omnilife health products in order to peddle them in a vaguely pyramidal scheme. According to Cahn, the publicity for Omnilife endows the items for sale with sacred qualities, which means to lift the products from the realm of "crass materialism," in a gesture reminiscent of Pfau's analysis of Wordsworth's attention to audience (433). On an intuitive level, a fundamental similarity conjoins Omnilife's message of aspiration and that of the reading campaigns. Vergara markets not just vitamins, but optimism: customers hope to make money, and rise in status, by taking the supplements which give the health to sell them, in a possibly deluded but effectively self-perpetuating cycle that many literature professors may recognize when they total the costs incurred to support their professional reading habit. The attraction of Omnilife vitamins and Wordsworth's lyrics involves suspended disbelief in the uncertain payoff of faith, or as Cahn puts it, the possibly misplaced trust in "nebulous promises of access to consumption" (431). Among those with a reasonably adequate diet and competent literacy skills, neither ingesting vitamins nor reading books is strictly necessary. Ergo, the vitamin pitch and the recent pro-reading publicity seek to convince observers that by investing precious resources in vitamins (especially on top of good health) or by reading (drawing on already extant literacy skills), the disciplined customer manifests admirable aspirations; he or she gambles on the shadow of statistical hope of becoming a better producer, and thus a more powerful consumer, which is to say, a more legitimate and less vulnerable member of the ambitioned middle class.

In the end, the anxiety-producing image of the entrenched happy gambler in capitalism, whose most foolish risks put us all in financial danger, brings me full circle to 2010, with the start of the reading campaigns undertaken by the Council of Communication. Another Council-sponsored campaign began around the same time: the pro-Mexican entrepreneurship and small businesses ads of the "Pepe y Toño" series. This message is ongoing with the pro-reading publicity, and for example during the months surrounding June 2014, Mexico City news kiosks, such as those along the Paseo de la Reforma, the Zona Rosa, and the Historic Center, featured images of elderly Mexican writer Elena Poniatowska promoting reading, or images of anonymous models testifying as to the advantages of having taken the leap of starting a business. To review the origins of the pro-business campaign, a spot from 2010 shows fictional business owners Pepe and Toño, and eventually many others, laying hands on one another's shoulders in single file, which in the initial shots seems playful (Pepe y Toño). The final, marching band-inspired trick imagery, as perceived in the insinuated camerawork of an extreme long shot, reveals the pattern formed by this mass of people: a system of gears. A similar spot appears from the Televisa Foundation (Fundación Televisa), the charitable counterpart to the Mexican communications powerhouse Televisa, which created the video "Because there are more and more of us" (Porque cada vez somos más); there, a backwards domino effect shows single-file lines of people magically rising from the ground and back onto their feet. The voice-over explains the effect of what happens when one person decides not to do drugs and convinces someone else to abstain, and as one person refuses to accept corruption and encourages someone else to repeat the act, and so forth. The benevolently framed pitch for the Council of Communication's notion of happy citizen-cogs and Televisa Foundation's idea about vulnerable citizen-dominos who on a good day enjoy reversed gravity, hints at the risks of good faith citizenship.

The very dreaminess of committing to a daily reading habit if one cannot afford books or the time to read them, and the notion of founding a business, if one lacks startup resources and knowledge, suggests that this publicity is perhaps not directed at changing a daily reality but at managing hope and fear. On this note of functional escapism, it is interesting to trace a parallel between the campaigns and commercial Mexican film. Ignacio Sánchez Prado points out that domestic box office hits, *Sólo con tu pareja* (1991), *Ladies' Night* (2003), which incidentally stars Ana Claudia Talancón, *Cansada de besar sapos* (Tired of Kissing Frogs, 2006), and *Amores perros* (2000), use the figure of the publicist or the setting of the advertising agency to connote glamorous Mexico—or at least a glossily middle-class Mexico City (Kindle Locations 1624–1625). In other words, successful Mexican movies promoted the profession of advertising, whose real-life results appear for middle-class moviegoers as they step outside the movie theater and onto the street level in Mexico City. (The same screen-to-sidewalk parallel appears for those Mexicans who cannot afford the movie theater ticket, but consume the same cinema on inexpensive pirated DVDs and then travel to set locations such as the Historic Center of Mexico City.) Now the smash hit *Nosotros los Nobles* (The Noble Family, 2013) follows a wealthy Mexican character with aspirations to start his own business, as he takes entrepreneurial lessons from a street-smart lower-class youth who instantly dismisses unprofitable (read: impractical) ideas. After hearing Sánchez Prado's and Bruce Robbins's musings regarding the contemporary idealization of the entrepreneur at the Modern Language Association's annual conference in January 2015, I am inspired to ask if the figure of the Mexican publicist in film is evolving into the entrepreneur, a message that would find reinforcement in the Pepe y Toño campaign.

Despite the fantasy aesthetics and contradictions, the twenty-first-century publicity campaigns and films remind us that contemporary Mexican statistics provoke real ambitions and anxieties. On the one hand, healthy capitalism does not trust that it will be around forever—and on the other hand, we have to keep the faith. In point of fact, the first line of actor Mauricio Barcelata's testimonial in the Council's reading campaign claims: "For me, reading is ... magic." An animated fish illustrates the point by jumping out and back in the open picture book that Barcelata holds. The implicit lesson suggests that you can teach a man to read a fish, but you can't expect him to eat it. The middle class must constantly reimagine itself, always optimistically training for the best, always anxiously "accumulating hours" as protection from the worst. Government and business interests are probably well advised to continue to channel the faith of the non-reading 50 percent into a public dream, as if into a glass half-full, all the while benefitting from an almost imperceptible stasis amid the volatile fashions that the middle-class mindset helps to conjure. That mindset sustains this delicate arrangement.

Notes

1. All translations are mine. To find the publicity materials discussed, use the campaign catchphrases as keywords in Google search. The "images" section of the Google search engine and the YouTube website turn up the posters and videos, whereas general Google searches will lead to more text-rich materials. The main relevant websites are listed in the bibliography.
2. My description refers to the version of this poster on the Web. During my comings and goings at the TAXCO bus station in Mexico City, from the end of January through the end of June 2015, I spotted an eye-level and plexiglass encased poster of the storm trooper image near a street corner. The poster adds another line to the "What Matters ..." slogan: "Armour protects you. Reading too." This argument still does not make much sense. The storm troopers' armour protects the soldiers so that they may work, mindlessly, for Darth Vader, the antagonist of Star Wars.

Works Cited

Aguilar Sosa, Yanet. "SEP quiere lectores de 20 minutos." *El Universal* Feb 15 2011 Google. Web. 4 Dec 2014.

Bravo Varela, Hernán. "Malversaciones." In *Escribir poesía en México*. Ed. and prologue by Julián Herbert, Javier de la Mora, Santiago Matías. México: Bonobos, 2010. 39–55. Print.

Brouillette, Sarah. *Literature and the Creative Economy*. Stanford: Stanford University Press, 2014. Kindle Edition.

Bunker, Steven B. *Creating Mexican Consumer Culture in the Age of Porfirio Díaz*. Albuquerque: U of New Mexico P, 2012. Print.

Cahn, Peter S. "Consuming Class: Multilevel Marketers in Neoliberal Mexico." *Cultural Anthropology* 23.3 (2008): 429–452. Print.

Calderón Alzati, Enrique. "¿Hacia la privatización de la educación?" *La Jornada* Opinión 5 de octubre de 2013. Google. Web. 10 Nov 2014.

Calomiris, Charles W., and Stephen H. Haber. *Fragile By Design: The Political Origins of Banking Crises and Scarce Credit*. Princeton and Oxford: Princeton UP, 2014. Print.

Castañeda, Jorge. G. *Mañana Forever? Mexico and the Mexicans*. New York: Alfred A. Knopf, 2011. Print.

Conaculta. Encuesta Nacional de Lectura. (Hacia un país de lectores) 2006 Google. Web. Oct 5 2013.

El Consejo de la Comunicación recibe el Premio EFFIE Social 2011. Evento n 21 Oct 2011. 7 Dec 2011. Google. Web. 11 Nov 2014.

Córdova, Carlos Acosta. "Reforma hacendaria de EPN: No IVA alimentos y medicinas; propone eliminar IETU." *Proceso* 8 Sep 2013. Google. Web. 10 Nov 2014.

"Cuantificando la clase media en México: Un ejercicio exploratorio, Resumen." *Instituto Nacional de Estadística y Geografía* (2010): 1–13. Google. Web. 20 Feb 2015.

De la Calle, Luis, and Luis Rubio. *Clasemediero: Pobre no más, desarrollado aún no*. México: Centro de Investigación para el Desarrollo, 2010. Print.

———. *Mexico: A Middle Class Society. Poor No More, Developed Not Yet*. 2010. CIDAC and Woodrow Wilson International Center for Scholars, 2012. Web. 20 Feb 2015.

Diviertetelеyendo.com. "Campaña." (www.divertetelyendo.com.mx) Google. Web. 13 Mar 2015.

Domingo Argüelles, Juan. "Al compás de la OCDE (educación y cultura en México)." *La Jornada Semanal* 743. May 31 2009. Google. Web. Jul 19 2013.

———. "Educación y lectura en México: Una década perdida." *La Jornada Semanal* 835. Mar 6 2011. Google. Web. Jul 19 2013.

Eineigel, Susanne. "Revolutionary Promises Encounter Urban Realities for Mexico City's Middle Class, 1915–1928." In *The Making of the Middle Class*. Eds. A. Ricardo López and Barbara Weinstein. Kindle Edition.

Ervin, Michael A. "The Formation of the Revolutionary Middle Class during the Mexican Revolution." In *The Making of the Middle Class*. Eds. A. Ricardo López and Barbara Weinstein. Kindle Edition.

Escobar Latapí, Agustín, and Laura Patricia Pedraza Espinoza. "Clases medias en México: Transformación social, sujetos múltiples." *Las clases medias en América Latina: Retrospectiva y nuevas tendencias*. Coordinado por Rolando Franco, Martín Hopenhayn, Arturo León. México y Buenos Aires: Siglo XXI, 2010. 355–408. Print.

Ferreira, Francisco H.G., Julián Messina, Jamele Rigolini, Luis-Felipe López-Calva, María Ana Lugo, and Renos Vakis. *La movilidad económica y el crecimiento de la clase media en América Latina*. Washington D.C.: Banco Mundial, 2013. Print.

Franco, Rolando, and Martín Hopenhayn. "Las clases medias en América Latina: Historias cruzadas y miradas diversas." *Las clases medias en América Latina: Retrospectiva y nuevas tendencias*. Coordinado por Rolando Franco, Martín Hopenhayn, Arturo León. México y Buenos Aires: Siglo XXI, 2010. 7–41. Print.

Enlace. Resultado Prueba ENLACE Nacional Julio 2013. PDF. Web. Google. Oct. 5 2013. Fundación Mexicana para el Fomento de la Lectura. "De la penumbra a la oscuridad." (www.lector.mx) 2012. PDF. Google. Web. Oct. 5 2013.

Gandhi. "Publicidad." (www.gandhi.com.mx) Google. Web. 5 Oct 2013.

Gay, Peter. *Schnitzler's Century: The Making of the Middle-Class Culture, 1815–1914*. New York: WW Norton, 2002. Print.

Gilbert, Dennis. *Mexico's Middle Class in the Neoliberal Era*. Tucson: U of Arizona P, 2007. Print.

Gonzales, Michael J. "Imagining Mexico in 1910: Visions of the Patria in the Centennial Celebration in Mexico City." *Journal of Latin American Studies* 39.3 (2007): 495–533. Print.

González, Ívaro. "Visita Fox La FIL, y Se Va Sin Libros." *El Norte* 2. Dec 04 2004. ProQuest Central; ProQuest Newsstand. Web. 24 Aug. 2013.

Graeber, David. *Debt: The First 5,000 Years*. New York: Melville House, 2011. Print.

Greer, Thomas V. "An Analysis of Mexican Literacy." *Journal of Inter-American Studies* 11.3 (1969): 466–76. Print.

Guevara Ramos, Emeterio. *Los medios en la democracia: Enrique Peño Nieto Presidente*. Bloomington, IN: Palibrio, 2012. Print.

Hopenhayn, Martín. "Clases medias en América Latina: Sujeto difuso en busca de definición." In *Clases medias y desarrollo en América Latina*. Eds. Alicia Bárcena and Narcís Serra. Santiago de Chile: CEPAL, Barcelona, España: CIDOB, 2010. 11–37. Print.

Hornstein, Jeffrey M. *A Nation of Realtors: A Cultural History of the Twentieth-Century American Middle Class*. Durham: Duke UP, 2005. Print.

James, Lawrence. *The Middle Class: A History*. London UK: Little, Brown, 2006. Print.

Joseph, Gilbert M., and Jürgen Buchenau. *Mexico's Once and Future Revolution: Social Upheaval and the Challenge of Rule since the Late Nineteenth Century*. Durham: Duke UP, 2013. Print.

"Libros ¿qué ha leído? Peña Nieto." Video on YouTube posted by El Respetable Diario Digital. 3 Dec. 2011. Google. Web. 10 Nov 2014.

"'Lo que importa está en tu cabeza': Nueva campaña del Consejo de la Comunicación para impulsar el hábito de la lectura." 5 Nov 2014. Consejo de la Comunicación Website. Google. Web. 10 Nov 2014.

López, A. Ricardo, and Barbara Weinstein, eds. *The Making of the Middle Class: Toward a Transnational History*. Afterword Mrinalini Sinha. Duke and London: Duke UP, 2012. Kindle Edition.

Martin, Rubén. "Y Peña Nieto movió a México ..." Opinión y Análisis. *El Economista*. Google. Web. Nov 29 2013.

Martínez, Nurit. "Leer 20 minutos al día mejora 30% rendimiento escolar." *El Universal* Sep 26 2011. Google. Web. Oct 5 2013.

Meyers, Susan. *Del otro lado: Literacy and Migration across the U.S.-Mexico Border*. Carbondale: Southern Illinois UP, 2014. Print.

Monsiváis, Carlos. "Laughing Through One's Tears: Popular Culture in Mexico." Transl. Suzanne D. Stephens. In *Literary Cultures of Latin America: A Comparative History*. Vol I. *Configurations of Literary Culture*. Eds. Mario J. Valdés and Djelal Kadir. Oxford UK and New York: Oxford UP, 2004. 557–597. Print.

Moreno-Brid, Juan Carlos, and Jaime Ros. *Development and Growth in the Mexican Economy: A Historical Perspective*. Oxford: Oxford UP, 2009. Print.

Nuñez Siller, Roxana. "Lo que importa está en tu cabeza." *Revista Neo: Marketing on the Go*. Voces de Neo. 6 Oct 2014. Google. Web. 10 Nov 2014.

Organization for Economic Cooperation and Development (OECD). Education at a Glance 2012. Country Note: Mexico. Google. Web. 5 Oct 2013.

Ortiz, Paola. "Quién lee más y mejor en el mundo: Cantidad y calidad los distingue." Univision. Web. 2006. Google. Web. Sep 7 2013.

Pepe y Toño. (www.pepeytono.com.mx) Google. Web. 13 Mar 2015.

Pfau, Thomas. *Wordsworth's Profession: Form, Class, and the Logic of Early Romantic Cultural Production*. Stanford CA: Stanford UP, 1997. Print.

Plan Nacional de Desarollo, 2013–2018. Diario Oficial de la Federación. Government of Mexico website. 20 May 2013. Google. Web. 10 Nov 2014.

"Publishing in Latin America: A Literary Deficit." *The Economist* The Americas. Dec 10, 2011. Google. Web. 10 Nov 2014.

"Reto 'Leer MAS' 2013." 11 Feb 2014. Google. 11 Nov 2014. Web.

Ruiz, Ramón Eduardo. *Mexico: Why a Few Are Rich and the People Poor*. Berkeley: U of California P, 2010. Print.

Sánchez Prado, Ignacio. *Screening Neoliberalism: Transforming Mexican Cinema, 1988–2012*. Nashville: Vanderbilt UP, 2014. Kindle Edition.

Walker, Louise E. *Waking from the Dream: Mexico's Middle Classes After 1968*. Stanford CA: Stanford UP, 2013. Print.

Woodward, Kathleen. "Statistical Panic." *Differences: A Journal of Feminist Cultural Studies*. 11.2 (1999): 177–204. Print.

UNESCO Institute for Statistics (UIS). "UIS Statistics in Brief: Education (all levels) profile: Mexico." Google. Web. Oct 5 2013.

Yeh, Rihan. "A Middle-Class Public at Mexico's Northern Border." *The Global Middle Classes: Theorizing Through Ethnography*. Eds. Rachel Heiman, Carla Freeman, and Mark Liechty. Santa Fe, NM: School for Advanced Research, 2012. Kindle Edition.

Zaid, Gabriel. *De los libros al poder*. Mexico: Océano, 1998. Print.

———. *Los demasiados libros*. Mexico: Océano, 1996. Print.

3 Conflicted Images

Producing and Consuming Images of the Middle Class in China's Media

Xin Wang

Introduction

China's emerging middle class, which numbers 150 million people, has drawn both academic and media interest from scholars in both China and overseas. A number of studies have examined the political, social, and cultural tendencies of this class. The new modern middle class is born out of economic reforms and the restructuring of the labor market. The Chinese Communist Party institutionalized the "Three Represents" theory in 2001 to admit private entrepreneurs, freelance professionals, scientific and technical personnel employed by Chinese and foreign firms and other newly emerged social groups to the party (Lawrence 32–35). The CCP's "Three Represents" idea declares that the Party represents the most advanced productive forces, the most advanced culture and the broadest cross-section of the people. According to the Three Represents theory, the interests of different classes are not in conflict with one another and that the Party can harmoniously represent all classes simultaneously. In addition, China's national legislature, the National People's Congress (NPC), passed the Property Rights Law in 2007. This new law, which undermines the socialist tenet of state ownership of property, intends to protect individuals' ownership rights to all legally obtained properties. These examples of new policies and laws represent ideological changes in class discourse among both CCP leaders and the country's political elites.

In cultural and imaginary space, the construction of social identity of the middle class has become a field of intense symbolic struggle. On one hand, the middle class has been imagined by state media as well as popular media. The image of the middle class has become a popular subject for cultural consumption in Chinese media, film and literature. State media and cultural apparatus have readily given recognition to the rising middle class. On the other hand, State-run and commercial media outlets have targeted the middle class as their primary viewers and audience. They have created productions specifically for the tastes of the middle class. It is precisely against these political, economic and cultural conditions that media and other state cultural apparatus, including the television and film industries, have participated in the construction of social identity of the middle class and played a pivotal role in shaping middle-class consciousness and identity. This chapter intends to examine the role of media in cultural politics of representation, specifically the representation of the middle stratum. Following this broad line of inquiry, this essay intends to answer the following questions: How is the middle class as a social stratum constructed in media? And, how have the media and entertainment industries contributed to public discourses of the middle class in contemporary China?

The article analyzes the 2009 TV series *Dwelling Narrowness* (woju) and the 2010 hit white-collar office worker film *Go! Lala, Go!* (*Du Lala Shengzhi ji*) in order to shed light on the understanding of the social identity and cultural attributes of China's new middle stratum. The plots of both productions are centered on the middle stratum in China and both have received high ratings of viewership. However, two conflicted images of the middle class are produced in the two visual media productions: one successful image and one stressful image of the middle class in pursuing materialistic wealth and home ownership. The chapter juxtaposes the two productions in order to provide a nuanced analysis of the contemporary imagining of the middle stratum.

In the last thirty years of economic reform, Chinese mass media and the entertainment industry have embraced marketization, commercialization, and internationalization. Although the party-state still keeps control over ideology and content of mass media, the profit-driven communication industry has submitted to the capitalist system of consumption and production (Zhao). The state, the market, and independent parties have participated in cultural productions. Meanwhile, the consumption of such media content and productions has become increasingly stratified in order to feed the interests of a more stratified Chinese society.

It is precisely for this reason, the configuration and construction of middle-class identity needs to be understood and explored, particularly in regards to how media have shaped and formed public discourses on class identity and how the Party-state, media, and capital participate in the formation of such class identity. After offering a reflection on the changing relationship between the state and media in China and a discussion of how middle-class status is categorized in China primarily according to profession, I explore in comparative perspective how middle classness is developed in the fiction film *Go! Lala, Go!* (2010) and the television series *Dwelling Narrowness* (2009).

Media in China: The Party-State, Market and Capital

The media founded in the People's Republic of China serve as the embodiment of Mao's ideology of the mass line. It was the duty of the media to draw information "from the masses" and to educate "the masses" with Communist ideology (Zhao). Scholars have noticed how the role of media has changed since the 1980s and how economic development and administrative reform has weakened the Party's control over mass media (J. Chan

70–88). Scholars argue that market reforms have unintentionally liberalized China's media system by stressing the media's entertainment function (Chu 4–21; H. Liu 31–41). Indeed, market reforms have required the media to be financially independent by increasing entertainment content and advertising income. Consequently, the content of the media has shifted from pure political propaganda to an integrated pursuit of political, social, economic, entertainment, and cultural interests (A. Chan 35–51).[1]

Many scholars have described that the Chinese media reform has gone through an experiment of a two-track system (Yu 33–46). That is, a state-controlled news sector worked in combination with a market-oriented entertainment business. While market power has dictated the domestic media and communication industries, the party still controls the backbone of China's media and communication infrastructure and its logic dominates how media are managed. In the rush toward marketization, digitalization and internationalization, the party-state organ media, such as CCTV, People's Daily, the Xinhua News Agency, China Radio International and the China Film Group Corporation, are encouraged and supported by the central government to establish new ventures into the Internet, mobile and other digital broadcasting production and distribution platforms. Private equity and capital have flowed into the media and entertainment industries. State-run media and news agencies are allowed to raise capital through stock markets. For instance, People.com.cn, the Internet portal of the People's Daily, raised 1.4 billion yuan (US$220 million) in its IPO at the Shanghai Stock Exchange Market. China's state-run Xinhua News Agency's Xinhuanet went public in 2014.[2] By raising private capital, the party-state hopes its propaganda arms can help promote China's soft power as well as to develop a thriving domestic media industry.

The triangular relationship between the media, the Party-state, and the market often creates tensions between political goal of the Party-state and the demands of the market. For example, the TV drama *Dwelling Narrowness* was produced as a result of market demand and the logic of the market economy of the Chinese media industry. However, the TV drama was also under political scrutiny and censorship. The show was pulled off the air on Beijing TV and criticized for exploiting the themes of sex and political corruption to seek profits by the director director of the State Administration of Radio, Film and Television (SARFT), Li Jingsheng. In order to survive in the dual logic of the neoliberal market and the socialist state, the media tends to focus on profits and produce media content for entertainment. Entertainment culture dominates the media market. Media productions focus on entertainment values rather than political and moral didactic functions. As Ruth Huang noted in her research that entertainment programs and TV shows are becoming apolitical, lack of moral standards from both the producers and the characters in the productions (155–188). She argues that there is a new kind of Chinese realism in popular media culture. TV productions emphasize living conditions, hedonism and materialism. The media and entertainment industry have walked a fine line when working with the state, censorship, the market and audiences.

Meanwhile, media and cultural forms and practices, including journalism, film, television drama, cinema and Internet portals, have proliferated, while remaining highly sensitive to both the vagaries of state control and regulation and the drive for profitability. New media forms and technologies have enabled mass communication and provided Chinese citizens with new opportunities to access information. Online reporting sites and message boards challenge government controlled media and facilitate conditions for the growth of civil society and the emergence of free press. Both state media and commercial Internet portals have begun online media reporting as well as online forums and message boards. Research shows that online forums and message boards have challenged the official monopoly of information and censorship (Qiang 70–75). Yang argues that through the use of bulletin boards and forums, Chinese Internet users are "engaged in the discursive construction of an online public sphere ... in a new type of political action, critical public debate" (Yang 474). Yang also believes that civil society and the Internet energize each other in their co-evolutionary development in China as the Internet facilitates civil society activities by offering new possibilities for citizen participation and civil society facilitates the development of the Internet by providing the necessary social basis for communication and interaction. Some scholars argue that the Internet will be a "key pillar of China's slow, evolutionary path toward increased pluralization and possible even nascent democratization" (Chase, and Mulvenon 90).

The microblog sphere has become an important communicative and discursive space for constructing middle-class identity. In the special issue "Communication and Class Divide China" of Javnost-The Public, the editor notes that the micro-blog Weibo, a Chinese version of Twitter, has around 300 million accounts and has emerged as the newest means of popular communication for China's middle class in the last several years. The article by Wu Changchang in the same issue provides a detailed account of how China's microbloggers rally around the middle class toward a neoliberal reform agenda after the high-speed rail accident in July 2011 (Wu 43–62).

China's media, therefore, has to operate and function under the dual logics of the neoliberal market and the socialist state. It has to serve two goals: the party's political "main melody" (*zhu xuanlu*) and audience-pleasing entertainment. Precisely under such macro-political and economic environment, media and entertainment industries have participated in the production of media content about consumption-oriented popular culture that are favored by the state and the market. The discourses and the content produced by the media are for entertainment, at the same time, and meeting the requirement of the party's political propaganda. However, study of media's role in forming cultural and class identity is still limited in the field of China studies.

Defining the Chinese Middle Class

The middle class is a complex group to define and categorize. In the recent book *The Making of the Middle Class*, the editors Lopez and Weinstein acknowledge that the "middle class" is a fuzzy term characterized by an "overabundance of meanings," which brings up more complexities and problems than it offers conceptual and analytical usefulness (446). Thus, it is important to define as best as possible what constitutes the middle class.

Conventionally, the middle class is defined based on its economic capital (income, business ownership, occupations and property ownership) and its social capital (education as well as social and political networks). Though divergent opinions exist on how to define and distinguish China's middle class from the rest of the society, Chinese scholars agree that occupation is a primary factor as it has already reflected income levels and social-economic status and, therefore, can be used as the main denominator to identify the middle class.[3] Although some scholars may argue that class as an identity linked to labor has become obsolete, labor retains a certain degree of legitimacy in examining the middle class in China as China's middle class is born out of the expansion of the service sector and professional work. This in turn has shaped the formation and identity of the middle class in China.

The formation of China's emerging middle class shows a strong connection to type of occupation, including a wide range of professions. It primarily includes intermediate-level business professionals, mid-level managers, and private business owners. Business professionals, also known as the so-called "white collars," are office workers of businesses and enterprises in China. They often have a high level of education, professional training, and living standard. It also includes a public servant stratum, which consists of government employees, who exert strong influence in public and social sectors as the result of the administrative reform in the Chinese government system. Some government cadres have transferred from administrative positions to managerial positions in business and economic arenas. They are referred as the "quasi middle class" due to their employment status and social ties with the state and the ruling party (Li 35–44). Some of them are senior managerial staff of state-owned enterprises (SOE) who gained income and control over state properties and production materials as the result of the privatization of state enterprises. They, often regarded as "red capitalists," are shareholders of transformed state enterprises and control the production materials of the SOEs (Dickson). Meanwhile, a wide spectrum of professions has emerged in the transition toward a market-oriented economy. New professionals with knowledge in special areas, such as certified public accountants, lawyers, biotech and IT engineers, judicial workers, and medical staff, are regarded as the typical middle class. They have a stable income, a high-level education and professional training and promising career prospect. In addition, China's intellectuals, including university professors, writers and artists, are recognized as the middle class (Zhou). In the post-Mao reform era, the intellectual group has gained political recognition and social prestige as well as financial privileges.

Different from lower-income strata, which include rural residents, the urban working class, and laid-off laborers, China's middle class possesses a relatively high level of education, professional skills and a relatively stable and high income. Chinese Academy of Social Sciences (CASS) research shows in a recent study that about 73 percent of the respondents have a postsecondary-level education or above, which gives this group an advantage in acquiring other social, economic, cultural and political capital (Lu, 2004 79). However, previous studies have also pointed out that China's middle class is moderate in its political participation. It tends to be more interested in activities associated with its own immediate personal interests rather than the social wellbeing yet (Cai 31–56; Wang, "Divergent Identities"; Wang, "Seeking Channels").

An Upward and Westward Class in *Go! Lala, Go!*

China's middle class has become a popular subject in China's visual media, especially for the screen arts such as TV shows and films. Visual media productions are created about the middle class and for middle-class viewers. The image of the middle class has been created for consumption in the visual media market. Some recent popular films and TV dramas about China's middle class have generated heated discussions in society, including the middle class itself.

One hit film about white-collar office workers is *Go! Lala, Go!* (*Du Lala Shengzhi ji*), released in 2010 and directed by Jinglei Xu. It was adapted from a popular Internet novel *Du Lala's Promotion* by Li Ke in 2007.[4] The author claims that the book is based on her real work experience in a multinational company in China. She states in the preface that the book is written about the white-collar middle class and for middle-class readers. The primary discourse of the film frames members of the middle class as social climbers and well-to-do consumers under the neoliberal economic system. The success of both the book and film is due largely to the portrayal of the career experiences of the protagonist, which resonates with contemporary Chinese white-collar office workers.[5]

More importantly, the film creates a narrative of career success and social mobility, which is based on the logic of global capitalism and neoliberalism. On Lala's first day of work, the chief secretary informs Lala of the social stratification in the office telling her:

> "By the way, this company has really different personnel levels. People below manager are small potatoes. This means they are poor, making less than 4,000 yuan. The managers are the middle class. They have their own cars, and an annual salary of over 200,000. Directors are upper class. Their annual incomes are over 500,000. They take their

> vacations abroad ... The CEO of the company, typical upper class, makes more than a million a year."

This narrative confirms that occupation and income are predominant economic markers to constitute the middle class. What is more, it shows that middle-class socioeconomic status is imagined being closely associated with social mobility and lifestyles (i.e., owing cars, foreign travel, etc.).

Globalization and the Middle Class

Such imagination of being the global middle class and being Western dominates the rest of the narrative in the film. The film portrays China's white-collar middle class as being Westernized or globalized. They generally have higher levels of English proficiency and education and can afford and pursue a "petty bourgeoisie" lifestyle (*xiaozi*) (Xu, 261). Characters in the film go by English names yet they communicate in both English and Chinese. They travel and vacation overseas. They are not only employees of global capitalist enterprises, but they also participate in global capitalist production and consumption. All these factors define the basic characteristics of China's middle class, born out of neoliberalism and nurtured by the culture of global consumerism. Thus, they tend to have strong ties with global capitalism. In fact, they cheer the success of neoliberal global capitalism in China (Dai 129–150). They are part of the global middle class, which is defined by their profession, income and lifestyles. Subsequently, they place high value on materialistic success, wealth accumulation and career mobility. They are consumers of global luxury brands and global media content. For instance, the global luxury brands such as Gucci, Dior, Chloé, Chanel, Valentino and many others that appear in the film *Go! Lala, Go!* have become symbols of socioeconomic status and aspirational lifestyles of China's middle class. The film portrays that the new middle class imagines itself as the part of the new global middle class and as the representative of Western modernity. In sum, they consume global products and goods and espouse Western cultural predispositions and consumption patterns as part of their new lifestyles.

The association between the middle-class status and consumption is imagined especially through fashion in the film. For example, each time the female protagonist receives a promotion, she changes her attire and shoes with heels higher and higher. As she appears in her new wardrobe, intertitles on the screen state her new professional positions and salary. Her upward consumption of fashion matches her upward mobility in career and an increase in earnings.[6] Lala's fashion choices not only mark her material status but also her class status and her tastes and symbols of identity. In Lala's case, fashion is a social process of acquiring and asserting her middle-class status. In this way, the film's narrative asserts that the middle class is a socioeconomic group defined by cultural and material products its members consume and share. It confirms the argument made by some sociologists that consumption practices and choices are closely associated with social and economic status.[7]

Middle Class and Urban Space

In addition to consumption and fashion, middle-class identity is constructed and imagined through the representation of space. China's new (neoliberal) middle classes have emerged in tandem with the neoliberal economy. They tend to be clustered around new centers of global finance and commerce, such as Beijing and Shanghai, which are built to become global cities. Public spaces represented in the film include glistening glass skyscrapers, Western coffee houses, clubs, trendy shops and modern shopping malls filled with international brands. These places are frequently visited by middle-class consumers. Notably, it is within and through these spaces that middle-class identity and image are produced and reproduced. Eating, drinking, consuming and working at these spaces become symbols of middle-class lifestyle. And, going to these places is as much an expression of middle-class identity as it is a consumption choice.

Such urban space in the film displays the rapid urban transformation that Chinese cities have experienced over the past two decades. Beijing, as the backdrop of this film, is a modern cosmopolitan world city rather than a historical and political capital city. The landmarks in the film are the newly constructed Central Business District (or CBD) and buildings designed by world-renowned architects. These modern buildings are not only symbols of spatial development of this global city but also symbols of urban consumerism stimulated by neoliberal development in China. In addition, these buildings are often the office buildings for multinational corporations in China. Therefore, these new urban spaces represent opportunities for social mobility as well as consumption to assert middle-class status.

Another important space represented in the film and consumed by the middle class are overseas travel sites. For instance, Lala and Wang Wei, a sales director of the company, realize their affection for one another on a beach in Thailand. Indeed, tourist sites have become new spaces for cultural production and consumption. Some of the beach resorts portrayed in the film have become popular among Chinese middle-class tourists. The travel destinations visited by the middle class reveals that the middle-class consumers have developed an interest in leisure activities, including travel and vacations. These leisure activities are also ways of manifesting middle-class lifestyle and its distinctive taste. Indeed, the tourism industry in China has embraced the middle class by offering various travel products and instigated cultural consumerism such as theme parks and cultural entertainment performances. For example, Shen-Zhen-based Jinxiu Zhonghua claims to be the world's largest Chinese culture theme park that includes miniature Chinese tourist sites and ethnic cultural performances on a daily basis.

The rise of tourist consumerism is also in line with the state's economic interest in increasing domestic travel. In addition to a Spring Festival holiday, the state created two Golden Week holidays in 1999, the May Day holiday and the National Day holiday in October. Both new holidays are intended to encourage public spending to boost the domestic economy. Notably, it is estimated that about 480 million Chinese went on holidays during the National Day holiday in 2014.[8] Additionally, a relaxation of visa restrictions on Chinese travelers by many destination countries also gives Chinese middle-class tourists an opportunity to visits European countries and the United States and be exposed to elite and popular culture as well as middle-class lifestyles in the West.

The taste and the lifestyle of the middle class are manifested through domestic and international leisure travel as well as fashion in the film. As Anthony Giddens has asserted, lifestyle is the core of self-identity.[9] Tastes and lifestyles through consumption of fashion and space in the film are essential elements of China's middle-class identity (1991). The film *Go! Lala, Go!* has contributed to the formation of the middle-class identity and consumption behaviors by using the method of "product placement" (such as luxury items and tourist destinations), which is defined by Robert McChesney as an instance when a product is "woven directly into the story so it is unavoidable and its messages can be smuggled in when the viewer's guard is down" (147). To nurture and captivate the class consciousness of China's urban middle class, the film has accentuated the significance of career mobility and lifestyles as class distinction. Over twenty different brands are placed in the plot to exhibit values and distinctions in tastes and lifestyles of the social elite and the middle class. The majority of the product placements are Western luxury brands and commodities. In this, the film functions "as a lure or bait to catch and keep people paying attention" to advertising messages (Smythe 232). The film thus reproduces middle-class identity and culture by capitalizing on their labor and their role as an active "audience commodity," encouraging them to pay attention to appropriate middle-class lifestyles and materialistic culture. The middle class is thus contained and their political potential is thus neutralized through the profit-seeking mechanism of China's entertainment industry. The media, including both film and television, are simultaneously a commodity and an artifact, presenting ideology and culture that is manufactured and created for consumption and interpretation by an audience.

This also reminds us that the construction of China's middle-class culture is created by the interplay of the market, capital, media as well as the party-state. The middle class is imagined as cultured, hardworking, successful, global, westward and upward. Values such as material success, career and social mobility as well as individual successes are endorsed by the party-state, media and the market. Ultimately, the film shows that the middle class is a "connected class." Not only is the middle class connected to Western markets, products, cultures, languages, ideologies and values, but it is also connected to opportunities to participate in globalization. Such a relationship to globalization allows the middle class to create its own dreams; whether the Chinese dream or American dream, it is the dream of individual success. Its participation in globalization also makes China's middle class part of the global middle class. The middle class is also strongly socially and politically connected with the ruling elite as is evident in the 2009 TV drama *Dwelling Narrowness* (*woju*).

A Struggled and Stressed Class: "*Dwelling Narrowness*"

If the middle class is imagined as a middle class seeking its identity and asserting its status through occupation, consumption of leisure, fashion, Western commodities and luxury brands, ironically, a hit TV series in 2009 reveals a much less glamorous lifestyle of the middle class in big cities. The thirty-five-episode TV drama *Dwelling Narrowness* (*woju*) offers a less-sanguine look at the social struggles and the plight of two sisters, Haiping and Haizao, in a fictional city resembling Shanghai where they pursue their middle-class dream of homeownership. The show's plot, which is also adapted from the Internet novel *A House of Romance* (2007) by the Chinese cyber writer Liu Liu,[10] centers on a white-collar couple Haiping and her husband Su Chun and their lofty desire to buy an apartment in the city. The couple represents a typical middle-class citizen/consumer who has a college degree, a white-collar job, a stable income and a desire to own private cars and houses. They both come from small towns but have migrated to urban China to pursue their education, which provides them with opportunities to participate in the neoliberal economy.

Middle Class and Homeownership

The identity of the middle class in the TV drama is imagined through the consumption of housing and domestic space. The cityscape is viewed through rows of drab stone-gated houses along narrow lanes (or, *nongtang*), gentrified neighborhoods and glitzy malls against a broader backdrop of an urban space teeming with demolition and new construction projects. In juxtaposition with the portrayal of exterior urban space, interior domestic space of the middle-class couple is portrayed as a cramped living area with simple furnishings and unhygienic living conditions in houses along the *nongtang*, where a middle-class dream for homeownership is nurtured and sought by the protagonists.

For middle-class families, the exterior urban space signifies opportunities, possibilities, materialistic wealth and comfort and the promise of a better life for their children. Reflecting aspirations to social mobility, Haiping states emotionally to her husband Su Chun:

> "In such a large city, so many people can come and settle down, why can't we? So many people can survive, why can't we? Not only will I survive, I will live well. I believe that I will not spend my future in

> this shabby alleyway with old shop assistants living on the first floor, hourly maids on second floor, cooks on the second and half floor. My future will definitely be better than theirs" (in Episode 1).

Not only does the protagonist express her disdain of her poor neighbors, but she also shows her ambition for success in the city.

In contrast to the portrayal of urban space in the film *Go! Lala, Go!*, the city is portrayed in the TV series *Dwelling Narrowness* as a space filled with anxiety and tension. The urban middle-class experience multifaceted stresses, including those related to finances, work, marriage and social interactions. In one instance, Haiping confessed her stress to Haizao:

> "Every morning when I wake up, a string of digits just pop up in my head. The house mortgage costs about 6000 yuan; food, clothes and household necessities cost about 2500 yuan; daycare for Ranran (her daughter) is about 1500 yuan; gift money (for interpersonal and social *guanxi*, or relationships) 600 yuan; transportation expenses 580 yuan; property management fee 340 yuan, cell phone 250 yuan, and utilities, 200 yuan. In other words, from my first breath when I wake up, I have to make 400 yuan every day to break even. This is my cost of living in this city. These numbers have forced me not to relax and lay back every day and not to even think about the next ten years" (in Episode 35, Finale).

In this particular instance, the protagonists of *Dwelling Narrowness* illustrate that China's middle class experiences high levels of stress in its social and economic life. Some stresses arise from an obsession for wealth, materialistic success and the homeownership in China's large cities (Yang and Chen, 8–9). In an Internet survey about the TV drama, about 73 percent of the viewers finds the drama "realistic."[11] Yet, despite causing great frustration, these aspirations are prioritized in social relationships. For example, the character Haiping teaches her younger sister Haizou how to measure a man's true love when she states, "If a man loves a women, ... the first thing he should provide is a pile of money, neither his heart nor his body, second, a house (Episode 16)." The obsession with homeownership and the desire for materialistic possessions has created the new class of *fangnu* (house slaves), the middle class with high mortgage payments for housing. What is more, the TV drama shows how the middle class has also become "enslaved" to cars, educational costs and securing quality healthcare. In other words, middle-class households are under the oppression of the "three new mountains" – the costs of housing, healthcare, and children's education.

China's middle class may be the product and beneficiary of a neoliberal market-oriented economy, but the program suggests that this comes at a personal cost. In the TV series, the identity of the middle class is closely associated with its educational achievement, career success and economic status. The protagonists gained their social and economic status through education. In fact, education is regarded as a means to gain social mobility and social capital. To middle-class families, education has helped them achieve their economic and professional success. They also see their educational attainment as their cultural capital to distinguish themselves from other social classes. For instance, Su Chun, the husband in *Dwelling Narrowness*, regards their education from a prestigious university as their middle-class credential that differentiates them from the working class. He holds a negative attitude toward the working class and regards the working class as uneducated "petty urbanites" (*xiaoshimin*). It is evident that the middle class hopes to acquire and transfer cultural capital through their children's education.[12] It shows that education is a process of social reproduction for middle-class parents, who are keenly invested in the cultural and social reproduction of their children to become the next generation of successful members of the middle class.

Yet, there are tensions, disappointments and frustrations with the proposed paths to achieving middle-class status. Haiping expresses to her husband at one point, "At least we are university graduates. People would see us as white collar or middle class. Why couldn't we afford to purchase a house? I heard that in the United States, you would be considered middle-class when you own a house" (in Episode 11). Haiping's understanding of middle-class status is clearly based on her perception of the middle class in the U.S. and its levels of homeownership. She justifies her middle-class status and her obsession with homeownership with an American standard though she is located in a Chinese city. This suggests that the Chinese middle class shares similar ambitions as the middle classes of other societies. Even though the middle class varies from one society to another, property ownership has become a frequent criterion for defining one's social class.

New Social Relations: The Middle Class, the Working Class and the Political Elite

The TV drama identifies that the middle class defines itself in contrast to the working class and the political elite. The middle class is imagined as above a working class and below the capitalist ownership class and the bureaucratic elite. Locating a middle class in this particular way, on one hand, assumes that the middle class is a distinctive social stratum with its own identity in contemporary China. The middle class does represent new social relations, values, and forces of production and consumption. On the other hand, the TV drama reveals bluntly the stratified urban society and complex relationships among the working class, the middle class and the political elite as the result of the neoliberal economic system. The three classes have formed a social pyramid in China, and the TV drama offers multiple perspectives to understand how individuals from all three classes imagine their class position in the changing society.

The working class is imagined as the lower layer of urban society. The middle class' relation to the working class is imagined as one of overt conflicted interrelationship in *Dwelling Narrowness*. The middle class as portrayed in the TV drama distances itself from the working class but closely associated with the ruling elite for its own economic and social benefits. For example, the working class, through the life of Grandma Li and her family, is portrayed as conniving, uneducated, and greedy for demanding unreasonably high compensation and relocation fees and resisting the demolition of their residence for the cause of urban renewal. The TV drama reveals the challenges the working class is facing, including low incomes, being laid off at a fairly young age, the lack of a social security net, social injustice and increasing disparity in urban China. Grandma Li is portrayed as the "stuck-nail household" (*dingzi hu*) of the relocation process by the government and real estate developers in the drama. She candidly describes the ongoing urban development as a "class struggle" and demolition as "a business that would make the poor cry and put a smile on the faces of the rich. The developers are businessmen. How could you possibly gain any advantage from them?" (in Episode 4). Generally speaking, the working class is portrayed as "petty urbanites (*xiaoshimin*)", a loser of China's miracle economy. Workers and peasants, who were the pillars of the proletarian and the political backbone of socialist China, have now been marginalized and disenfranchised during China's economic and social transformation and become the disadvantaged groups. The TV drama reflects on this shift as it portrays increasing disparity and divides between the middle class and the working class. The attitude of the middle class toward working class residents, who are forced out of their homes when their homes are demolished, is indifferent. The middle class seems to be more concerned about their own social and economic wellbeing. What is more, the middle class is portrayed as superior to the working class. They boast about their achievements in education, occupation, and their social, cultural and economic advantages.

Meanwhile, the middle class shows strong ties with the ruling elites. In the TV series, both groups share similar interests in attaining economic wealth and enjoying a materialistic lifestyle. The middle class admires the lifestyles of the ruling elite. In the drama, the relationship of Haizao and the corrupted official Song Siming reveals how the middle class identifies with the ruling class and how Haizao benefits as a mistress of Song Siming. The union between the corrupted official and Haizao (as a member of the middle class) reveals how they share similar moral and social values. For instance, while Song used his political power to assist the two sisters in acquiring their middle-class status, the middle-class sisters are, in turn, fascinated by the ruling elite's economic prestige and lifestyles, including the luxury cars and countryside villas. What is more, Song is extremely popular among the middle-class audience and netizens.[13] About 30 percent of over 46,000 viewers rated him as their favorite character of the TV drama, the highest ranked among all characters.[14] He is portrayed as an insightful politician with global perspectives. His views and narratives on china's society and politics are popular among Chinese viewers and often quoted on the Internet.[15]

In addition to identifying with the Chinese elite, the middle class is also portrayed as identifying with global capital. Whereas this is clearly developed in the TV drama *Dwelling Narrowness*, the film *Go! Lala, Go!*, also has a subtext on relationships between the Chinese middle class and the transnational capitalist class. In *Dwelling Narrowness*, Mark, an American lawyer and Song's close friend, represents the transnational capitalist class. He helped Haiping become an entrepreneur with his own financial resources and social network with the transnational middle class who works in China. He also assisted Haizao in relocating to the U.S., thus furthering Haizao's entry into the transnational middle class. The transnational capitalist class, represented by Mark in the series, is well-connected with corrupted officials, members of the middle class and other transnational capitalists in China and overseas. Just as Mark assisted Haizao, he himself has benefited from China's participation in the neoliberal global capitalism. The transnational capitalist courts the ruling political elite and the middle class to capitalize on its investments in China. The TV series shows how the three classes are intimately linked based on economic relationships. Both the ruling class and the global capitalist class are viewed as being well-connected and globally mobile by the middle class.

Related to its identification with transnational capital, the drama *Dwelling Narrowness* shows that the middle class in China is obsessed not only with the ownership of private cars and houses and consumption of luxury goods but also global middle-class lifestyle and status. Infomercials in the TV drama feature luxury brands from the West. For instance, the infomercial about Land Rover (*Luhu*) is built into the plot and is described as "the British royal family designated vehicle." In a way that recalls the film *Go! Lala, Go!*, the middle class is imagined as being connected with global capitalist production and consumption as well as materialistic possessions and economic success. Also similar to the protagonist in the film, the career of the protagonist Haiping in the TV series *Dwelling Narrowness* represents the connectedness of the middle class with globalization. The career trajectory of Haiping, who started as a member of the office staff at a Japanese firm, worked as a private Chinese language tutor for foreign businessmen in China. She eventually became the boss of her own language school to teach Chinese to foreigners, revealing how she has benefitted from the neoliberal economy and globalization. Her upward social mobility is the result of the globalization era rather than the socialist era.

Socialist Housing Reform and the New "House Slaves"

The primary plot of the TV drama is centered on China's urban housing reform. The TV drama reveals the subtle and sensitive relations among the government, the profit-seeking real estate developers and the residents through the demolition-and-relocation process. The TV drama has drawn wide attention and generated controversy in Chinese society as it comments on contemporary social issues for the middle class in urban China, including the increasing disparity in wealth, skyrocketing real estate prices, pervasive political corruption and eroding traditional Chinese family values. What the TV series created is the image and the new term "house slaves" (*fangnu*), which portrays the middle-class families who are paying a high mortgage and eating from inexpensive lunch boxes. Such a contrast in lifestyle the middle class faces is supported by research studies. According to the report from the China Index Academy, a domestic real estate research institute, as of 2009, the average housing price in Beijing has reached 16,057 yuan per square meter, a 54 percent increase from the average price of 10,403 yuan in January 2009. In Shanghai, the average residential price for October 2009 was 16,954 yuan per square meter, up 22 percent since January 2009.[16] The Green Report of the Housing Market in China published by the Chinese Academy of Social Sciences pointed out that despite new measures by the Chinese government to emphasize construction of low-cost houses, low- and middle-income families are "not well-covered" by the current residence-guarantee system (CSSA).

Comparative Views of Class Construction: *Dwelling Narrowness and Go! Lala, Go!*

The study of *Go! Lala, Go!* and *Dwelling Narrowness* shows that the party-state, the market and visual media have all participated in and contributed to public discourses on the middle-class identity as well as subjectivity.[17] Both views of the middle class in visual media – that of a successful career women and a family pursuing ownership of a house – have resonated well with the middle-class viewers. Both productions have generated heated discussions among middle-class viewers, especially in the blogosphere. Sina.com, one of the largest Internet portals in China, has created surveys and blogging space for both shows for viewers to express their opinions. For example, the image of the "house slaves" and the term "*fangnu*" have become the focal issue of many online postings and discussions. Such an image of the middle class is widely accepted by the middle class itself and the broad spectrum of society. According to the online poll conducted by Sina.com, about 59 percent of 46,000 respondents agreed with the statement that the drama reflects the public's sentiment on "house slaves."[18] The poll also shows that audiences attributed the drama's success to its "realistic" portrayal of the hardships of everyday urban life. Seventy-four percent of the viewers agree the drama reflects their experiences accurately and another 23 percent feel the reality is disheartening. Such widely accepted images created by media and entertainment industry demonstrate how media have acted as agents of socialization in class identity acquisition of the newly emerged middle class.[19] For the film *Go! Lala, Go!*, about 50 percent of the respondents say that they have gained professional experience and lessons from the film. About 59 percent feel that the film provides some ideas for their professional practice at work.[20] This also means that media and entertainment industries have provided alternative discourses to the state discourse and ideology. The state discourse on social stratification, urban development, social harmony and socialist ideology is challenged by media content about social discord and income disparity presented by visual media. In other words, state discourse is no longer the only dominant and popular ideology of society. Media also become a space for middle-class viewers to provide their own opinions about middle-class identity based on their own experience and values. The case of Sina.com illustrates how it has mobilized viewers with its own online surveys.

Not only have the visual media participated in the discourses about the middle-class identity, they also have participated in the discussion about the social relationship of the middle class within the larger social order, particularly the middle class' relationship with the upper ruling class and the working class. The media's discourse on these social relationships has challenged socialist notions of class, which is largely determined by one's position in the relations of production and political consciousness. In both the film and the TV series, middle-class characters are closely associated with the elite ruling of domestic bureaucratic-capitalists and transnational capitalists in order to secure their middle-class lifestyles. The class alliance with the elite ruling class and the transnational capitalist shows that middle class greatly admires the lifestyles of the ruling and the transnational capitalist elites. On the other hand, the TV drama *Dwelling Narrowness* portrays proletarians as uneducated, conniving, greedy, and at the bottom of the social and economic ladder. The show also presents a distant relationship between the middle class and the working class as well as the indifference and contempt of the middle class toward the working class. The TV drama *Dwelling Narrowness* reveals that a stratified society has been formed as the result of the neoliberal economic development (Lu 2002). Studies have shown that Chinese class formation has shifted from a rigid status hierarchy under Mao to a stratified class system in the post-Mao reform era. The society under Mao was primarily structured based on the rural-urban residential status, the cadre-worker occupational classification, party and non-party membership, and the revolutionary-antirevolutionary political grouping. The post-Mao society in the reform era is stratified into multiple classes in both rural and urban China. In urban China, scholars have found that Mao's protected working class of state-sector workers became differentiated and disempowered (Whyte), while state officials and managers gained executive control and income rights over state properties and became capitalized (So). Private entrepreneurs rose in the growing market economy but lacked any political interest or autonomy (Pearson 1997). Of particular relevance here is the relationship between the middle class and the working class. This relationship is more problematic than it was in Mao's era because Mao's ideology placed the proletariat, the working class and the peasantry with high status in the social order. By contrast, neoliberal economic reform tends to place professional employees and white collar experts with higher status based on their occupational and technological expertise essential to economic revitalization and modernization.

In addition, both productions have demonstrated how social and cultural values, tastes, and lifestyles of the middle class are imagined by visual media for middle-class viewers. As both media productions have woven certain types of products into the storylines and intentionally delivered the values, tastes, and lifestyles to viewers, the middle class has become the desirable "audience commodity" for the entertainment and media industry (Huang 23–42). As noted above, visual media have employed the method of "product placement" to include the advertisement of luxury brands into the story. Both *Dwelling Narrowness* and *Go! Lala, Go!* have explicitly inserted infomercials to exhibit imagined aspirational lifestyles of the middle class. Visual media have worked closely with capital and market and reproduced the right kind of content for the right kind of middle-class audience. For example, the film *Go! Lala, Go!* received 6 million yuan from advertisements and 0.8 million yuan from the Thailand Tourism Promotion Bureau for the beach vacation scene in Thailand. Both productions show how media has created and communicated strong intertwined messages of consumption and self-identity for the middle-class viewers, and eventually formed a consumer culture for the middle class through product placement. The Western luxury brands and glitzy shopping malls are visible in both media productions. Both works demonstrate how profit-seeking entertainment, visual media industries and the market have made the middle class into a targeted audience for an imagined upwardly mobile lifestyle and as consumers for certain types of commodities.

Finally, the portrayal (albeit conflicted) of the middle class in visual media, has also contributed to shaping outward class identity as well as the self-consciousness and subjective identity of the middle class. Both productions present a middle class asserting its identity and self-consciousness through its cultural, economic, and social capital as well as its consumerist predispositions. Haiping and Duchun in *Dwelling Narrowness* developed their self-consciousness and subjective identity based on their education and homeownership while Lala imagined her class identity and self-consciousness through her professional success, spaces she occupied, fashions and modes of consumption. As the economic and social status of China's middle class is not inherited, the self-consciousness of class identity is often developed from a variety of factors, including career, spaces, education, homeownership, wealth, lifestyles, tastes and modes of consumption.

Conclusion

Taken together, the visual media productions discussed in this chapter reveal that the formation of China's middle class has occurred in multiple registers and dimensions, including profession, consumption, space, fashion, education, and social relations. Members of the middle class are imagined as hardworking, well-educated, entrepreneurial and aspirational citizens who long for middle-class membership and a good quality of living. However, this longing comes with the anxiety and the desire for a feeling of security or belonging, through homeownership, marriage or through work and consumption.

This chapter has aimed to contribute to theorizing the emerging middle-class culture in the context of globalization and China's socialist logics. It offers a nuanced analysis through the lens of visual media to study the middle class and the practices, ideologies, and meanings associated with middle classness. Middle classness is manifested through everyday life activities, including how people make meaning in their everyday lives, what products they consume, where they choose to shop, travel and go on vacation, and how they raise their children. As discussed here, the classness of the middle stratum is imagined through the ideas of status, conspicuous consumption, habitus, cultural and social reproduction, and the consumption of space rather than the Marxist and socialist ideas of economic relations based on the ownership of production materials, capital, and labor. These ideas enable us to see how the emerging middle stratum, born out of China's neo-liberal market economic reform, has gained its social status based on its education and its command over the skills, expertise and knowledge essential to industrial and economic progress. Therefore, China's middle class is a fruitful research site to understand the new relations of production and consumption that involves new classed subjects as consumers and cultural reproducers rather than material labors and workers, and understand how consumption has become the new dominant marker of middle classness. The visual media show that middle class and its culture are defined by the lived experiences of particular kinds of socioeconomic relations that arise under neoliberal economic conditions. Their styles of consumption, approaches to cultural and social reproduction, and aspiration for middle classness – along with the anxieties that accompany the process of class formation – are shown as being connected with global middle-class practices and subjectivities through consumption and access to global commodities.

However, China's middle class and its experience and meaning are both uniquely Chinese and global. As discussed in this chapter, middle-class life is mediated by both China's socialist logics and the global neoliberal logics that, in turn, shape middle-class identity, self-consciousness, and its culture and practice. On one hand, China's middle-class life is formed around ideologies of global consumption, individual professional success and ownership of private property. To belong to the middle class means having access to global goods and being able to participate in global consumption. It is formed in the global context of larger relations of production, circulation and consumption rather than labor. China's middle class has begun to emerge as a critical site for considering the implications of the rise and spread of neoliberal logics.

On the other hand, China's middle class does not follow the footprint of the Western middle-class process. China's middle-class experience is never a reliving of the Western social past. It is born out of both socialist ideology and its promotion of economic development and "getting rich first." The middle class has emerged and become more central to the state's efforts to develop its new markets through new forms of labor, to promote new forms of consumption, and to protect the interests of the party and the state. For instance, domestic consumption (generally) and home ownership by the middle class reflects the state's discourse regarding the improvement of people's living standards in the 10th Five-Year Plan. The Plan was intended to expand domestic demand and boost domestic consumption, especially in the sectors of tourism, education and housing. Such policy to accelerate domestic consumption has continued during the recent global financial crisis as China's exports declined sharply. Stimulating domestic consumption became the focal point of the state's economic recovery strategy to move from an export-led economy to consumption-led economy.[21]

The socialist party-state has deep interests in maintaining and privileging the middle class. That the party-state adopted new policy in 2001 to induct entrepreneurs, and middle-class white-collar office professionals into the party demonstrates the CCP's promotion of the middle class and its class interests. It passed a new law in 2007 to protect the social and economic elite's property rights. Meanwhile, middle-class lifestyle is shaped by the state's promotion of consumption to boost the domestic economy. These policies show that the socialist state intends to maintain its political stability and legitimacy by promoting middle-class interests and social status, and manage classes and class relations in the interests of capital, market and socialist ideology. These political, social, cultural, and economic factors discussed in this chapter make it clear how the conflicted visual imaginations of the middle class on screens are the mediated result of tensions between the state and the market, and between the local and the global.

Notes

1. China Central Television's evening TV news magazine, *Jiaodian Fangtan* (Focus Interview), has been a popular program with its criticism of local cadres and attracts a daily audience of 300 million, though it remains conservative in its subtle and cautious control of the frequency, timing, level, and content of the criticism; *Nanfang Zhoumo* (Southern Weekend) has published a series of reports on poverty and social injustice and revealed social issues such as AIDS, SARS, and homosexuality. *Nanfang Zhoumo* (Southern Weekly) reported a protest organized by the Xiamen citizens against a proposal of building a chemical industry in the city in 2007. Though local news media mainly focused on the economic benefits of the proposed project, the central government intervened. A front-page editorial on People's Daily urged local officials to abandon this project to preserve the environment. Such pattern is also seen in a recent collective

action taken by Shanghai citizens to hold a protest march against an expansion plan of the magnetic levitation train, or maglev, in 2008.

2. See "Xinhua's Internet Arm Seeks an IPO," *Wall Street Journal*, Jan. 7, 2013. http://online.wsj.com/article/SB100014241278873234825045782265210524l2836.html.
3. A study by the Chinese Academy of Social Science (CASS) in 2001 used occupation as the primary indicator to define Chinese middle-income stratum. The estimate number of middle-class households in China was 80 million. The CASS report adopted the term *zhongchan jieji*, which means "the middle property stratum," to deemphasize the income and the ownership of private assets and properties but use the occupational characteristics as the criteria for the new social class. Some scholars define the middle class as the socio-economic group with annual household earnings of 30,000 RMB ($3,600) (see Yang, Yiyong, ed. *Equality and Efficiency: The Issue of Distribution of Income in Contemporary China* [in Chinese]. Beijing: Today's China Publishing House, 1997. Print; China's National Bureau of Statistics posits the annual income of middle-income households in a range from 60,000 RMB (US$7,500) to 500,000 RMB (US$62,000) in its 2005 report (People's Daily, *China's Middle Class Defined by Income* [in Chinese], January 20, 2005). Li Chunling used multiple factors to define the middle class: the middle class would be 15.9 percent of the whole population when using professions and occupations, 24.6 percent when using income, 35 percent when using consumption, 46.8 percent when using self-identification (subjective cognition). In "The Composition and Proportion of the Present Chinese Middle Class." *Chinese Journal of Population Science* 6 (2003) Beijing.
4. The book was also adapted to a TV drama series in 2010 and a stage play in 2009.
5. The term "white collar" was widely adopted by Chinese scholars and citizens in the late 1980s to refer to Chinese office workers for foreign companies. American sociologist C. Wright Mills used the term "white collar" to refer to the new office workers as the new middle class in his seminal work *The American Middle Classes*. Mills observed the shift in the American labor force and argued that office workers, "white collar" people on salary, was the new middle class of the mid-twentieth century. He explains that the white-collar middle class has new "styles of life," which form the middlebrow culture in American society. See Mills, C. Wright. *White Collar: The American Middle Classes*. New York: Oxford University Press, 1951. Print. Mills' book was translated into Chinese and published in China by Zhejiang People's Press in 1987 and by Nanjing University Press in 2006.
6. The costume designer of the film is the celebrated American costume designer Patricia Field, who has won several awards for designing costumes for the stylish television series "Sex and the City."
7. In his seminal book *The Theory of the Leisure Class,* the economist and sociologist Thorstein Veblen first introduced the concept of *conspicuous consumption*. Veblen defined conspicuous consumption as the use of money or other resources by people to pursue, display and assert their social status. This also echoes Herber Blumer's trickle-across theory.
8. China Tourism Academy, http://www.ctaweb.org. Web. 6 Dec. 2014.
9. Other scholars also shared similar ideas about lifestyles of middle classes from various societies. Marina Moskowitz argues that middle-class identity in the

U.S. was "based on notions of cultural capital, luxury, material aspiration, and credit." Daniel Walkowitz's study of the participation of the professional managerial workers in the folk dance movement in the U.S. demonstrates how "middle class is more about style and status claims—cultural capital—than about political or economic power." Sociologist Pierre Bourdieu argued that all tastes are acquired and tastes are based on social class. He presented tastes as an individual and collective resources used to mark social distinctions. In Western society "good taste" is the symbol appropriated by economic and social status and educational levels. In Paul Fussell's book on class, he described how social class status could be revealed by symbols, styles, and intellectual proclivities. Fussell pointed out that class in America is not decided exclusively upon finances; it is also a matter of taste, what one does with one's recreational time, what one reads, what schools one has attended and how well one speaks.

10. The TV adaption of the novel marks the third collaboration between director Teng Huatao and the writer Liu Liu, following their earlier collaborations of two popular TV series, *Double Adhesive Tape* (2008) and *Wanggui and Anna* (2009). The TV drama offers snapshots of everyday life as well as insights into contemporary moral and ethical thoughts and social values, particularly the life of the middle class in urban China.
11. see http://survey.ent.sina.com.cn/result/39451.html.
12. Bourdieu defines the cultural capital as the forms of knowledge, skills, and education, which give families or individuals a higher status in society. He points out that cultural capital is initially passed down by the family. In Pierre Bourdieu, "The Forms of Capital." Ed. Richardson, J.G. *Handbook of Theory and Research for the Sociology of Education*. New York: Greenwood. 1986. Print.
13. The English word "Netizen" is widely and frequently used by mainland China-based English language media to refer to "Internet users" (wangmin, literally "net-people"); Sina.com, "Woju Broke Records of Audience Rating and Provoked Discussions among White-Collar Workers" 《蜗居》创收视新高 引发白领阶层大讨论, August 10, 2009, http://ent.sina.com.cn/v/m/2009–08–10/13342646466.shtml.
14. See "Woju: Survey," Sina.com, real time and ongoing, http://survey.ent.sina.com.cn/survey.php?id=39451&dpc=1 and, for survey results, see http://survey.ent.sina.com.cn/result/39451.html.
15. These online articles provide detailed accounts about how the TV show is received by the audience. See Time Weekly 时代周报, "*Awaking the Pain of the Era*," Nov. 26, 2009. http://www.time-weekly.com/html/20091126/6096_1.html; See "Most Popular Modern Chinese Drama of 2009," in Interactive Age 时代互动, www.325000.tv, real time and ongoing, http://www.325000.tv/movie/tv.aspx?ord=2&class ID=54&years=2009.
16. Data available at http://fdc.soufun.com/Report/CIAReport.aspx. Web. 10 Aug. 2013.
17. *Go, Lala! Go!* is invested and produced by DMG Entertainment, a private media company and one of the largest advertising agencies. *Dwelling Narrowness* is co-invested and co-produced by Shanghai Media Group (SMG), Huayi Brothers Media Group, Jilin TV, Beijing Jindun Film and Television Company. SMG is one of the largest media conglomerate in China.
18. Data retrieved from http://survey.ent.sina.com.cn/result/39451.html on 20 Jul. 2010. Web.

19. "*Woju* Broke Records of Audience Rating and Provoked Discussions among the White-Collar Class." 10, Aug. 2009, http://ent.sina.com.cn/v/m/2009–08–10/13342646466.shtml. Web.
20. http://survey.edu.sina.com.cn/result/45215.html.
21. China's Prime Minister Wen Jiabao stated that China would emphasize the domestic demand, particularly consumer demand, as the driving force of economic growth in his government work report at the opening of the second session of the 11th National People's Congress (NPC) on March 5, 2009 (http://news.xinhuanet.com/english/2009-03/05/content_10945808.htm).

Works Cited

Blumer, Herbert. "Fashion: From Class Differentiation to Collective Selection." *The Sociological Quarterly*. 10.3 (1969): 275–291. Print.

Bourdieu, Pierre. *Distinction: A Social Critique of the Judgment of Taste*. Cambridge, Mass: Harvard University Press, 1984. Print.

———. "The Forms of Capital." Ed. Richardson, J.G. *Handbook of Theory and Research for the Sociology of Education*. New York: Greenwood. 1986. Print.

Buckley, Christopher. "How a Revolution Becomes a Dinner Party: Stratification, Mobility and the New Riches in Urban China." *Culture and Privilege in Capitalist Asia*. Ed. Michael Pinches. London: Routledge, 1999. 208–29. Print.

Chan, Alex. "From Propaganda to Hegemony: Jiaodian Fangtan and China's Media Policy," *Journal of Contemporary China* 11.30: 35–51. Print.

Chan, J. M. "Media Internationalization in China: Processes and Tensions." *Journal of Communication* 44 (1994): 70–88. Print.

Chase, Michael S., and James C. Mulvenon, *You've Got Dissent! Chinese Dissent Use of the Internet and Beijing's Counter-Strategies*. Santa Monica: RAND (2002): 90. Print.

China Social Science Academy (CSSA). *Annual Report on Development of Housing Market in China*. 2009, Beijing: China Social Science Documents Press. Print.

Chu, Leonard L. "Continuity in China's Media Reform." *Journal of Communication* 44 (1994): 4–21. Print.

Dai, Jinhua. "I Want to Be Human: A Story of China and the Human." *Social Text*. 29.4 (2012): 129–150. Print.

Dickson, Bruce. *Red Capitalists in China: The Party, Private Entrepreneurs, and Prospects for Political Change*. Cambridge, UK: Cambridge University Press, 2003. Print.

Fussell, Paul. *Class: A Guide Through the American Status System*. New York: Simon & Schuster, 1992. Print.

Giddens, Anthony. *Modernity and Self-Identity: Self and Society in the Late Modern Age*. Cambridge: Polity Press, 1991. Print.

Goodman, David S. G., "The New Middle Class." *The Paradox of China's Post-Mao Reforms*. Eds. Merle Goldman and Roderick MacFarquhar. Cambridge, Mass: Harvard University Press, 1999. 241–61. Print.

Huang, Ruth "The State and the Market: Chinese TV Serials and the Case of Woju." *Boundary* 2 38. 2 (2011): 155–188. Print.

Huang, Ying-fen. "The Case *of Dwelling Narrowness:* Audience Commodity, the Spectacle, and Class Formation." *Javnost-The Public* 19. 2 (2012): 23–42. Print.

Lawrence, Susan V. "Three Cheers for the Party." *Far Eastern Economic Review* 26 Oct. 2000. 32–35. Print.

Li, Chunling. "Middle Stratum: The Group of the Chinese Society Needs Attention." *2004: The Analysis and Forecast of the Condition of the Chinese Society* [in Chinese]. Ed. Zai Ruxin. Beijing, China: Social Science Documentation Publishing House, 2004. Print.

Li, Qiang, "Market Transition and the Generation's Alteration of China's Middle Class." *Strategy and Management*, 3 (1999): 35–44. Print.

Liu, Hong. "Profit or Ideology: The Chinese Press between Party and Market" *Media, Culture & Society*, 20 (1998): 31–41. Print.

Liu, Qing, and Barrett McCormick. "The Media and the Public Sphere in Contemporary China." *Boundary 2* 38.1 (2011) *101–134*. Print.

Lopez, A. Ricardo, and Barbara Weinstein, eds. *The Making of the Middle Class: Toward a Transnational History*. Durham, NC: Duke University Press, 2012. Print.

Lu, Xueyi, ed. *Research Report on the Social Strata in Contemporary China* [in Chinese]. Beijing, China: Social Science Documentation Publishing House, 2002. Print.

———. *Research Report on the Social Mobility in Contemporary China* [in Chinese]. Beijing, China: Social Science Documentation Publishing House, 2004. Print.

Lynch, Daniel C. *After the Propaganda State: Media, Politics, and Thought Work in Reformed China*. Stanford, CA: Stanford University Press, 1999. Print.

McChesney, Robert W. *The Problem of the Media: U.S. Communication Politics in the 21st Century*. New York: Monthly Review Press, 2004. Print.

Moskowtiz, Marina. "'Aren't We All?' Aspiration, Acquisition, and the American Middle Class." *The Making of the Middle Class: Toward a Transnational History (Radical Perspectives)*. Eds. López, A. Ricardo & Barbara Weinstein. Durham: Duke University Press, 2012.75–86. Print.

Pearson, M. *China's Business Elite: The Political Consequences of Economic Reform*. Berkeley: University of California Press, 1997. Print.

Qiang, Xiao. "Cyber Speech: Catalyzing Free Expression and Civil Society." *Harvard International Review* 25, 2 (2003): 70–75. Print.

Smythe, Dallas. "After Bicycles? What?" *Counterclockwise: Perspectives on Communication*. Ed. Guback, T. Boulder: Westview Press, 1994. 230–244. Print.

So, A. Y. 2001. "The State, Economic Development and Changing Patterns of Classes and Class Conflict in China." International Conference on Money, Growth, and Distribution, Academia Sinica, Taipei, September 5–8. Print.

Veblen, Thorstein. *The Theory of the Leisure Class: An Economic Study of Institutions*. New York: Penguin Book, 1994 [1899]. Print.

Walkowitz, Daniel. "The Conundrum of the Middle-Class Worker in the Twentieth-Century United States: The Professional-Managerial Workers' (Folk) Dance around Class." *The Making of the Middle Class*. Eds. López, A. Ricardo & Barbara Weinstein. Durham: Duke University Press, 2012. 121–140. Print.

Wang, Xin. "Divergent Identities, Convergent Interests: The Rising Middle-Income Stratum in China and Its Civic Awareness." *Journal of Contemporary China* 54, 17 (2008): 53–69. Print.

———. "Seeking Channels for Engagement: Media Use and Political Communication by China's Rising Middle Class." China: An International Journal 7, 1 (2009): 31–56. Print.

Whyte, M. K. "The changing role of workers." *The Paradox of China's Post-Mao Reforms*. Eds. Goldman, M. and MacFarquhar. Cambridge, MA: Harvard University Press, 1999. 173–196. Print.

Wu. Changchang. "Micro-Blog and the Speech Act of China's Middle Class: The 7.23 Train Accident Case." *Javnost-The Public* 19.2 (2012): 43–62. Print.

Xu, Rong. "Taste: Symbolic Lifestyle of the Middle Class." Zhou, Xiaohong. Ed. *Survey of the Chinese Middle Class*. Beijing: Social Sciences Academic Press, 2005. 259–298. Print.

Yang, Guobin. "The Internet and Civil Society in China: A Preliminary Assessment." *Journal of Contemporary China* 12, 36 (2003): 453 – 475. Print.

Yang, Zan, and Jie Chen. Housing Affordability and Housing Policy in Urban China. 2014. New York: Springer. Print.

Yu, Haiqing. "Dwelling Narrowness: Chinese media and their disingenuous neoliberal logic." *Continuum: Journal of Media & Cultural Studies* 25.1.(2011): 33–46. Print.

Zhao, Yuezhi, *Communication in China: Political Economy Power, and Conflict*. Lanham, MD: Rowman and Littlefield, 2008. Print.

Zhou, Xiaohong, ed. *Survey of the Chinese Middle Class* [in Chinese]. Beijing, China: Social Sciences Academic Press, 2005. Print.

Section II

Economics and Consumers

4 Meanings Attached to Cruises by Emerging Consumers

A Study Using Participant Observation

Ana Raquel Coelho Rocha and Angela da Rocha

Introduction

This research aimed to study the meanings attached to cruises by consumers who recently moved from poverty to the middle class in Brazil. Marketing scholars have only now started to study this new segment of consumers in order to understand better their desires and aspirations, as they increasingly have access to credit and expand their consumption. The behavior of upwardly mobile consumers is becoming an important research topic because this phenomenon – the emergence of a large middle class from poverty – has become increasingly apparent and manifests in several developing countries, such as China, India, Turkey, South Africa, and some Latin American countries. It is estimated that over 1 billion people have recently entered consumer markets. In the case of Brazil, an estimated 30 to 40 million (15 to 20 percent of the Brazilian population) have moved up from the bottom of the pyramid into the middle class.

Several criteria have been used in Brazil to define those who belong to the middle class. For the Secretariat of Strategic Affairs (Brazil 2012), the Brazilian middle class comprises those families whose income per capita falls between the 34th and the 82nd percentile of the population's income distribution. Another classification used by firms and research institutes is the *Critério Brasil* (The Brazil Criteria). Both classification systems divide the middle class into three segments: low-middle class, middle-middle class, and upper-middle class. Table 4.1 compares the average monthly income used by both classification systems for each middle-class stratum.

Table 4.1 Middle-Class Strata in Brazil (Average Monthly Family Income in USD)

Strata	*SAE Classification*	*Critério Brasil*
Low-middle class	845	950
Middle-middle class	1,056	1,582
Upper-middle class	1,544	2,724

Source: Brazil 2012: 8.
Note: converted from *reais* to dollars based on the April 1, 2012 exchange rate.

This study looks at a specific phenomenon resulting from the emergence of a substantial number of individuals from poverty to the middle class. We adopt the term "emerging consumer" to designate this group. Although they tend to belong to the lower income stratum of the middle class, this is not necessarily the case. The relevant issue for the present study is not, therefore, the segment of the middle class they now belong to, but rather the fact that they only now have access to new types of leisure consumption and, specifically, to maritime cruises.

In fact, the consumption of leisure products is one of the characteristics of the phenomenon under study. Poor consumers do not have access to leisure products, and their consumption is often defined as pre-industrial; that is, limited to public spaces and family gatherings. Therefore, as consumers emerge from poverty, leisure is one of the areas in which they want to spend part of their discretionary income. Cruises are an outstanding example of a leisure product that has recently attracted the attention of this segment of the Brazilian population. A market study by Abremar, the Brazilian Association of Maritime Cruises (2012), showed that 63 percent of cruise travelers during the years 2010 and 2011 had their first experience with cruises and 87 percent intended to repeat. Approximately 45 percent of the travelers had a monthly family income of less than US$ 2,500, and 15 percent of less than US$ 1,250.

However, despite the growing importance of interpretive research in marketing (e.g. Denny 2006; Holbrook 2006), few studies have looked at the meanings of leisure, and even fewer have focused on how consumers from emerging markets create meanings from leisure. Venkatesh (2006) looked at meanings associated to leisure trips and devised a model that views leisure as a function of personality, motives, attitudes and context. However, although the author based part of his arguments on phenomenological studies, the proposed model was positivist, and, therefore, incapable of grasping the meanings consumers attach to leisure. In contrast, the work of Celsi et al. (1993) and Moutinho et al. (2007), exemplify the interpretive approach in marketing studies. In fact, there is a growing interest in the use of interpretive methods in the area of leisure studies (for example, Sharpe 2005; Shipway and Jones 2008; Yarnal 2004) as well as in other areas of social studies (e.g. Markula 1997; McDonald et al. 2011; Sletten 2010).

Scholars have called for more research on the consumption patterns of emerging middle-class consumers from developing countries (e.g. Üstüner and Holt 2010). This study looks specifically at the meanings attached to maritime cruises by emerging consumers belonging to the Brazilian middle class. Given the goal of understanding symbolic aspects of consumption, participant observation followed by in-depth interviews was the research method elected for the study.

Theoretical Background

Symbolic meanings attached by consumers to products and services change the nature of the offer to incorporate elements that, to a large extent, surpass its pure utilitarian value (Barbosa and Campbell 2006; McCracken 2003; Sherry Jr. 1995). Meanings associated to products and services can include issues such as identity, identification, self-image, distinction, socialization, or belonging. Consumers use products and services to speak about themselves and their relationship to others, as well as to participate in a socially constructed world. Consumption is, therefore, used both as a means of constructing social reality and as a means of (re)constructing the self. Because consumers typically have limited resources at their disposal, they have to be discerning in the choice of meanings to consume (Elliot 1997). Elliot calls attention to the intrinsic difficulty of studying symbolic representations, claiming that (i) they involve not only the symbol itself but also what the individual attaches to the symbol, and (ii) these representations can only be partially verbalized.

Holt (1995: 1) recognizes the use of three metaphors in the interpretive literature on consumer behavior – consumption as experience, consumption as integration, and consumption as classification – to which he adds a fourth, consumption as play. He used these four dimensions to study how spectators consume a baseball game. In this study, we started from these four categories to structure our analysis of participants in a maritime cruise.

Consumption as Experience

As pointed out by Holt (1995), the literature on hedonic consumption focuses more on the psychological processes (e.g. emotional states) associated to consumption and, therefore, looks at consumption more as an individual than a social phenomenon. Research on experiential consumption was pioneered by Hirschman and Holbrook (1982). Although still anchored, to some extent, in the traditional consumer behavior literature, with foundations in the fields of psychology and psychoanalysis, their work on hedonic consumption is mainly rooted on a phenomenological perspective of consumption. The key issues associated to hedonic consumption, according to this stream of research, are that (i) consumption has meanings that transcend the utilitarian value of a product or service; (ii) consumers' emotions prevail over rationality; and (iii) hedonic consumption is attached to a subjective construction of reality. The consumption experience was summarized by these authors as "fantasies, feelings and fun" (Holbrook and Hirschman 1982: 132). Campbell (1987: 85) suggests that a modern view of hedonism (which he named "autonomous imaginative hedonism") places the individual "as an artist of the imagination, taking images from memory or the environment and rearranging them." Such process, according to Campbell, is completed with the possession of the object or the usage of the service. However, consumers may or may not be satisfied depending on whether their expectations were met. When dissatisfied (which will be often the case since reality rarely meets anticipated imageries of an experience), consumers engage in the pursuit of "a new object of desire" (86). Campbell's view implies that consumers tend to be constantly frustrated and to substitute one dream by another in an almost unending search for pleasure, or satisfaction.

Emerging middle-class consumers should have an anticipatory view of the experience on a cruise, which is, to some extent, an elaboration of previous images collected from the social environment, as well as those produced by the media (including advertising and movies). These consumers will tend to elaborate further on this image by adding elements or rearranging those already in the memory to construct an anticipated image of a cruise. Once the cruise experience is over, they may be satisfied or dissatisfied, resulting in their desire for further cruises or their seeking other experiences.

Consumption as Integration

The second metaphor, consumption as integration, refers to how consumers actively engage in the process of creating and transferring social meanings. McCracken (1986) proposed an explanatory framework to describe the process, whereby meanings residing in the culturally constituted world are transferred to goods. Consumers then take possession of goods and transfer those meanings to their own selves. The instruments of meaning transfer from the culturally constituted world to products and services are advertising and the fashion system, through several agents that "gather up cultural meaning and effect its transfer to consumer goods" (77). Advertising as a cultural product is seen as providing consumers "with the opportunity to construct, maintain and communicate identity and social meanings" (Elliot 1997: 285). Once product "qualities" are incorporated into goods, the final step has to be taken by the consumer, who is the one responsible for transferring these meanings to their own life via ritualistic behavior.

According to McCracken (1986), rituals are activities performed by consumers to transfer to their lives symbolic properties that are associated to consumption artifacts (i.e. products and services). Rituals have specific norms that give directions as to how people should engage and behave during the ritualistic event (Üstüner, Ger, and Holt 2000). While performing rituals, consumers may use symbolic artifacts, follow predefined scripts, and perform specified roles to an audience (Rook 1985). Whereas not all these elements are necessary for a set of symbolic activities to be considered a ritual, their presence is considered an indication of the vitality of a ritual.

Rites of passage are one of the ways by which consumption is used to express the passage from one state to another, such as wedding ceremonies (Holt 2000), or plastic surgery by women undergoing role transitions (Schouten 1991). Shared celebratory occasions, such as Christmas (Tynan and McKechnie 2009) and Thanksgiving (Wallendorf and Arnould 1991), are also occasions in which consumers actively engage in ritualistic behavior to construct social meanings. Whereas traditional rituals are typically more stable and rigid, in modern societies, although more flexible and plastic, rituals are often the loci "where conflicting world-views converge." Accordingly, rituals may be used "as cultural resources to define new social boundaries" (Üstüner, Ger, and Holt 2000: 213). Integration can be achieved also by "adapting one's identity to fit institutionalized meanings through assimilating and producing practices" (Holt 1995: 14), as consumers adjust their selves to perform certain roles and follow existing scripts.

In the case of emerging middle-class consumers, one can expect that certain events – such as the participation in their first maritime cruise – be used symbolically to commemorate the passage from poverty to the middle class. We also expect that emerging middle-class consumers should be concerned with three elements of ritual behavior (artifacts, scripts, and roles) in maritime cruises insofar as they are novices in this type of consumption.

Consumption as Classification

The third metaphor, consumption as classification, looks at "consuming as a process in which objects – viewed as vessels of cultural and personal meanings – act to classify their consumers" (Holt 1995: 2). The classificatory nature of consumption, inspired by a long-standing tradition of sociological studies (e.g. Bourdieu 1979), has been used in interpretive consumer research to show how possessions are used by consumers to say something about themselves and to distinguish themselves from others (e.g. Mehta and Belk 1991). It should be noted, however, that traditional economic theory also has taken into account positional consumption, which is described by economists as demonstration effects, impacting more heavily on those with relatively low incomes (Frank 1985; Veblen 2000).

Bourdieu (1979) posited that economic capital and cultural capital are behind the differences among classes. People belonging to the higher classes tend to have a larger amount of economic and cultural capital than those belonging to the lower classes. Cultural capital is a key element to understand how consumption differs among social classes. Cultural capital permits one to choose, use, or consume products that require certain knowledge and learned skills. Taste, that is, is "the propensity and capacity to appropriate (materially or symbolically) a given class of classified, classifying objects or practices" (Bourdieu 2006: 295), is the mechanism by which material and cultural goods are changed into signs of a distinctive lifestyle. The choice of objects and the ways of using or consuming them are, therefore, quite homogeneous within a social group. Those that come from the same social standing have similar cultural capital and similar lifestyles and, therefore, "have every chance of having similar dispositions and interests, and thus of producing practices that are themselves similar" (Bourdieu 1989: 17). Accordingly, a system of differences is built around the ways an individual relates to the world, to others, and to his/her own self; moreover, such differences define the position one occupies in the social space.

Holt (1997) suggests that differences in social meanings embedded in consumption patterns can be used to create symbolic boundaries, which can be used to include some individuals and exclude others. In his study of consumption practices of individuals with low and high cultural capital in an American county, Holt found that it was not the consumption of products or services that distinguished the two groups, but rather the ways groups extracted meaning from them. For example, people with low cultural capital consumed leisure for the experience itself, while those with high cultural capital used leisure to express their individual creativity and achievement. Üstüner and Holt's (2010) study with upper middle-class female consumers in Turkey supported Bourdieu's (1979) contention that people use consumption to express their social standing and that their acquired cultural capital defines the meanings attached to consumption. Nevertheless, they found differences (in relation to the United States) on how social capital is acquired and how each group used consumption to mark differences.

In the case of emerging middle-class consumers, one expects that products and services be used to mark their upward social mobility, as well as to differentiate themselves from those that remained in poverty.

Consumption as Play

The fourth metaphor, play, refers to the use of consumption to interact with other consumers, "interaction for interaction's sake" (Holt 1995: 9). Play includes communing (sharing experiences with others) and socializing (a consumer assuming a more active role and entertaining another consumer). Holt (1995: 3) showed how "consuming as play" is also an important dimension, and can happen in private consumption (self-play) or in group consumption. Emerging consumers are probably eager to share their experiences with others and to socialize as they participate in a cruise.

This study starts from Holt's four metaphors to understand how consumers from the emerging middle class use cruises, simultaneously, to consume experiences, transfer symbolic properties to their selves, classify themselves as part of the middle class, and play. As the work progressed, we identified a fifth metaphor, which we called "consumption as achievement," which is probably typical of emerging consumers.

Methodology

The nature of the phenomenon under investigation suggested that participant observation, a method used in ethnography, might be appropriate to attain the goals of the study. The method entails the researcher spending a period of time to experience the situation under study as if he/she were a regular participant (Berreman 1990; Elliot and Jankel-Elliot 2003). The researcher acquires a more detailed and complex understanding of a social phenomenon because he/she has to experience it with others. It is particularly desirable to use the method when the experience of participation is considered critical to arrive at an understanding of the problem investigated (Jorgensen 1989). As preached by Geertz (1973), ethnography affords an understanding of the insiders' viewpoint from a microscopic perspective. This is exactly the case of a cruise experience.

Therefore, one of the authors embarked on a cruise to do the fieldwork. The selection of the cruise was based on the advice of cruise agents in order to select one that would better fit the desired profile of the target clientele. An eight-day all-inclusive cruise off the coast of Brazil was the locus of the participant observation. The researcher used a covert approach (Hammersley and Atkinson 1995); that is, she did not inform the others of her purpose, and acted as a regular traveler in the cruise. Interviews were informal and did not follow any specific guide, although a list of topics was prepared in advance – used mostly as a guideline for the fieldwork as a whole, and not for each specific interview. These casual conversations provided valuable information, since informants were not defensive. In addition, it was possible to take photos that could later serve as an additional element for the analysis. Several times a day, the researcher went back to her cabin to write a detailed account in a field diary of what she observed. Sometimes, when time was short, the researcher's observations were recorded (and later transcripts were made). By observing and conversing with people in the cruise, it was possible to get a general understanding of the situation, as well as a more in-depth understanding of the issues that the study intended to uncover.

The choice of informants was a difficult process because one could not ask directly questions related to family income. Therefore, indirect data were used to determine whether the informant belonged to the target population. Several criteria were applied to verify whether a cruise participant was a member of the "new" middle class: (i) type of work/job; (ii) neighborhood where he/she lived; (iii) whether the cruise was paid in installments; and (iv) other indications that emerged from informal conversations. At the end, 24 informants who were informally interviewed complied with the selection criteria.

After the end of the cruise, contacts were made with several participants. At this point, the researcher revealed her purpose with the cruise and asked for an additional interview. Six of the ten people approached at that point agreed in giving their time to discuss several aspects related to the cruise. These interviews, which followed a guide, were recorded and afterwards transcripts made.

Analytical work followed an abductive approach (Dubois and Gadde 2002), moving from deductive to inductive reasoning and back to deductive. A first round of analysis was done after the cruise ended, using field notes, photographs, and notes from interviews. Only after the first analysis was done, in-depth interviews were conducted and analyzed. Pattern-matching logic was employed to compare results with the literature.

Results

Results are described using Holt's four metaphors of consumption, and a fifth proposed metaphor, "consumption as achievement."

1. Consumption as Experience

Emerging consumers recognized that they were living an experience that did not jibe with their "real" lives, as if reality had been suspended for a few days. The limits of the ship, the isolation from outside interferences (except in the ports and short visits to the cities in the tour), the multiplicity of leisure activities occurring simultaneously within the ship, the rhythm and intensity of these activities, as well as the fact that they would start quite early and only end very late, created an atmosphere of "suspension of reality." On the cruise, everyday rules are suspended in the sense that there is no routine, no work, no responsibilities. Ana, one of the passengers interviewed after the cruise, described the experience as follows:

> It is a wonderful journey, a dream, a fantasy that lasts seven, eight days, but it's a dream. Because you have no commitments there. By commitment I mean schedules, paying bills – all these things that are part of everyday life. You see different people, even if occasionally you meet somebody you already know, but most people you meet on the cruise you had no access to before. You make new friends, different relationships, you get to see new places, new cities. In a very short period of time you have shows, movies, swimming – you have everything in there. You feel like a queen, Alice in Wonderland. An out-of-world experience. You pretend you don't care about prices, you pretend you don't have any problems, that nothing bad ever happens. You forget all these things. You get out of your routine and you create a moment that belongs to you. I say it's a dream because after a while it ends, right? After eight days, you wake up.

The rules of the "world outside" do not apply. One can do things that would not be considered appropriate in everyday life, such as eating too much, drinking too much, or dancing despite not knowing how to do dance: there are no official rules or limits. To some extent, the cruise experience presents similarities with the Brazilian Carnival (as analyzed by Brazilian anthropologist Roberto DaMatta 1983), in which there is also a suspension of reality.

Abundance was another aspect of the experience valued by consumers. Because it was an "all-inclusive" cruise, everything one could wish – food, beverages (including alcoholic beverages), a large variety of onboard entertainment, music, sunny days – was available in seemingly unlimited quantities and variety. Ana liked to try foods that she had not experienced before, and she felt there was no risk in trying different foods because if she did not like a dish, she could just ask for another: "Not satisfied for any reason? You have the option of eating meals or snacks in another space. I loved that." She had however ambivalent feelings toward the abundance of food. At the same time that she enjoyed the food, she felt uneasy with the waste: "For me this is not right, throwing food away … There are so many people in the world without food – they would certainly eat that dish without even knowing what it was … And here I was turning up my nose, throwing food away …"

Because abundance was not something these consumers experience in their daily lives, the cruise brought a once in a lifetime experience – for those on first cruise – an experience of wealth and complete satisfaction. In fact, the cruise simulates for a short period of time the life of the "leisure class," as portrayed by Veblen (2000), with its conspicuous consumption – and wastefulness. Waste is, in fact, an aspect that one notices at every moment of the cruise: the large amounts of food and beverages displayed and left over, the attractions that have a small number of participants but are still available.

2. Consumption as Integration

One of the issues examined in this study was how emerging consumers became aware of cruises and how they developed their imagery of a cruise. Word of mouth seemed to be the most common way by which these consumers became aware of the cruise. Maria saw cruises as something that "everybody is going on": "It's terrific to go on a cruise: it's fashionable, very fashionable. I do know it is the fashion now." Mariana heard from friends who "were dazzled" by the experience: "They talked about everything: food, fun, cleanliness, and how friendly the crew members were. They told so many things that I wanted to go too. An adventure, to see different places." Laura "always" wanted to go on a cruise and the opportunity came when she and two friends decided to share the same cabin:

> Cruises are now fashionable. Many of my friends have been on cruises. And we see a lot in magazines. So I had heard many stories of people who had been on cruises and everyone gave rave reviews. I went on the cruise already thinking of the parties, the dinners, the Captain's Party. I wanted to have fun.

Yet, it was clear that the images of a cruise preceded these recent experiences and stories told by friends and relatives who had already been on a cruise. For all our informants, a cruise carries an image of glamour, which seems to have been built from movies and TV shows. Laura described why she found the rooms glamorous: "Decoration, carpeting, objects, velvet, colors … The red refers to Hollywood, to what we're used to seeing on television." In fact the term "glamour" was frequently used to refer to the cruise, to the ship, or to the events during the cruise.

Ritualistic occasions, with their artifacts, scripts, and roles (Rook 1985), could be easily identified. One of the highlights of the cruise that most contributed to glamorize the experience was the "Captain's Night," with its formal dress code. To the event, the passengers used what was their finest attire, and took photographs to commemorate. The informants were anxious for the experience, and seemed to be prepared: dresses, suits, accessories, and hairstyles – the artifacts – were different from the casual style used every day. In this ceremonial occasion, people tried to emulate behaviors they considered appropriate for the event. They tried to eat in a more formal (and careful) way, they sat at the table according to stricter rules of etiquette, and so on. The photograph with the captain was specially prized – long lines formed with this purpose. It would, in the near future, provide tangible proof of having been on a cruise, something to be shared with others.

Informants attributed different status to different places in the ship. For example, the "gala restaurant" was designed for the wealthy, whereas the self-service restaurant was for everybody. Accordingly, one had to dress up and follow the appropriate etiquette rules when eating at the "gala restaurant," while there was no need for pretentiousness at the self-service.

Novice cruisers often felt uneasy because they did not know how "to behave properly," that is, they were not aware of the right scripts. This was often the case with food, because emerging consumers were unfamiliar with several of dishes served on the cruise. Julia, who saw the variety of food options as a source of embarrassment, also made them into an opportunity for fun and camaraderie:

> It made us get closer to other people on the trip because every night we would sit with the same people and get served by the same waiter. On the first night, no one knew the name of the dishes. Then everyone ordered without even knowing what they were ordering. And when the dish arrived, the waiter would set it on the table, on one small plate, with just a little food in the middle of the plate ... It was very funny, but also disappointing. But this is how we made friends with the others, because everyone looked at the dish, and then looked at each other. Well, the friendship was made right there. Because the situation was very funny. So from that night on we've wondered what everyone else is eating: 'What is that on your plate?' 'Can I try some?' And one was already passing the fork to another. Sometimes we already knew the dish, but by a different name. I ordered one meal that when it came, it was pods. So simple, but they used mega names. It was a very funny thing. Afterwards, we had no problems in choosing, because we became friends with the waiter. So we would ask, 'Hey, what's that?' And he would reply, 'Madam, it is duck in orange sauce.' Then, on the third night, the waiter knew exactly who we were and what kinds of things we liked.

Maria noticed that some passengers did not know what to eat, but they felt embarrassed to ask the waiter: "I think they did not know the names of the dishes, but they seemed shy about it. They did not ask the waiter, they asked each other. But there is no reason for embarrassment: you paid for it, then you can ask."

Selecting the proper attire was a major concern for our informants. McCracken (1986) sees the careful preparation for a gala evening, a dinner, or a party, as grooming rituals performed by consumers before they expose themselves to "public scrutiny" (79). Julia brought too many clothes and accessories with her to use during the cruise, because she was not aware of how people dressed in such a situation:

> I did not know the routines on a cruise. I always think of all the possibilities. So the first day, I and my sister dressed very well, because we thought: 'We are poor, we paid the cruise in installments, but nobody knows, and the first impression is what sticks.' One of the young men at the table looked at us from top down, and I thought he was thinking 'these are two black women pretending they are something else.'

Mariana had a similar experience; she also took with her a lot of clothes to be sure she would dress properly for every occasion, only to find out later that they were not needed: "I had an image of how people behave on a cruise; I expected people to be very well dressed, very elegant. And then you get there and see that things are much simpler." Nevertheless, she was proud of being well dressed for the Captain's Night; she knew the script: "I already knew what was going to happen, so I was prepared. I made a dress especially for the Captain's Night. The dress was all a glow, all sparkly."

Packing and unpacking can be seen as the initial and final rituals associated to the cruise. For example, Laura was very careful in preparing her bag: "I packed my bag a month before. I thought of everything I would wear. Because there are many options. There are the combinations, the options for the day and the night." Claudia went with friends and she explained that they carefully discussed what they should take with them:

> We were very excited, anticipating everything would be great. We couldn't wait to go. 'We have to take a lot of clothes for the cruise – we have to be well-dressed – we don't want to be embarrassed.' We separated all the clothes well in advance. We started by selecting the bikinis: bikini X was to be used with the outfit X, and with the sandals X. We bought new beach hats to protect ourselves from the sun. We also took a lot of night dresses, and in fact ended up by using them all.

And Julia had a final ritual of cleaning all her clothes after the cruise ended: "I had to wash, because everything was mixed up in the suitcase, and I had to wash and clean all the dirty clothes." Unpacking the objects used on the trip, washing them and placing them back in the closet are a type of divestment rituals (McCracken 1986). By cleaning and washing clothes, the consumer brings her objects back to her daily life: they no longer belong to the realm of the cruise.

3. Consumption as Classification

To go on a cruise meant to be part of a select group of people that had the chance (and the means) to buy the experience. One informant mentioned that "the cruise is great, it has high-status people." Several of our informants were impressed by the opportunity to experience a cruise with "upper-class" cruisers. Mariana said: "Honestly, I found the people on the cruise quite select. Everyone played; everyone had fun; but at no time did you see any disorderliness or fights." And Maria described the passengers on the cruise according to their appearance in a quite homogeneous group: "I think most people were there for the first time. A few pretended they were wealthy, sophisticated, but most people behave naturally. The way they dress, the way they talk, their behavior: the people on the cruise were neither rich nor too poor."

Interestingly, one of the characteristics stressed by several passengers was the omnipresence of service on the ship. Service was one of the attractions to these emerging consumers, who often worked, or had worked, in service jobs, in which they were the ones serving upper-class consumers. Therefore, the constant service was highly appreciated, and was seen as an inversion of their everyday reality. Julia mentioned that before she decided to buy a cruise, one of the attractions people mentioned was the service: "It is a different thing with people doing things for you ... For you know that it is a service, and the money was well spent."

One specific way of stressing differences was by those that had already been on a cruise, like Maria: "people like us, who have already been on a cruise, we are used to it ..." They played the role of "experts," showing the others how to do things, where things were, or how to use the facilities. Typically, they would claim that "the other cruise was better," and described features (such as better facilities, or more disciplined passengers) to support their claim.

Yet the cruise was also perceived as a space where social differences were temporarily removed: all passengers were equal, all had access to exactly the same services, and all were treated by crew members as equals. Therefore, the cruise is also perceived by emerging consumers as democratic, equalitarian, unlike the "world outside," which is hierarchical. Being a black woman, Julia was very aware of this feeling of equalitarianism:

> It is an environment with all kinds of people, but people are the same. There is none of this 'Oh, I will wear these clothes to show up, so and so.' No, there you are yourself and you are a person. Even if you see

> wealthy people, with their whole family, they still are like everyone else. You don't know the other passengers. I mean, the lives they live. If they made a sacrifice to buy [the cruise], if somebody paid for them, or if they are just enjoying it. Everybody shares the space in the restaurant, the space in the elevator, so there's no such thing as division.

The experience can be compared to a visit to a shopping center, where the outside world is for some hours left behind, and "the equality of 'everyone'" becomes the rule (Fiske 2000).

4. Consumption as Play

Holt (1995: 3) suggested that "consuming as play" be considered another metaphor for consumption. He proposed two processes by which consumers use consumption to play: socializing and communing.

Socializing is a key feature of a cruise for several informants. Sometimes people enjoyed socializing with other passengers, but others preferred to socialize within their own group (family members or friends that embarked together). Some informants reported that there was a sense of camaraderie among the cruisers. Ana explained: "You make friends on a cruise, and you do not feel alone ... On the first day you start by making friends in the waiting line. At the check-in, you already make friends ..." Claudia, a younger woman, found the experience of socializing with her friends on a cruise highly pleasurable: "To go with friends, to have fun, not to worry about anything, staying in the pool sunbathing, the rite of getting ready everyday – it was terrific."

As stressed by Holt (1995), consumers were not only observers who participated in the cruise, but also active players who co-constructed the spectacle. Julia described how audience and actors became the same:

> Customers were part of everything. It was all very interactive. We participated in everything, both at night and during the morning in the pool. Everything engaged the public. See, it was not a show that excluded us. We were part of the show. The show started, the performance took place, and then the presenter turned to the public as well, and we were just kind of taking part on it all. [...] And they say your name, they invite you to participate. And I was shy, I was wondering, 'Is he going to call me?' So you are not just one more person, you are a part of the whole thing. And everybody – the crew, the staff, the passengers – everybody was part of it.

Although the cruise could be seen as a spectacle performed every day, every moment, were both cruise members and passengers were actors, the Captain's Night was the supreme moment of the cruise. More than ever, passengers became actors performing the ongoing play, as described by Ana:

> The night before we arrived in Rio de Janeiro, there was the Captain's Party. At some point, the lights dimmed. There was music in the background and lights went off. It was dark. And then they entered, each carrying an ice cream cake like a volcano. All the waiters were in costume gala and they were introduced to the passengers. Then they light up this volcano, the candle coming out of the cake. The waiters serve the tables; they bring the cake to your table for you to take a picture, to honor you and to thank you for coming.

Mariana referred to a specific activity in which the passengers were both organizers and participants as one of the most attractive parts of the cruise:

> It goes on all the time. From the time you wake up until the time you go to sleep, it is pure fun. I particularly enjoyed the show "The Tourist is the Artist." It is a show that the passengers organize. They choose something they know and then they make a presentation in the theater, and the other passengers get to watch. It is very entertaining.

5. Consumption as Achievement

Emerging consumers used the cruise as a way to build their new social identity by choosing a glamorous, sophisticated leisure activity. To be part of a cruise was, therefore, seen as a tangible expression of achievement: "I can afford it and I deserve it," Julia explained in the interview after the cruise:

> And so it happened. It was not something I dreamt of, but it happened. I could afford it, and I did. I had heard other people talking about cruises. ... Then one day I entered the site and took a look. And then I went up to the girl in the agency. We signed the contract and paid the installments. Everything the right way. Back home, I still had installments to pay. But I was glad to pay because I had the experience, one that I could afford.

Several informants were aware of the sacrifices necessary to book a cruise, but they felt rewarded by the experience, and were desirous of repeating it. One passenger said, "This is the first time I do something for myself ... But from now on, even if I have to work 365 days a year, I am going to take one week off every year for a cruise."

The sense of achievement was reinforced after the cruise ended, when consumers had the chance to tell their stories to others. Claudia explained: "After I did the cruise, everyone said, 'oh, I envy you.' ... Even though [a cruise is] more accessible today, it is still something that everyone wants, to be different and to enjoy all these attractions."

Yet there seems to be a lot of encouragement for others to experience a cruise too. Mariana saw her experience as something she fought for and conquered, but that was also accessible to others like her: "When I tell others about the cruise, they ask how much it costs. But it is not expensive: it can be afforded by anyone who works and battles for a better life."

Several informants expressed their careful financial planning to be able to go on the cruise. Emerging consumers were aware of the costs of a cruise in relation to their budget. They seemed to reduce the dissonance of spending a considerable amount of their budget on a cruise by evaluating the experience as extremely rewarding and the cruise as "a good deal." The rationale was that if one were to pay separately for all the shows, food and drinks, and other aspects of the cruise, the total cost would be much higher. Also, they tended to regard themselves as smart buyers, since they had booked the cruise well in advance (often as much as year), a decision that enabled to get a better deal.

Conclusion

Consumption choices, particularly those related to lifestyle (of which leisure is an essential part), serve as markers of social identity. We explored in this study five metaphors of consumption to explain how consumers from the emerging middle class in Brazil consumed maritime cruises. Besides confirming the four metaphors suggested by Holt (1995) to study a baseball game, we identified a fifth metaphor used by emerging consumers, one we called "consumption as achievement."

This study contributes to the literature on the consumption of individuals who have emerged from poverty to the middle class in the last two decades. Because of the importance of this segment, which represents approximately one sixth of the world population, and the dearth of research on the phenomenon, the study opens new windows to the understanding of how ascending consumers may use their discretionary income to buy leisure products and the meanings they ascribe to them.

Consumption is an essential element of life in contemporary societies. As pointed out by Douglas and Isherwood (1979:12), goods "can be used as fences or bridges," to exclude or to include. Societies exclude individuals that have no access to consumption; they are invisible to the other members of their own society. Access to consumption is therefore a symbol of achievement, a beacon of distinction, and a defining feature of middle classness for emerging consumers.

Much research remains to be done in order to expand our knowledge of this phenomenon. Changes in lifestyle as consumers ascend in the social structure are a key issue for marketers. Among the topics that could interest future researchers in marketing, the acquisition of other symbols of middle-class status, such as the first car, a home in a more selective neighborhood, a health plan, or private school for the children could reveal new facets of how emerging consumers use consumption to enact their new social status, to affirm identities, and to change lifestyles.

In addition, one should not underestimate the political and social impacts of this phenomenon. As these individuals have access to other types of consumption, several changes will pose new threats to politicians, urban planners, and the private sector, such as urban mobility and pollution, caused by the large increase in the number of cars; rising property prices, due to the increased demand for homes in upscale neighborhoods; or insufficient private hospital infrastructure and services due to a substantial increase in the number of health plans. Consequences of the consumption of the "new" middle class in emerging markets, therefore, also pose a challenge to researchers in several other fields.

Works Cited

Abremar. "Cruzeiros Marítimos: Estudo de Perfil e Impactos Econômicos no Brasil." 2012. Brasilcruise.com.br. Web. 23 Sept.2013.

Barbosa, Livia, and Collin Campbell. *Cultura, Consumo e Identidade*. Rio de Janeiro: FGV, 2006. Print.

Berreman, Gerald D. "Etnografia e Controle de Impressões em uma Aldeia do Himalaia." *Desvendando Máscaras Sociais*. Ed. Alba Z. Guimarães. 3rd ed. Rio de Janeiro: Francisco Alves, 1990. 123–174. Print.

Bourdieu, Pierre. *La Distinction: Critique Sociale du Jugement*. Paris: Les Éditions de Minuit, 1979. Print.

Bourdieu, Pierre. "Distinction." *Inequality: Classic Readings in Race, Class, and Gender*. Ed. Grusky, David B. and Szonja Szelényi. Boulder, Colorado: Westview Press, 2006. 287–318. Print.

Bourdieu, Pierre. "Social Space and Symbolic Power." *Sociological Theory*, 7.1 (1989): 14–25. Print.

Brazil, SAE. Secretariat of Strategic Affairs. Office of the President. "Perguntas e Respostas sobre a Definição da Classe Média." 2012. Sae.gov.br. Web. 6 Nov. 2013.

Campbell, Collin. *The Romantic Ethic and the Spirit of Modern Consumerism*. Cambridge, Mass.: Backwell, 1987. Print.

Celsi, Richard L., Randall L. Rose, and Thomas W. Leigh. "An Exploration of High-Risk Leisure Consumption through Skydiving." *Journal of Consumer Research* 20.1 (1993): 1–23. Print.

DaMatta, Roberto. *Carnavais, Malandros e Heróis: Para uma Sociologia do Dilema Brasileiro*. 4th ed. Rio de Janeiro: Zahar, 1983. Print.

Denny, Rita M. "Pushing the Boundaries of Ethnography in the Practice of Market Research." *Handbook of Qualitative Research Methods in Marketing*. Ed. Russell W. Belk. Cheltenham, U.K.: Edward Elgar Publishing, 2006. 430–439. Print.

Douglas, Mary, and Baron Isherwood. *The World of Goods: Towards an Anthropology of Consumption*. London: Allen Lane, 1979. Print.

Dubois, Anna, and Lars-Erik Gadde. "Systematic Combining: An Abductive Approach to Case Research." *Journal of Business Research*, 55.7 (2002): 553–560. Print.

Elliot, Richard. "Existential Consumption and Irrational Desire." *European Journal of Marketing* 31.3/4 (1997): 285–298. Print.

Elliot, Richard, and Nick Jankel-Elliot. "Using Ethnography in Strategic Consumer Research." *Qualitative Market Research* 6.4 (2003): 215–223. Print.
Fiske, John. "Shopping for Pleasure: Malls, Power and Resistance." *The Consumer Society Reader.* Ed. Juliet B. Schor and Douglas B. Holt. New York: The New York Press, 2000. 306–328. Print.
Frank, Robert H. "The Demand for Unobservable and Other Nonpositional Goods." *American Economic Review* 75.1 (1985). 101–116. Print.
Geertz, Clifford. *The Interpretation of Cultures.* New York: Basic Books, 1973. Print.
Hammersley, Martyn, and Paul Atkinson. *Ethnography: Principles in Practice.* New York: Routledge, 1995. Print.
Hirshman, Elizabeth C., and Morris B. Holbrook. "Hedonic Consumption: Emerging Concepts, Methods and Propositions." *Journal of Marketing* 46.3 (1982): 92–101. Print.
Holbrook, Morris B. "Photo Essays and the Mining of Minutiae in Consumer Research." *Handbook of qualitative research methods in marketing.* Ed. Russell W. Belk. Cheltenham, U.K.: Edward Elgar Publishing, 2006. 476–493. Print.
Holbrook, Morris B., and Elizabeth C. Hirshman. "The Experiential Aspects of Consumption: Consumer Fantasies, Feelings, and Fun." *Journal of Consumer Research* 9.2 (1982): 132–140. Print.
Holt, Douglas B. "How Consumers Consume: A Typology of Consumption Practices." *Journal of Consumer Research* 22.1 (1995): 1–16. Print.
Holt, Douglas B. "Poststructuralist Lifestyle Analysis: Conceptualizing the Social Patterning of Consumption in Postmodernity." *Journal of Consumer Research* 23.4(1997): 326–350. Print.
Holt, Douglas B. "Does Cultural Capital Structure American Consumption?" *Journal of Consumer Research* 25.1 (1998): 1–25. Print.
Jorgensen, Danny L. *Participant Observation: A Methodology for Human Studies.* Newbury Park: Sage (Applied Social Research Methods Series, v.15), 1989. Print.
Markula, Pirkko. "As a Tourist in Tahiti: An Analysis of Personal Experience." *Journal of Contemporary Ethnography* 26.2 (1997): 202–225. Print.
McDonald, Paula, Barbara Pini, Janis Bailey, and Robin Price, R. "Young People's Aspirations for Education, Work, Family and Leisure." *Work, Employment & Society* 25.1. (2011): 68–74. Print.
McCracken, Grant. *Cultura & Consumo.* Rio de Janeiro: Mauad, 2003. Print.
McCracken, Grant. (1986) "Culture and Consumption: A Theoretical Account of the Structure and Movement of the Cultural Meaning of Consumer Goods." *Journal of Consumer Research* 13.1 (1986): 71–84. Print.
Mehta, Raj, and Russell W. Belk. "Artifacts, Identity, and Transition: Favorite Possessions of Indians and Indian Immigrants to the United States." *Journal of Consumer Research* 17.4 (1991): 398–411. Print.
Moutinho, Luiz, Pedro Dionisio, and Carmo Leal. "Surf Tribal Behaviour: A Sports Marketing Application." *Marketing Intelligence & Planning* 25.7 (2007): 668–690. Print.
Rook, Dennis W. "The Ritual Dimension of Consumer Behavior." *Journal of Consumer Research* 12.3 (1985): 251–264. Print.
Schouten, John W. "Selves in Transition: Symbolic Consumption in Personal Rites of Passage and Identity Reconstruction." *Journal of Consumer Research* 17 (1991): 412–425. Print.

Sharpe, Erin K. "Delivering Communitas: Wilderness Adventure and the Making of Community." *Journal of Leisure Research* 37.3 (2005): 255–280. Print.

Sherry Jr., John F. "Anthropology of Marketing and Consumption: Retrospect and Prospect." *Contemporary Marketing and Consumer Behavior: An Anthropological Sourcebook*. Ed. John F. Sherry Jr. Thousand Oaks: Sage, 1995. 435–445. Print.

Shipway, Richard, and Ian Jones. "The Great Suburban Everest: An 'Insiders' Perspective on Experiences at the 2007 Flora London Marathon." *Journal of Sport & Tourism* 13.1 (2008): 61–77. Print.

Sletten, Mira A. "Social Costs of Poverty; Leisure Time Socializing and the Subjective Experience of Social Isolation among 13–16-Year-Old Norwegians." *Journal of Youth Studies* 13.3 (2010): 291–315. Print.

Tynan, Caroline, and Sally McKechnie. "Hedonic Meaning Creation through Christmas Consumption: A Review and Model." *Journal of Customer Behavior* 8.3 (2009): 237–255. Print.

Üstüner, Tuba, and Douglas B. Holt. "Towards a Theory of Status Consumption in Less Industrialized Countries." *Journal of Consumer Research* 37.1 (2010): 37–56. Print.

Üstüner, Tuba, Güliz Ger, and Douglas B. Holt. "Consuming Ritual: Reframing the Turkish Henna-Night Ceremony." *Advances in Consumer Research* 27 (2000): 209–214. Print.

Veblen, Thorstein. "Conspicuous Consumption." *The Consumer Society Reader*. Ed. Juliet B. Schor and Douglas B. Holt. New York: The New York Press, 2000. 187–204. Print.

Venkatesh, Umashankar. "Leisure – Meaning and Impact on Leisure Travel Behavior." *Journal of Services Research* 6.Special Issue (2006): 87–108. Print.

Wallendorf, Melanie, and Eric J. Arnould. "'We Gather Together': Consumption Rituals of Thanksgiving Day." *Journal of Consumer Research* 19.1 (1991): 13–31. Print.

Yarnal, Careen M. "Missing the Boat? A Playfully Serious Look at a Group Cruise Tour Experience." *Leisure Sciences* 26.4 (2004): 349–372. Print.

5 Conjectures on Global Virtual Economies

Discretionary Consumption, Online Gaming and the Rise of the Global Middle Class

Manuel (MJR) Montoya

Introduction

On June 2012, Blizzard Entertainment, a subsidiary of well-regarded video game developer Activision, launched a "Real Money Auction House" (RMAH) within its massively successful Massive Multiplayer Online Role Playing Game (MMORPG), *Diablo 3*[1]. The RMAH served as an online sales component within the game, allowing customers to purchase special items (i.e. weapons, armor, relics) that provided advancement in the game. While the game provides opportunities to "mine" gold (a virtual currency within the game) for the purchase of items, those customers unwilling or unable to invest the amount of time needed to cultivate these resources were given an opportunity to exchange real money either for the virtual in-game gold or directly for valuable items. What makes this process interesting is that any gamer could ostensibly go into business for him or herself mining gold, crafting weapons or a combination of the two. While other games have had components of this before, *Diablo 3*'s RMAH served as the first trading system fully-immersed within the reality of the game. Rather than being an external unit of account, the system (vis-à-vis a complex interface with monetary intermediaries such as PayPal, Bitcoin, and other digital exchanges) was able to exchange currencies while making the consumer participate in a distinct and fully realized parallel economy. *Diablo 3*'s four million subscribers from almost every part of the planet produced an unprecedented economic phenomenon. In 2012, gamers represented 143 nations and all seven continents (there were four instances of gameplay in Antarctica) and the gaming pool constituted nearly 130,000 people at any given point throughout the day[2]. Not only were consumers trading with a currency that was supranational, the theatricality of video-game gold combined with the omnipresence of foreign exchange created the circumstances for a currency that was universally signified in-game while being internationally traded out-of-game.

Diablo 3 is an interesting case study not because of its popularity, but because it introduced problems that exemplify the complexity of the social realities we have and the social realities that mediate our economic behavior.

As Lopez and Weinstein argue, we must resist the "tired teleology of first here, then there" when describing the experiences of people throughout the world (Lopez and Weinstein 7). The problem with historicizing the experiences of people is that the geographies that mediate our identity are prioritized and placed in a hierarchy of meaning. We believe ourselves to feel more deeply in our local spaces, and thus we tie ourselves to the idea that we belong more meaningfully to local spaces. But virtual spaces are not local. They don't subscribe to a "first here, then there" hierarchy. Moreover, Diablo 3 had a fully realized and self-contained economy that connected the forces of global capital without relying on conventional spaces wherein these exchanges were understood. The RMAH closed in March of 2014, for many reasons, most publicly that the software could not sustain the complicated and nuanced market it tapped into.[3] The short lifespan of the auction house highlights the popularity of the exchanges within the game, but also provides insight into a problem that has challenged the discourse on the global middle class. In some countries, the RMAH was banned.

Studies of the global middle class are complicated, mostly because each term ("global," "middle" and "class") contains qualities that are difficult to contextualize. Recent attempts to describe the global middle class have employed ethnography, focusing on the encounter between local communities and global capital (Heiman, Freeman, and Liechty 14). However, the emphasis on the global's impact on the local still leaves the "global" without its own distinctive content. Instead, global capital is still assumed as an invisible force that impacts well-defined communities, and does not account for the consumption patterns that shape the global.

The "middle" part is a little more established. In 2002, Prahalad and Hart established groundbreaking work on the distribution of global income worldwide (53). At that time, they produced striking numbers: 1 billion of the world's population earned above $20,000 adjusted USD, 1 billion earned between $2,000 and $20,000, and 5 billion earned below $2000 adjusted USD. What can be gleaned from this information is complicated. While one can rightly cultivate systemic poverty and social justice issues that have developed over many centuries, one can also see the immense amount of opportunity for growth (in the multiple ethical frameworks this can be conceived). Some projections estimate that income distribution will shift dramatically over the next fifteen years. By 2030, European and American middle-income groups will constitute only 22 percent of the world's middle-income population whereas Asia will constitute 64 percent of that middle-income grouping (Kharas 15). This group will total 4.9 billion people. However, most scholars have been confounded by the difference between a global middle *class* and global middle *income*.

"Class" implies a cultural category that is relatively difficult to describe. As discretionary income rises within the global economy, issues of class will follow. As consumption patterns translate into other cultural practices, so too will groups of people "enact the collective programming of the mind that will differentiate one group of people from another" (Hofstede, 26). Class is a cultural category that may include income, but is the result of a much more nuanced socio-economic process. Prahalad and Hart's famous work on the base of the global income pyramid (often referred to as "BoP") reveal that discretionary income is on the rise across the world and across a diverse cross section of societies (55). The concept of the BoP has been used to describe new economic and political dynamics of the twenty-first century, coming from people that had been perceived as limited in their ability to shape the global agenda. As global consumers enact global culture, they will create class structures that have previously not been seen, which requires that we frame the emergence of these consumption patterns into new communities, which by extension, will bridge the presently dubious conflation of global middle class and global middle income. This brief exposition seeks to contribute an understanding of what is "global" in global culture, by focusing on phenomena that let the global appear in a meaningful way. Virtual economies have the ability to contribute content to the global experience in a unique way, and herein the study of a consumption pattern drawn within a virtual experience will contribute conjectures on how the "global" contributes to the concept of a global middle class.

Theoretical Background

Discussions of the global middle class have been emergent for over a decade. The following background information tries to refine what is meant by "global" in relation to the term "middle class" to clarify any redundancies in the usage of those terms as they have traditionally been employed.

What Is the Global Middle Class?

The majority of discussions around the middle class revolve around several basic concepts. Banerjee and Duflo contend that the middle class is conceptualized by three basic things: democracy, defined largely by tolerance and civil liberties; entrepreneurial values, measured and refined by the mobilization of human capital and savings; and lastly a sense of consumption that emerges from access to a marketing culture and information about the quality of goods (5–6). This is reinforced by scholars who find significance in these three factors and find that the confluence of these factors create an environment wherein discretionary income becomes a mobilized component of an individual's economic possibilities (Barro 43; Acemoglu and Ziliboti 734; Easterly 24). To varying degrees, the middle class around the world is measured either as a rigid economic variable (an economic factor) or as a composition of values and systemic features that make it possible for individual choice to converge with political, economic and social values (Murphy, Shleifer, and Vishny 544). In each case, the debate between middle income serving as middle class is a central theme. It is notable that in these discussions, it is rarely if ever discussed what is "global" about either middle income or middle class, respectively. Heiman, Leichty, and Freeman describe this behavior as a constellation of forces that are creating cultures of work, structures that change "consumption patterns, reproduction and citizenship," each of which contain the subjectivities that construct class and more specifically, the "aspirations" that mobilize the social construction of class (6). The problem remains that in those aspirations, such subjectivities are still bound by local geographies. The global rarely, if ever, emerges as a relevant geography that contains its own subjectivity. Hence, global ethnographies are elusive because the container (the global) is not a dimension with any depth and therefore is rarely seen as a legitimate space that shapes our experiences. For example, the lack of a global currency (the USD is used as a proxy if not the International Monetary Fund's SDR index) demonstrates the economic dominance of the more particularistic features of our economic experiences. Thus, the processes of class (the subjective work needed to create habitus) excludes the global.

What Is Global?

Boli and Lechner define global culture as:

> ... certain ideas and principles ... presented as globally relevant and valid and are seen as such by those who absorb them ... grows alongside of, and in complex interaction with the more particularistic cultures of the world ... encompasses different domains and contains tensions among its different components ... is a crystallizing phenomenon with its own content and structure ... is a socially shared symbolic and meaning-making system ... and is open to new ideas, vulnerable to new conflicts, and subject to continual reinterpretation (25–29).

We like to mark as global anything that interacts across boundaries. So long as we put together a "greatest hits" of civilizations when talking about history, culture, life, society, we superficially mark it as global. A person traveling to a new country claims to participate in some form of global citizenship simply because they have left the borders they associate with "home." But being global, if it is to have its own structure and content, must be more than the sum of its parts. It must have qualities that make the time and place of the world seem more real, more specific, and directly tied to what belongs to the planet. Scholte argues that we use redundant frameworks when discussing globalization. What we commonly refer to as globalization is more likely explained by internationalization, universalization, Westernization, imperialization, and liberalization (Scholte 51). All these processes matter deeply to the formation of the world, but they only explain parts of what makes the world have its "own thing." Those who participate in global culture then are participating in enacting a set of practices that have crystallized into a distinct set of traits and properties that are largely associated with the body of the planet as a realized object. How does one define a global middle class when the concept of a global economy, much less a global community, remains relatively incoherent? What we commonly refer to as "globalization" has become a term that means everything and nothing at once. On the one hand, globalization is a fast moving process of interactions that connect us to the world and has in some instances provided a new vocabulary to describe emergent social realities. On the other hand, it is a force that has stratified the people, places, and things of the world so much, that even the most common social vocabulary is rendered without deep substance.

Virtual economies provide great insight into the way that global culture has crystallized. Because the world and its people are understood through a lens of countless cultural categories, we experience an environment we call global that both has no sense of place and also still imagines itself as participating in an amorphous global village that somehow has substance and tangible cultural content (Appadurai 35). In the words of Arjun Appaurai:

> The world we live in seems rhizomatic, even schizophrenic, calling for theories of rootlessness alienation, and psychological distance between individuals and groups on the one hand and fantasies (or nightmares) of electronic propinquity on the other ... if a global system is emerging, it is filled with ironies and resistances, sometimes camouflaged in the Asian world by all things Western (29).

The curious case of *Diablo 3*, an online game with a Western narrative derived largely from medieval Judeo-Christian mythology, represents the cultural framework that Appadurai and others propose. While the fantasy produced by the game (or the nightmare as one would encounter it) may have been uniquely Western at one point, it has been appropriated by numerous sets of social imaginings. The hunt for the "primevals," the fallen angels and demons that loom ominously in the game are no longer the indices of Western traditions found in a twelveth century epic poem. One could argue that the works of Dante or Milton, whom much of the source material for the game is owed, was Western only to the extent that it marked the complex and incoherent encounter of Christianity with the innumerable images and beliefs of the world around it. Even 800 years ago, these narratives were as much about the collision of Western ideas (and the ethnocentrism inscribed therein) with a new and barely understood world (Berlin 78). Since then, the narratives of Gothic knights errant hunting down evil in the name of a Christian god is only the thin veneer whereby a world of customized heroes and constantly evolving characters interact. It is no coincidence that *Diablo 3* has a subscription base that spans every part of the planet, and is paid for by almost every known currency therein. Those who play Diablo 3 are not consuming a Western platform; they are merely standing upon it and appropriating it with a nearly limitless set of materials to invent and reinvent the realities of the game. The era of the avatar is the era of the "re," "de," and "counter" appropriation of what the world is and was. It is a playground, much like the fantastic world that Alice encounters in Wonderland, where everything is familiar, but maddeningly unfamiliar at once. What Diablo players consume is a much more complex set of cultural interactions that are more consistent with the rootlessness and rhizomatic processes that Deleuze and Guattari mark as a fundamental problem of the modern world system (*Plateaus* 157). *Diablo 3* represents a game that imagines itself in this equally constructive and disjunctural process. The game's properties help us understand why "global" (as a category) is an elusive term.

If the game itself is a constant revision of its own narrative, despite the strong aesthetic elements within the game, how then, does it produce anything but a post-modern condition whereby anything is meaningful and can be seen as global? One cannot deny the compelling image of a Europen-Alp borne barbarian wielding a sword from Japanese legend fighting alongside an Incan-like community against a horde of demons drawn from Sumerian lore. In the case of *Diablo 3*, the answer may lie less in the post-modern imaginings that the game permits, but instead in the machinations that produce such imaginings. Fighting demons within a fully contained universe doesn't necessarily produce global culture (although the cross-pollination of images and objects does matter deeply). It is the structure of the Massive Mutli-player Online Role Playing Game (MMORPG) itself, the subscription to an online gaming service that provides the ingredient that turns that universe into something global. By 2014, frustrations with the game caused several governments to ban the use of real money exchanges, for reasons similar to the concerns with Bitcoin[4]. Sovereign governments are increasingly having to contend with non-sovereign exchanges. The "first here, then there" is not merely is historical problem. It's a political urgency prompted by nations to ensure that it can retain control over economic decisions, which translates into cultural practices. Ultimately, *Diablo 3*, at the height of its popularity contained the economic forces of global capital while also serving as a place where global behavior could produce meaningful communities and cultural practices. It represents a place where "global," "middle," and "class" crystallize in a unique and valuable way.

Methodology: Applying the "Imagined Community" to the RMAH

Benedict Andreson's concept of the "imagined community" becomes useful to help articulate this point further. In his exploration of nationalism and the power nationality has in mediating our social identity, Anderson suggests that all communities are:

1. Imagined – meaning that communities are large and complex and therefore require shared signs and symbols to represent being and belonging to these complex communities.

2. Limited – meaning no one community is coterminous with humanity, hence, identity politics produce limits across all levels of being and belonging.
3. Sovereign – meaning every community has a "higher power" or an authentic placeholder for the ability to make rules matter to people. Much like the Hobbesian concept of the "Leviathan," every community must have a "Sovereign"—something great to believe in so that power and the ability to abide by rules (some social contract) is worth believing in it (Hobbes 17).
4. Communities – meaning there is a deeply felt connection amongst people who share these symbols, produce these limits, and contribute to the self-determination of that community (Anderson 10, 48).

This exercise is quite simple. If culture is about the way we imagine it, one must first begin the work of building conceptual frameworks that identify the distinctiveness of those social imaginings.

Discussion: The RMAH as an "Imagined Community"

If a class is anything, it is a community. To begin what is essentially a "Gordian" prospect (a term Anderson applies quite genuinely to the naming of complex communities) one may apply the concept of an imagined community as a way to prompt a refined definition of the circumstances to produce a given cultural framework. In this regard, we will apply this to virtual economies and the consumption patterns that emerge from thinking about a game and the gamers as an imagined global community. Effectively, the *Diablo 3* game and its RMAH can utilize Anderson's model to help us refine how virtual economies become global. In the following discussion, we will ask four fundamental questions that correspond with each of Anderson's categories:

1. Imagined – how does the game create a space whereby "being global" is given value?
2. Limited – how does the game expose the boundaries that prioritize our social behavior? In other words, how does the game expose and reconfigure the "first here, then there" problem?
3. Sovereign – how does the game ignite questions of sovereignty both inside and outside of the game?
4. Community – how does the game create a community that then produces cultural practices? What does this tell us about the "class" part of "global middle class?"

Imagined

Like any virtual landscape, the game's self-contained narrative is imagined as a fully realized space. Those people who understand terms such as "grinding," "farming," "corpse runs," "medding," "twinking" or other esoterica that comes from gaming culture participate in the meaning making system of the game. In Act 1 Quest 1 of the game, the player is introduced to the mythological town of New Tristram.[5] A falling star from the heavens has caused the dead to rise, and as a result, the character, must venture into the depths of the caverns beneath the town to discover that the demonic forces of the cosmos have threatened the planet once more. The use of castles and inns frame the narrative in a medieval space, which quickly moves into more ancient aesthetics. The haunting, double-string guitar of the town of Tristram theme (one of the most popular parts of the soundtrack) produces an immediate nostalgia for the previous games (Tristram was a sanctuary within the game that was later devastated by the villains within the game). The game was choreographed by Russel Brower, who indicated that his inspiration for the music of the game was to "create a primal experience, something that you felt existed at the beginning of time."[6] The game's images and sounds were produced to appeal to have ancient properties,[7] which Vidal Naquet argues is a form of nostalgia intended to escape the linearity of being modern and nationalistic (45). The character classes themselves tell us much about the question of "class." Within the game, barbarians, monks, demon hunters, wizards and witch doctors constitute the initial "classes" of characters that the player may then customize.[8] Each of these characters is conceived as ancient and uses imagery drawn from mythologies that are "atlantean," meaning they come from stories and places that are familiar, but located in places that have very little association with who we are today (55). More than escape fantasies, these characters empower the player to occupy a world that is completely deterritorialized. One can have the whole world as their playground without the burden of the borders, inscribing symbolic meaning for gamers that uses the ingredients of the ancient to form a new world. It is here that fantasy games are at the cusp of creating new images and narratives. But more importantly, the gold in the game, this ancient fantasy realm is given real world economic credibility through the RMAH. The RMAH, albeit short-lived, was a threshold between the fantasy world of Diablo and a unique trading system built on the complicated and often overwhelming world of the global foreign exchange market. There would have been a subtle but important difference if the RMAH allowed a consumer to trade items exclusively in the currency of the customer. This would have created the same experience as anything else bought or sold online, virtual or otherwise. However, the act of thinking about the trading experience in relation to virtual gold served as a placeholder of imagining the trading mechanism in relation to one symbolic currency. This is similar to what Alexander Hamilton once asserted. He argued that one sovereign currency should replace the many colonial currencies in circulation in order for the United States to form a more cohesive social and political environment (Mises, 39). The same problem was noted in the formation of the European Union and the development of the Euro. The Euro was not only proposed as a means of reducing the translation and transaction costs associated with the regional integration of Europe; it was seen as a way to imagine a stronger sense of "European-ness" (Tilly 240). Similarly, Bitcoin has tried to address these high translation and transaction costs by side-stepping sovereign currency altogether. Diablo gold (though the RMAH) was not merely a unified medium of exchange, but it also gave consumers a way of connecting the self-contained fantasy of a fully realized world (with a fully imagined set of communities within the game) with the complex realities of global foreign exchange. The Euro, like the U.S. dollar before it, helped people of its time imagine the redrawing of Europe and the United States particularly at a time when those communities were searching for the vocabulary to define the substance of their respective realities. Although the world of Diablo is merely playfulness, it is important to remember that the same kind of playfulness allowed very real currencies to emerge. It is the kind of playfulness that hints toward the emergence of a world unified by a common currency.

In terms of the gaming experience, let's summarize this into some important points. First, the aesthetics of the game are ancient or "atlantean" in nature, giving people an environment immediately familiar but grand enough to connect to a cohesive sense of planetarity. Second, the nostalgia for the ancient produces a tension between the feeling of belonging in the modern sense with a sense of newness that can contain the ambivalence of being "in the world" and defined by structures such as nationality, but also allows for escaping it. Third, the economic exchanges are shaped by a space that is ancient and is traded with ancient currency, but is also meaningful because it is connected to real money. These tensions create an imagined world that, in a sense, invites a sense of belonging that is global, economically and aesthetically.

Limited

Even if everyone was global "in name" there are people throughout the world who wake up every morning and consider the urgencies of the planet less important than their more visible, more locally perceived obligations. Critics argue that nationalism represents the sort of provincialism that makes solving global problems a greater challenge (Fan 91). Being global may be the right of every sentient creature on the planet, but it has not yet been rendered self-evident. Despite having documents like the Universal Declaration of Human Rights and the Rome statute, documents like the International Covenant on Civil and Political Rights and the International Covenant on Economic Social and Cultural rights still demonstrate that the limits whereby we define our belonging to a global community are delineated by nationality and other complex community relationships (Carter 288). If we consider the rarity whereby social, cultural, economic or political issues register as a "global problem," the extent whereby people consider themselves active participants in global issues is less than self-evident. Being global is small in the sense that participants in globally derived phenomena are not readily seen as distinctly global. The romanticization of the pirate in the nineteenth century in art and literature represented, at least partially, the anxiety felt over the byzantine rules that merchants encountered as the world became increasingly connected by maritime trade (Moretti 199). "Belonging to the sea" became part of the fantasy that writers such as Jules Vernes and Daniel Defoe used imagine non-national spaces made possible by the ocean and other places that were difficult for nations to appropriate (Apter 55). In Act 3 Quest 5 of the game, characters are forced to fight giant squid-like creatures as part of an attempt to destroy a plague that is destroying the planet.[9] Upon completion of the quest, the game upgrades the character into a class that can move beyond the gate "at the edge of the abyss" (Act 3 Quest 6). This moves the character out of the "real world" and into the demonic territories. This is fascinating, because the game employs the same aesthetics popularized by the "atlantean" narratives of the nineteenth century to move into the unknown, places not appropriated by any space at all.

Stories of alien invasions, zombies and other horror/science fiction/fantasy stories all participate in the modern fantasy of destroying the barriers that prevent us from belonging to the world as the most prominent feature of our social realities (Montoya 14). The undead characters in the game employ these ingredients in every aspect of the game. It then allows the environment to let virtual class structures evolve within the game based on the limitations of each character class. The appeal can be understood as a non-linear way of destroying the teleological boundaries of the real world with the fantasies in the game. Players can use the ingredients of a fictional past (a shared universal mythology) to recreate and re-order the world around them. The "first here, then there" problem that Lopez and Weinstein describe does not apply in the game. It reifies the transnationality of the player by using the atlantean aesthetics which define the environment within the game. In October 2010, *Diablo 3* subscriptions reached nearly 12 million, 6.5 million who joined the network in its first week of its release.[10] Although this is a small number considering the seven billion of the world's population, it is a glimpse into the particular appeal of this kind of fantasy experience.

Sovereign

Anderson argues that a community does not have the power of self-determination without engendering a sense of awe and wonder (8). Communities have not power if they cannot capture the imagination of its people. This source of inspiration was once primarily located in religious systems. Gods were once the source of all authority, and one defined their ability to make choices in relation to the will of a god or gods. As civilization moved toward a secularized civil society, the awe and wonder once within the domain of deities was partly transferred to science and technology. One could argue that our modern fascination with fantasy games and the supernatural is partially connected to the desire to find awe and wonder in our civil and political life (Geertz 580). To be meaningful citizens – to be civil creatures that believe in and respect the rule of law – one must feel the "political urgency" and "political will" needed to prompt a larger sense of self-determination (Duara 47). This is partially why being global is not taken as seriously as attending to our more particularistic ways of being in the world. What does it mean for global sovereignty to take place?

Within the confines of the RMAH, the game allows the player to switch between a gold based economy and the currency which the player's subscription is located.[11] Through this process, the game creates a way to "close the door" on the use of sovereign currency by immersing the player in trade based on the fictional gold within the game. The ability to switch from any given currency and gold is a practical way to see how much money you actually spent in relation to how much gold you have in the game. However, this also has the added effect of making the trade within the game more serious. You know you are spending real money, but you are concurrently using fake money. The parallel process legitimates gold as a currency for the player and gives it a sense of urgency that gives it a sovereign quality.

Like the ambivalent tension the player experiences by playing the game, the trading within the game results in questions of legitimacy. Recently, discussions on the merit of digital currencies such as Bitcoin have received much media attention.[12] Bitcoin is a peer-to-peer software program that allows a chain of transactions between people who accept it as a legitimate currency. Like any other currency, it achieves value based on the robustness of the exchanges it represents. Like the RMAH and Diablo gold, these virtual forms of economic activity are prompted by an initial investment in an established, sovereign currency. Based on the momentum of those exchanges, the real money that provided the initial investment becomes more discreet, which is partly why many people are still confounded by the way these currencies work. An important index of these currencies is the way they force one to think about the function of money and the authenticity associated with money. This is a problem related in large part to sovereignty, a concept that is elucidated by the failures of both Bitcoin and the RMAH. When the Korean government banned all online trading activity within games, it noted that gamers were breaking very real laws which included illegal gambling, identity theft, and illegal labor usage, often referred to as "sweat mining" within the gaming community, and example that can be seen in this video.[13] By creating incentives within the game that had significant economic consequences outside of the game, the Korean government determined that it needed to intervene by prohibiting this behavior altogether.[14] The game's trading system produced a sovereignty issue that parallels the current problems with Bitcoin. If trade and other exchanges are mediated by non-sovereign currencies, the game itself exposes the legitimacy of sovereign institutions to govern behavior that is not clearly within its jurisdiction.

The connection between the culture of gaming and the production of non-state economies becomes clear when we see how digital currency first gained its popularity. Mt. Gox, the largest exchange of Bitcoin, traded nearly 70 percent of all Bitcoin exchanged worldwide. In February of 2014, trading of Bitcoin was suspended because the digital currency had been hacked and likely stolen. The closure of Mt. Gox exposed several problems with digital currency. Digital currency, while extremely versatile, was still operating within an environment where cybersecurity issues have been difficult to determine. Hence, it has been equally difficult to determine the extent to which one can have faith in such currencies.[15] The *Diablo 3* RMAH closed for similar reasons.[16] It became clear that hackers were able to digitally produce counterfeit items and gold. Mt. Gox and the RMAH closed nearly one month away from each other. Part of the concern around these exchanges, especially for Bitcoin exchanges, is the lack of institutional monitoring. It is important to note that "Mt. Gox" is a shorthand term for Magic the Gathering Online Exchange, an exchange system for the very popular fantasy-based card game.[17] In the case of the Korean restriction, the motives for banning gaming trade outright was prompted by the inability for any one government to measure, much less catch the brunt of potentially illicit or exploitative activity. These privately mediated economies were considered a hotspot for parallel economic activity. For example, within Bitcoin, an increased concern around potential money laundering caused speculation that digital currencies created a space where illicit activity could be funded without any oversight or regulation.[18] In the case of the RMAH, speculation came forth that mining gold could create "virtual sweatshops."[19] Given certain rules for mining, one could earn nearly $2.85 USD per hour "mining" within the game and selling that gold for real money. Gamers themselves have organized to discuss potentially illicit "gold farming" and have created a community around this issue.[20] Images of these virtual sweatshops have appeared among these communities and have mobilized members of the gaming community to expose these violations.[21] Black market traders used this as an opportunity to recruit already exploited laborers with the draw of a much higher wage ($2.85USD per hour is still a much higher wage than comparable labor in many parts of the world) to spend hours mining gold in inhumane conditions.

These currencies lack any centralized authority, and herein lies a fundamental insight – virtual currencies were not merely fantasies of an alternate social reality, they were the enactment of the belief that alternative economies are increasingly relevant in the lives of people around the world (or that current institutions are increasingly irrelevant). Although these currencies are decentralized, they are decentralized in the same manner that the non-national spaces of pirate lore and science fiction have slowly enacted a sense of global belonging Like *Diablo 3*, the exchange system that produced

Bitcoin was inspired by fantasy gaming communities. This is no coincidence. The way the game is imagined and the way the player transforms from an individual player to a member of a gaming community with shared experiences links the fantasy of a global community with a very real, very urgent set of economic realities. For the RMAH, the currency in the game serves as a mediator for what is urgent and important within the game. People in the game are willing to play by the rules of the game precisely because the system of exchange is worthy of their time and effort. Otherwise, the entire system of exchange within the game would fail. Consider that the average gamer takes nearly thirty hours to complete the main campaign in the game, and that amount increases if people participate in mining for gold and searching for treasure that will further immerse oneself into the tantalizing experience of the game. The gold is a central part of the game's "social contract." It represents an authentic medium of exchange, and moreover, it becomes the thing that connects the gamer's fantasy world with the costs of playing the game in the real world. The gold is a powerful but discreet intermediary between life in the real world and life in the Diablo world. In this regard, we can consider the function of money and, in this case, the function of Diablo gold as a symbolic placeholder for the sovereignty of a class of globally-minded people.

Georg Simmel referred to money as a "highly signified form of language" (Simmel 22). In addition to being a credible standard of account, a store of value, a medium of exchange and a standard for deferred payments, money is a way of authenticating the sum total of trade within a given economy (Jevons 110). Essentially, money becomes a story you tell about an economy. Notice how money fluctuates in relation to economic productivity and the factors that make an economy grow or contract. This is why many currencies still rely on divine objects or great moments in history to mark their authenticity. One needs look no further than the images imprinted on sovereign currency. "In God We Trust" becomes more than a passing phrase, it defines the level of faith we place in the standard whereby we measure the complexity of our world and the security wherein we trade with one another. If we think about money in this regard, the term "Sovereign debt" takes on a deeper meaning. We live in a world that has global problems and we long for globally derived responses. However, we locate our sovereignty nationally. Nationality is still a powerful (if not the most powerful) force in the shaping of the world (Myers 24). Hence, the virtual economies of the early twenty-first century are experiments in creating a separate space wherein the authority needed to make a global community meaningful. If money is a story you tell about an economy, the global economy receives a tale based partially on fantasy.

It would make sense that a global middle class would also then be partially responsible for the formation of new forms of sovereignty. As mentioned earlier, *Diablo 3*'s gold, albeit fantastic and divorced from the realities of the world, is still connected to by the pervasiveness with which the gold is perceived. Inside the game, it's the only currency that matters, and therefore doesn't suffer from "monetary nationalism" as it occurs in the real world (Stiell 27). In discussions about *Diablo 3*, this sentiment has been mobilized by gaming critics who have argued about the importance of this moment for gamers moving "gaming as a hobby, into gaming as a profession[22]. Again, the exposition outside the game, it is fully adaptive, so any and most currencies were openly traded for Diablo gold by consumers whose real lives are deeply influenced by the pluralities of currency.

Community

Virtual economies have the benefit of not being real and outside the purview of governments. Real life, as Mark Twain once coined, "is no more than a series of contemptible events, which is why I exaggerate everything." It just happens that this common vocabulary is being shaped in a gothic, mystical made-up place. This does not make the connection felt by the participants any less "real." If community (or as Anderson describes it "a deeply felt horizontal kinship) relies upon a cohesive set of shared experiences, then the world only gives us brief glimpse of a experiences that make people feel their commonality to the entire planet (Ong 22). The prevalence of the online gaming community is astounding. Diablo 3 alone has one official gaming portal where players can meet to discuss issues regarding the game, but more importantly, the shared experiences within the game have produced thousands of online discussion boards, discussing anything ranging from gaming strategies to the game's connection to contemporary social problems.[23] Note that the gaming forums themselves are adorned with images and aesthetics that replicate those found within the game. The virtual gamer never sees the person it communicates with, and in a manner of speaking, exchanges with people with money that doesn't mark itself in the real world. The community has real urgencies (as noted by major social issues the result from the gaming) but is visualized with ingredients that mark that shared experience in the game.

Conclusions

Virtual economies imagine a global culture, and therefore refine what "global" is. Discussions about the emergence of a global middle class are at a point of inflection. While many discussions on worldwide interconnectedness have lingered for decades (even centuries), those concepts have too often been mediated by more parochial dimensions. "Globalization" is often conflated with internationalism, and the phenomena mediated beyond the influence of nation-states are difficult to capture at a level that resonates as a meaningful part of our social realities. It is often the case that our ideas about the world are too big to specify; however, the rise of newly formed economic patterns (such as BRIC), the emphasis on "Base of Pyramid" business strategies and the evolution of technology are among the growing constellation of features whereby a global population, a global culture and a globally derived economy can be conceptualized (Prahalad and Hart 58).

Max Weber once noted that scientific analysis must refrain from viewing phenomena exclusively as an interconnectedness of "things" but rather as an interconnectedness of "problems" (Weber 113). This is where defining a global middle class often encounters its greatest challenge. One cannot merely use the interactions of people, places or things as the index of being global. The global middle class is not an object, but a problem. Moreover, it is a problem without an adequate vocabulary. What are needed at this point are thoughts that continue to understand the way that the world becomes legible to us. Far from being a number that quantifies income at a global-level, the BoP framework implies that these patterns have crystallized in a way that cannot be reduced to national averages. If that were the case, then studies of the BoP falls victim to the "like national income only bigger" thinking that makes understanding the global economy so problematic. The world has effectively become illegible, particularly because the work done to define it has primarily thought of the problem as a problem of scale. If we constantly think about political economy – only bigger – then we fail to capture the distinctiveness of the problems that make the planet its own cultural category.

Virtual economies allow the fantastic elements of being global to shape global consumption patterns and the global agenda. The "imagined" part of the rise of a global middle class is massively important to how we understand the evolution of the world and the issues the world will produce in the next century. Diablo 3 represents a very real "in-between space" between a fantastic landscape that can serve as a global playground while also connecting to contemporary social issues that are part of the basic realities of rising discretionary income. Diablo 3 gamers are the product of new discretionary income throughout the world, and are also the shapers of what that market's consumers look like. Although the RMAH was short-lived, it produced important social issues, including the possibility of exploited labor through online gaming. In the case of Bitcoin, the prospect of money laundering for illicit activity, including the drug trade and human trafficking connect how we imagine the world to the darker side of the tensions felt when global problems are mediated by smaller institutional frameworks. This has undermined national economic policy and thus, policies similar to the Korean ban are now appearing in Australia, Japan, China and the United States.[24] In the United States, the legal system is beginning to rule that virtual money is real money and may be subject to any economic policy governed within its jurisdiction.[25] The problem that will continually arise is the question of jurisdiction. Virtual economies are meaning-making spaces, and by extension they are also sites of resistance and exploitation. It may be that the gaming community will bridge the fantasy of being global with the way we govern ourselves in the real world.

It was not long ago that consumption patterns between the North and South in the United States produced a discourse on slavery and resulted in civil war. A century later, John Maynard Keynes, during the Bretton Woods conference of 1944, proposed the development of a global currency. He argued that at no point in modern world history would there be circumstances like the end of World War II to integrate economic activity worldwide (Stiell 48). This was prompted by the shared experience of the holocaust and the unprecedented death toll in wake of the war. In each case, the idea of a place, combined with the economic urgencies of its time produced a shift in the way we perceived our social realities. This, arguably, creates the class structures that made the North and South of the United States and the Global North and Global South emerge after the civil war and WWII respectively. After the 2008, most experts and media marked the financial collapse of the world banking system as the first modern global financial crisis, the response to it was anything but global. Nations quickly reverted to austerity measures and economic policies that protected their national interests. Yet, despite all the discussion about global economic crisis, it is difficult to know to what extent that crisis was global. This is partly because there is no unit of account commensurate with planetary economic activity (if there can be such a thing other than a theoretical form of that activity). Keynes' argument was not merely for the unification of economic trade policy. His argument implied that the Second Great War was an indication that the world had already produced a form of economic activity beyond the measure of current social standards. As we encounter more global issues including issues related to environmental sustainability, potable water, and pandemic contagion (to name a few), we will have to account for these problems in measures beyond nationally signified currency. *Diablo 3* gold certainly isn't that measure, but it helps us understand the process whereby that measure is derived. Future studies may consider challenging a fundamental assumption about how we measure economic activity across several boundaries. Is it possible to know a middle class without marking their consumption commensurate to their globally derived patterns? Such speculation is necessary to refine the descriptions that, frankly, confound us presently.

Virtual economies redefine "middle" through the formation of an emergent technocracy. This leads to an important question -- what is global about the global middle class? If we have somehow reached a point in our discussions of the world economy to talk seriously about the emergence of a global middle class, this implies that certain cultural frameworks have also emerged to mark a group of people within society as globally oriented. This implies a cultural framework is at play at the planetary level challenging the old "periphery/semi-periphery" model of the twentieth century. As consumers from "developing" or "big emerging economies" (a term used to replace the First World/Third World model) mobilize capital in new and unprecedented ways, so too do the resulting consumption patterns shape the way we perceive the world. We run the risk of assuming that the global middle class is merely an average index of nationally derived consumption patterns. It is already clear that a new transnational citizen is emergent, but it is unclear how these forces are recognizable as a global construct (Sklair 44; Ong 22; Carter 14). In the game, as more gameplay is mediated by economic exchanges, as more people are hacked, exploited, and wronged, so too will the community discuss and respond. Diablo 3, like other gaming communities have already done this, and as such, they are framing the future rules of a new idea of citizenship. Like Scholte's warning, the global middle class can be reduced to some internationalized or liberalized way of thinking that avoids understanding the globally relevant part.

It's not merely that people with lower-income have increased levels of income; it's the fact that over 2 billion of the world's population has acquired greater access to *discretionary* income. As Thorstein Veblen once noted, there is a certain "playfulness" that manifests in the practices of the leisure class." By purchasing what one wants (above what one needs), the consumer prescribes in their behavior an image of what they want their world to look like (Veblen 58). If Veblen's theories of consumption still hold, what is achieved at the discretion of these consumers is the meaning-making system that contributes to making the world legible. If that cultural framework is imagined as global, then there is a "structure of feeling" that renders the global a meaningful part of one's social reality (Williams 20). This is where global middle *income* participates in the construction of a global middle *class*.

It is also no small coincidence that the "playfulness" that Veblen refers to bears a deep aesthetic connection to the culture produced by online games and by virtual economies in general. The RMAH is a place where real money is converted into fantasy gold in order to purchase a wide variety of magical weapons, armor, and items. One can hire another gamer in the online community to forge a magical sword (with a playful name like "globe shaper") complete with a name and story that further connects the gamer to the "realities" of that universe. "Playfulness" is related to experimentation, and in a world where everything is perceived as virtual, and the social vulnerabilities associated with shaping the world are minimal, one can experiment broadly. When one plays an online video game like *Diablo 3*, they experiment with like-minded people in the formation of a new social imaginary – effectively a class of people who share a sense of horizontal kinship that is based on a common social vocabulary.

This social vocabulary is clearly mediated by the technologies that organize these complex social imaginings. Moreover, the "digital divide" present in most of the world is creating a gap between those who can participate in the playfulness that is creating this global social vocabulary and those that describe the world with more provincial language. While this is not a clear distinction, future studies must contend with the role that virtual media plays in the shaping of a global social consciousness and a global civil society. A recent study on virtual economies by the World Bank asserts that the video game industry is the largest sector of the entertainment industry. Moreover, it represents the largest growth of discretionary income from the middle of global income distribution (Lehdonvirta 33). If we accept that these forms of virtual economic exchange advance the way we connect the world in new and unprecedented ways, those who do not participate in such exchanges are subject to being marginalized from a future global agenda. Hence, the discretionary income evident in virtual economic activity is already producing a social class system – a middle class derived from a small but fast-evolving technocracy.

These discussions are necessarily conjectural, not because there is not merit in new and current empirical studies. It is important, however, to stop and evaluate the elusive qualities of our global political economy with appreciation for the modes of meaning making that will manifest as legible patterns. To repeat an important point herein: global legibility is not merely an object to be described, but a set of problems related to the complex interaction between the planet and its parts. Virtual economies are one way to see inside and outside of that problem to capture slivers of the reality this planet so clearly provides, but is so easily shrouded beneath the veneer of human complexity.

Notes

1. http://www.forbes.com/sites/insertcoin/2012/06/13/why-diablo-3s-real-money-auction-house-should-not-be-your-summer-job-2/.
2. According to statistics gathered for Blizzard entertainment by an external party. http://www.dfcint.com/wp/.
3. http://www.forbes.com/sites/insertcoin/2014/03/18/diablo-3-finally-exorcises-its-demon-the-auction-house/.
4. http://www.cinemablend.com/games/Diablo-3-Forces-Korean-Government-Ban-All-Virtual-Item-Trades-43620.html.
5. https://www.youtube.com/watch?v=yaP65WOzA2E.
6. http://www.originalsoundversion.com/blizzcon-2008-interview-with-audio-video-director-russell-brower/.
7. https://www.youtube.com/watch?v=4QAuF2LCBWY.
8. https://www.youtube.com/watch?v=3wLi9HJqmZ4.
9. https://www.youtube.com/watch?v=XZS_3ALt5P4 see time sequence 16:20 for a clear example.
10. http://www.eurogamer.net/articles/2012-08-03-activision-diablo-3-has-over-10-million-players.
11. https://www.youtube.com/watch?v=18zmWtFggS4.
12. http://www.wired.com/2014/04/dark-wallet/.
13. https://www.youtube.com/watch?v=gj8YYYdXXdQ.
14. http://www.cinemablend.com/games/Diablo-3-Forces-Korean-Government-Ban-All-Virtual-Item-Trades-43620.html.
15. http://online.wsj.com/news/articles/SB10001424127887324373204578374611351125202.

16. http://www.forbes.com/sites/insertcoin/2012/06/13/why-diablo-3s-real-money-auction-house-should-not-be-your-summer-job-2/.
17. http://www.eurogamer.net/articles/2012-08-03-activision-diablo-3-has-over-10-million-players.
18. http://www.reuters.com/article/2014/05/13/us-bitcoin-regulations-idUSBREA4C0LQ20140513.
19. http://www.pcgamer.com/2011/11/10/for-players-or-profit-activision-blizzard-at-odds-over-diablo-3s-cash-auction-house/.
20. http://www.gamefaqs.com/boards/930659-diablo-iii/59923100.
21. http://www.extremetech.com/gaming/131615-diablo-3-the-blizzard-sweatshop.
22. https://www.youtube.com/watch?v=_pc53tFAo1g see time sequence 2:20 for a discussion that represents the sentiment referenced.
23. A great example can be found here: http://www.pathofexile.com/forum/view-thread/54324.
24. See http://www.theage.com.au/news/biztech/virtual-world-tax-man-cometh/2006/10/30/1162056925483.html http://english.mofcom.gov.cn/aarticle/newsrelease/commonnews/200906/20090606364208.html.
25. http://time.com/money/2792901/play-money-is-real-money-says-high-court/.

Works Cited

Acemoglu, D., and F. Zilibotti. "Was Prometheus Unbound by Chance?" *Journal of Political Economy*, 105(4), 709–51, 1997. Print.

Andersen, Benedict. *Imagined Communities: Reflections on the Origin and Spread of Nationalism*. New York: Verso, 1983. Print.

Appadurai, Arjun. "Disjuncture and Difference in the Global Cultural Economy." *Public Culture* 2(2):1–24, 1990. Print.

Appiah, Kwame A. *Cosmopolitanism: Ethics in a World of Strangers*. New York: W.W. Norton, 2006. Print.

Apter, Emily. *Continental Drift: From National Characters to Virtual Subjects*. Chicago: University of Chicago Press, 1999. Print.

Banerjee, Abhijit, and Esther Duflo. "What Is Middle Class about the Middle Classes around the World?" *Journal of Economic Perspectives*, 22(2): 3–28, 2008. Print.

Barro, R. "Determinants of Economic Growth: A Cross-Country Empirical Study", NBER, 1996. Web. April 28, 2014.

Berlin, Isaiah, and Henry Hardy. *The Roots of Romanticism*. Princeton: Princeton University Press, 1999. Print.

Boli, John, and Frank Lechner. *World Culture: Origins and Consequences*. Malden, MA: Blackwell, 2005. Print.

Cabrera, Luis. *Political Theory of Global Justice: A Cosmopolitan Case for the World State*. London, Routledge. 2006. Print.

Carroll, Lewis. *Alice In Wonderland*. Norton Critical 2nd ed., New York: W.W. Norton, 1992. Print.

Carter, April. *The Political Theory of Global Citizenship*. London: Routledge Books, 2001. Print.

Defoe, Daniel. *Robinson Crusoe*. Cambridge: Harvard Classics, 2007. Print.

Deleuze, Gilles, and Felix Guattari. *Capitalism and Schizophrenia Vol. 1: The Anti-Oedipus*.

Trans. Robert Hurley, Seem, and Lane. Minneapolis: University of Minnesota Press, 1983. Print.

Deleuze, Gilles, and Felix Guattari. *Capitalism and Schizophrenia Vol. 2: The One Thousand Plateaus*. Trans. Brian Massumi. Minneapolis: University of Minnesota Press, 1987. Print.

Duara, Prasenjit. *Sovererеignty and Authenticity: Manchukuo and the East Asian Modern*. Oxford: Rowman and Littlefield, 2004. Print.

Easterly, W. "The Middle Class Consensus and Economic Development", Policy Research Working Paper 2346, World Bank, Washington, DC, 2000. Web. April 30, 2015.

Fan, Gang. "Currency Assymetry, Global Imbalances, and Rethinking of the International Currency System." Global Imbalances and the US Debt Problem: Should Developing Countries Support the US Dollar? 2006, pp. 87–105, The Hague: Forum on Debt and Development. Print.

Geertz, Clifford. "What is a State if it is not a Sovereign? Reflections on Politics in Complicated Places." *Current Anthropology* 45(5): 577–593, 2004. Print.

Heiman, Rachel, Carla Freeman, and Mark Leichty. "Introduction." *The Global Middle Classes: Theorizing Through Ethnography*. School for Advanced Research Press, 2012. Print.

Hobbes, Thomas. *Leviathan*. New York: Dover, 2006. Print.

Hofstede, Geert. *Cultures and Organizations*. New York: McGraw-Hill, 1997. Print.

Huntington, Samuel P. *The Clash of Civilizations and the Remaking of World Order*. New York: Simon & Schuster, 1996. Print.

Jevons, William Stanley. *Money and the Mechanism of Exchange*. New York: Appleton, 1876. Print.

Kharas, Homi. "The Emerging Middle Class in Developing Countries." OECD Development Center, working paper 285, January 2010. Web. April 30, 2015.

Lehdonvirta, V., and M. Ernkvist. Knowledge Map of the Virtual Economy. Washington DC: World Bank, 2011. Web. April 30, 2015.

Lopez, A. Ricardo, and Barbara Weinstein. "Introduction." *The Making of the Middle Class: Towards a Transnational History*. Duke University Press, 2012. Print.

Meyer, John W., John Boli, and George M. Thomas. "Ontology and Rationalization in the Western Cultural Account." *International Structure: Constituting State, Society, and the Individual*. Eds. Thomas, Myer, Ramirez, and Boli. 12–37. Newbury Park, Calif.: Sage, 1987. Print.

Mises, Ludwig von. *The Theory of Money and Credit*. New Haven: Yale University Press, 1953. Print.

Moretti, Franco. *Graphs, Maps, Trees: Abstract Models for a Literary History*. London: Verso, 2005. Print.

Murphy, K.M., A. Shleifer, and R. Vishny. "Income Distribution, Market Size, and Industrialization." The Quarterly Journal of Economics 104 (3): 537–64, 1989. Print.

Ong, Aihwa. Flexible Citizenship: The Cultural Logics of Transnationality. Durham, N.C., Duke University Press, 1999. Print.

Prahalad, C.K., and S. Hart. "The fortune at the bottom of the pyramid." Strategy + Business 26 (2002): 54–67. Print.

Robertson, Roland. *Globalization: Social Theory and Global Culture*. London: Sage, 1992. Print.

Scholte, Jan Aarte. *Globalization: A Critical Introduction*, 2nd Ed. New York: Palgrave Macmillan, 2005. Print.
Simmel, Georg. *The Philosophy of Money*. New York: Routledge, 2011. Print.
Sklair, Leslie. *The Transnational Capitalist Class*. Oxford: Blackwell, 2001. Print.
Steil, Benn, and Manuel Hinds. *Money, Markets and Sovereignty*. New Haven: Yale University Press, 2009. Print.
Tilly, Charles. *Coercion, Capital and European States*. Oxford: Blackwell Press, ch. 1–5 and 7, 1992. Print.
Veblen, Thorston. *The Theory of the Leisure Class*. New York: Dover, 1994. Print.
Verne, Jules. *20,000 Leagues Under the Sea*. New York: Scholastic, 2003. Print.
Vidal Naquet, J.P. "Atlantis and the Nations." *Critical Inquiry*, Vol 18, No. 2, 1992. Print.
Wells, H.G. *The War of the Worlds*. New York: Bantam, 2003. Print.
Weber, Max. "Objectivity in Social Science and Social Policy." *The Methodology of the Social Sciences*, New York, 1949. Print.
Williams, Raymond. *Marxism and Literature*. Oxford: Oxford University Press, 1977. Print.

6 An Investigation of Chinese Middle Class Attitudes Toward Sustainability

Yushan Zhao and Erin Cavusgil

Introduction

China's middle class has expanded rapidly over the last 30 years to become a major component both in China and in the world (Radjou and Prabhu 81). It is estimated that 25 percent of the overall Chinese population is middle class, larger than the entire population of the United States. By 2030, over 70 percent of China's population could be middle class (Barton, Chen, and Jin 54–60; Cui and Song 38–41). At the same time, the number of people with higher education has been increasing dramatically since the 1980s (Crabb 395–400). In 1982, about 0.6 percent of the population had completed some higher education. In 2010, this figure increased to 9 percent. The Chinese middle class is transforming the society, the environment and the economy and asserting great influence on the economic domain and domestic politics, as well as international behavior (Radjou and Prabhu 81–88). They have acquired modern education in China and abroad and are concerned about sustainable economic development.

This study explores the attitude of the Chinese middle class toward environmental sustainability. China has emphasized economic growth more than environmental issues over the last thirty years (Hubacek, et al. 1241–1242; Radjou and Prabhu 81–88). As the economy continues to develop, China faces tremendous challenges on resources and the environment. Sustainability has become a serious concern that requires the attention of the entire society (Hubacek, et al. 1241–1242; Nkamnebe 217–220; Sheth, Sethia, and Srinivas 21). As the relatively new middle class in China gains more power and influence in society, it is critical to examine its role in the sustainable development of the economy.

While much research has been conducted to explore the Chinese middle-class phenomenon, few studies have examined how the Chinese middle class regards environmental sustainability (Barkmann, et al. 283). We designed this exploratory study to examine the attitude of the Chinese middle class toward environmental sustainability and how attitudes influence their green behaviors. This study reviewed the literature on middle class and environmental sustainability, collected data from Chinese middle class, analyzed the results and discussed the implications of how the Chinese middle class influences the sustainable development of the Chinese economy.

As the world is in the throes of a major expansion in the middle class, particularly in China, this study will provide insights on the emerging middle class in China who are increasingly concerned about the quality of the environment and sustainable development of the economy.

Literature Review

Environmental sustainability is defined as meeting the needs of current generations without compromising the ability of future generations to meet their own needs. It refers to the effort to minimize the environmental damage of human beings (individuals, groups, businesses and other entities) (Choi and Sirakaya 380–391). Environmental degradation in developing countries, especially in China, signifies the need to give increasing attention to different social groups toward the environmental impacts of their activities, to recognize the importance of changing their social norms to protect the environment, and to voluntarily behave in an environmentally friendly way (Chan 25–44; Nkamnebe 217–220).

Attitude toward environmental sustainability refers to concerns over environmental sustainability issues. As the public is increasingly concerned about environmental quality, two philosophies have emerged in the public: the economic view and the balanced view (Dias-Sardinha, Reijnders, and Antunes 51–68). The prevalent economizing of society suggests that developed countries have the resources and technologies to control pollution and environmental degradation, and developing countries, whose development relies heavily on natural resources, cannot afford to focus on environmental quality during the developing stage since it may undermine economic growth (Munasinghe 89–90). The balanced view of society holds that the importance of economic development for developing countries cannot be overemphasized. Improvement of environmental quality is an inseparable part of poverty reduction in developing countries. The economic and environmental dimensions are equally important for the sustainable development of the economy (Epstein and Wisner 1–3). As the concerns for environmental quality are more pervasive among the Chinese middle class, it is interesting to investigate their views on the balanced development of the economy and environmental protection and examine their role in environmental sustainability (Shen and Saijo 42).

Who are the middle classes? There is no official definition of middle class. Broadly defined, middle-class living standards begin when poor ends (Ravallion 446) and the lower endpoint of middle-class income is significantly above the poverty level (Horrigan and Haugen 5). International standards for middle class include (1) ownership of a house, (2) ownership of a car and (3) the ability to take an annual foreign or prosperous domestic holiday (Chikweche and Fletcher 27–30). The Chinese National Bureau of Statistics categorizes middle class as households with an annual income ranging from 60,000 to 500,000 Chinese yuan. Table 6.1 summarizes the three definitions of middle class. In this study we adopt the definition of the Chinese National Bureau and also consider the internationally accepted standards (see Table 6.1). The households who meet one of these standards are considered middle class. Therefore, we consider households with an income of 60K to 500K as middle class. We also treat households who own a house, have a car, and take an annual vacation as middle class.

Table 6.1 Definition of Middle Class

Sources	*Standards of Middle Class*
Chinese National Bureau of Statistics	Household annual income 60,000 to 500,000 Chinese yuan
Internationally Generally Accepted Standards	Ownership of a house, ownership of a car, and ability to take an annual foreign or prosperous domestic holiday

Compared to developed countries, the middle class in China is a relatively new phenomenon. They have just escaped poverty and become an important power in society. Large population and rapid growth in China implies that the Chinese middle class becomes an important force that can shape patterns of consumption and the behaviors of business practices (Cui and Song 38–41). Some economists argue that theories and practices serving the middle class in developed countries may not be readily applicable to those in developing countries. There is research opportunity to expand the current theories in western countries to the emerging world to guide the people behaviors in a sustainable pattern. Based on the above discussion, we propose the research questions of this study:

1 What are the levels of awareness and attitude of the Chinese middle class with respect to environmental sustainability?
2 How do demographic factors account for differences in the levels of awareness of and attitude toward environmental sustainability for the Chinese middle class?

Method

A questionnaire was used to collect data from the Chinese middle class. The survey consisted of twenty-eight questions/statements related to the concept of sustainability, general attitude toward environment and sustainability, participation in the activities to support sustainable development and environmental protection, and recommended actions to enhance the sustainability. The survey also has questions on demographics and household information. The survey was designed based on literature review (Chan 25–44; Choi and Sirakaya 380–391; Kilbourne and Polonsky 37–48; Pressman 243–262), focus groups, and interviews. Most questions/statements were adopted from previous research (e.g., Choi and Sirakaya 386, 389; Lee, "Opportunities for Green" 579–581, "The Green Purchasing" 27–28) and modified based on unique conditions in China.

The survey was managed by four trained Chinese administrators. The data was collected in summer 2013 in four Chinese cities (Beijing, Shanghai, Xi'an, Chengdu). The Chinese administrators conducted the survey in train stations, shopping malls, shopping centers and streets by the mall-intercept method. The trained administrators met with people in the four cities, introduced the survey of sustainability, and asked them to complete the surveys.

In all, 2019 people were approached and 509 of them agreed to fill the questionnaires. The response rate is 25.2 percent. Thirty-nine of them were identified unusable due to missing values. Three were excluded because they did not meet the middle-class standards. A total of 467 surveys are used in the data analysis.

Respondent Demographics and Household Information

Of the 467 respondents, 51.8 percent are males and 48.2 percent are females (see Table 6.2). In regard to marital status, 22.1 percent are singles and never married, 74.1 percent are married, and 3.9 percent are divorced or widowed. Their ages are between 20 and 79. About 77 percent of them are between 20 and 50 years old.

Table 6.2 Sample Profiles

	N (Total N = 467)	*Percent*
Gender		
Male	242	51.8
Female	225	48.2
Age		
20–30	84	18.0
31–50	275	58.9
51 and above	108	23.1
Marital Status		
Single	103	22.1
Married	346	74.1
Divorced etc.	18	3.9
Education		
High School or Less	64	13.7
Some College or 4-Year College	294	63.0
Post Graduate	109	23.3
Income (Chinese Yuan)		
<99,999	185	39.6

(*Continued*)

	N (Total N = 467)	Percent
100K–199,999	192	41.1
>200K	90	19.3
Ownership of House		
Yes	363	77.7
No	104	22.3
Ownership of Car		
Yes	272	58.2
No	195	41.8
Ability to Take Annual Vacation		
Yes	463	99.1
No	4	0.9

In terms of education level, 13.7 percent had a high school education or lower, 63.0 percent had some or four-year college education, and 23.3 percent had post-graduate degrees. It can be seen that most middle-class people surveyed had a good education. The survey shows that 86.3 percent of them had some college education, attended a four-year college, or pursued a post graduate education. Thus, as in Western countries, education is one of the main indicators of middle-class status.

In regard to the individual annual income level, 39.6 percent make less than 99,999 Chinese Yuan, 41.1 percent have income between 100K to 199,999 Chinese yuan, and 19.3 percent of them have income more than 200K Chinese yuan. Most middle-class households consist of two working parents/couples. Ninety-four percent of them have household income ranging from 60,000 to 500,000 Chinese yuan.

About three fourths (77.7 percent) of respondents reported that they have their own house. Approximately 58 percent of them said they own a car. Almost all respondents (99.1 percent) indicated that they have the ability to have at least one annual vacation. It can be seen that the Chinese middle class is different from that of developed countries. Less than a quarter (22.3 percent) of them do not own a house, and 41.8 percent do not own a car. Less than half (47.3 percent) of them own a house, have a car, and have the ability to take at least one vacation in a year, which meets the middle-class standards of Western countries.

The Concept of Sustainability

Responses related to sustainability issues are summarized in Table 6.3. When asked how many years they have known the term sustainability, 32.3 percent of them indicated that they had known the concept for less than five years, 33.4 percent indicated that they had known about sustainability for six to ten years, and 34.3 percent indicated that they had known the concept for more than eleven years.

Table 6.3 Sustainability Related Issues

	N (Total N = 467)	*Percent*
Years Know about Sustainability		
1–5 years	151	32.3
6–10 years	156	33.4
11 years and above	160	34.3
About Concept of Sustainability		
Environment/natural resources	93	19.9
Conservation/recycling	72	15.4
Ability to sustain life on earth	102	21.8
Balance of environment, societal and economic issues	158	33.8
How long something lasts	29	6.2
Do not know	13	2.8
Most Troubling Environmental Issues		
Water pollution	80	17.1
Habitat destruction	25	5.4
Solid waste	14	3.0
Climate change	73	15.6
Air pollution	60	12.8
Urban sprawl	16	3.4
Biodiversity loss	14	3.0
Human population growth	46	9.9
Soil degradation	24	5.1
Mining depletion	28	6.0
Oil and gas impact	55	11.8
Hazardous waste	22	4.7
Overfishing of ocean	10	2.1

The respondents were also asked what came to mind when they heard the term sustainability where 19.9 percent related sustainability to the environment and natural resources. Fifteen percent of them indicated that they think of conservation and recycling when they hear sustainability. Less than a quarter (21.8 percent) of them related it to the ability to sustain life on earth. One third (33.8 percent) of them said it is the balance of the environment, societal and economic issues. Six percent of them think it is about how long something lasts. Only 2.8 percent have no idea about sustainability.

The respondents were asked to circle the environmental issues they were most concerned about having an impact on their local community or region. The top four concerns were water pollution, climate change, air pollution and oil and gas impact. Approximately 10 percent of them were concerned about human population growth. About 5 percent of them worry about habitat destruction, soil degradation, mining depletion, hazardous waste and overfishing of the oceans.

Analysis and Results

Factor Analysis

On a scale of 1 to 5, where 1 means strongly disagree and 5 means strongly agree, respondents were asked to indicate their responses to a set of statements related to environmental sustainability. Factor analysis with principle component analysis and varimax rotation was utilized to examine the measurement items. Three factors emerged (attitude toward sustainability, participation, law enforcement) explaining 58.8 percent of the variance in the data. Factor loadings less than 0.5 percent and with cross loadings were deleted in the analysis. The results are presented in Table 6.4.

Table 6.4 Rotated Factor Pattern for Sustainability Items

Items	*Factor 1*	*Factor 2*	*Factor 3*
Attitude Toward Environmental Sustainability			
The sustainability of a thriving economy is dependent upon a healthy environment.	0.91		
Sustainability must be addressed now and in the future.	0.89		
I believe that all citizens should be responsible for sustainability.	0.84		
The highest priority should be given to sustainability even if it hurts the economy.	0.79		
Our children's lives will be worse because of our generation's wasteful habits.	0.77		
It is important to protect the environment.	0.75		
Climate change is one of the most serious threats to the health and safety of my family and my community.	0.64		
Global warming has been established as a serious problem, and immediate action is necessary.	0.61		
Participation			
I would pay slightly higher taxes to help preserve the environment.		0.85	
For everyday needs I would buy environmentally friendly products even if they were slightly more expensive.		0.73	
I like to volunteer for activities related to sustainability.		0.71	
I would use more public transportation, less personal vehicles.		0.66	

Items	*Factor 1*	*Factor 2*	*Factor 3*
I would reduce the amount of waste.		0.62	
When doing big-ticket shopping (buying car, heating devices) I would choose only environmentally friendly items.		0.60	
I make a strong effort to recycle everything I possibly can.		0.52	
Law Enforcement			
Anti-pollution laws should be enforced more strongly.			0.85
The environment is valuable in itself and should be protected by laws.			0.83
Pollution laws have gotten too strict in recent years.			0.81
Tougher environmental legislation is required so that only businesses that are environmentally responsible will survive and grow.			0.71

Anova Analysis

ANOVA and T-test were conducted to explore the differences in attitude toward sustainability and participation among different demographic groups of Chinese middle class (gender, age, education level and income level). T-test results on gender were presented in Table 6.5. T-tests indicate that levels of attitude toward sustainability and law enforcement were significantly different between genders ($p < 0.01$). Females indicated a higher level of attitude toward sustainability and recommended more law enforcement on environmental protection. Gender differences were not found for participation ($p = 0.95$).

Table 6.5 T-Test Results by Gender

	Male		*Female*		*T-test Results*	
	Mean	*S.D.*	*Mean*	*S.D.*	*T-value*	*P-value*
Attitude Toward Sustainability	3.15	1.01	3.48	0.94	–3.70	0.00
Participation	3.35	0.74	3.34	1.12	0.10	0.95
Law Enforcement	2.94	0.94	3.22	1.01	–2.71	0.00

Test results on age were presented in Table 6.6. ANOVA results indicate no significant difference among the three age groups (twenty to thirty years old, thirty-one to fifty years old and fifty-one and above) for attitude toward sustainability and law enforcement recommendations. The results suggest a significant relationship with middle class's participation and their age ($p < 0.01$). Duncan's tests were performed to assess the differences between pairs of the three age groups. Duncan's tests show that participation in pro-environmental sustainability decreases as the age categories increase ($p < 0.05$). Participation is significantly higher for the age group of twenty to thirty years old than the age groups of thirty-one and fifty-one years old and above. Younger Chinese middle class are more active in participating in pro-environmental activities.

Table 6.6 ANOVA Results by Age

	20–30 Years Old		*31–50 Years Old*		*>51 Years Old*		*ANOVA Results*	
	Mean	*S.D.*	*Mean*	*S.D.*	*Mean*	*S.D.*	*F-value*	*P-value*
Attitude	3.17	0.95	3.32	0.98	3.37	1.12	0.96	0.38
Participation	3.61	0.84	3.37	0.79	3.08	1.15	10.32	0.00
Law	3.11	0.96	3.10	1.00	2.88	0.98	2.30	1.01

Test results on education were presented in Table 6.7. Results of an ANOVA for education level suggest that the main effects of education level on both attitude toward sustainability and participation were significant ($p < 0.01$). Post hoc analysis via Duncan's test indicates that attitude toward sustainability and participation are significantly greater as level of education increases. Attitude toward sustainability and participation of higher education level (post graduate, some college, and four-year college) is greater than that of the lower education level (high school or lower). The main effect of education on law enforcement recommendations is not significant.

Table 6.7 ANOVA Results by Education

	High School or Less		*Some College or 4-Year College*		*Post-Graduate*		*ANOVA Results*	
	Mean	*S.D.*	*Mean*	*S.D.*	*Mean*	*S.D.*	*F-value*	*P-value*
Attitude	2.73	1.02	3.29	0.98	3.70	1.11	21.05	0.00
Participation	2.86	1.12	3.37	0.75	3.58	0.79	16.82	0.00
Law	3.29	1.01	3.04	1.00	2.97	0.94	2.22	1.09

Finally, ANOVA results on income level were presented in Table 6.8. The main effects of income level on attitude toward sustainability and participation are not significant; so, income level has no significant effect on attitude and participation. However, the main effect of income level on law enforcement recommendations is significant ($p < 0.01$). Post hoc analysis via Duncan's test indicates that law enforcement recommendations are significantly less for income levels of 200K Chinese Yuan than for income levels of 199,999 Chinese yuan or less. People with lower income would like to see more law enforcement on environmental protection.

Table 6.8 ANOVA Results by Income (Chinese Yuan)

	<99,999		100K–199,999		>200K		ANOVA Results	
	Mean	*S.D.*	*Mean*	*S.D.*	*Mean*	*S.D.*	*F-value*	*P-value*
Attitude	3.32	1.15	3.31	0.97	3.27	0.93	0.74	0.93
Participation	3.34	1.16	3.36	0.78	3.34	1.15	0.42	0.96
Law	3.22	1.02	3.05	0.98	2.75	0.92	6.65	0.00

Discussion

This paper summarizes the survey results on attitudes of Chinese middle class toward sustainability. The Chinese middle class is dissatisfied with environmental conditions in general and environmental protection law enforcement specifically. Dissatisfaction stems mainly from the fact that Chinese development is unbalanced and that the highest priority has not been given to sustainability. The survey suggests that sustainability is a pressing concern for the Chinese middle class. The study shows that the Chinese middle class is taking pro-environmental actions to address environmental problems. They are willing to contribute time and resources to support sustainability initiatives and the sustainable development of the economy. They also suggest that the government should put more law enforcement on environmental protection. The key findings are summarized below:

1 More than half of the Chinese middle class do not meet the international middle-class standards, i.e., ownership of a house, ownership of a car, and have the ability to take an annual foreign or prosperous domestic holiday. Less than half (47.3 percent) of them meet these standards.
2 The survey shows that 30.2 percent of them own a house and do not have a car. Ten percent of them own a car and do not own a house. For most Chinese middle class, purchasing a house is the most important and expensive investment, followed by car purchasing.
3 Almost all Chinese middle class (99.1 percent) can have an annual foreign or prosperous domestic holiday.
4 On average, the Chinese middle class has heard the term sustainability for 8.63 years. One third of them understand that sustainability is the balance of environment, society, and economic issues.
5 Female middle class, middle class of younger generations, middle class with higher education, and middle class of low income (less than 99,999K Chinese yuan) are more concerned about the environment, more active in pro-environmental behaviors, more worried about the environmental protection law enforcement.
6 Education is one of the main indicators of Chinese middle-class status. Most Chinese middle class have a good education. Results show that 86.3 percent of them had some college, a four-year college degree,

or post-graduate education. ANOVA analysis supports this view and confirms that people with a higher level of education (post-graduate, some or four-year college) are more concerned about the environmental sustainability and more likely to participate in pro-environmental practices. They also would like to see more law enforcement on environmental protection then people with lower educational levels.

7 Gender effects are significant for attitude toward sustainability and law enforcement. Females are more inclined to concern about the environmental protection. This is consistent with previous research that females are more environmentally aware and have a more favorable attitude toward green consumption. Environmentalists are more often females than males (Bask, et al. 391).
8 Younger generations are active in participating in pro-environmental behaviors. The results show that the younger generations are more supportive of preserving the environment. They are more competitive and ambitious and will be the main force of environmental protection in the future.
9 The survey indicates that the Chinese middle class are concerned about various environmental issues. The top five environmental concerns are water pollution, climate change, air pollution, oil and gas impact and human population growth. About 5 percent of them worry about habitat destruction, soil degradation, mining depletion, and hazardous waste.
10 In regard to the attitude toward sustainability, more than 40 percent of the Chinese middle class think that the highest priority should be given to sustainability even if it hurts the economy. They agree that sustainability is very important and must be addressed now and in the future. They are also anxious that the next generation's lives will be affected by this generation's wasteful habits. ANOVA results also demonstrate that females are more concerned about the environmental issues.
11 The Chinese middle class are very active in supporting the sustainable development of the economy. Based on the survey, 42.4 percent of Chinese middle class said they would pay slightly higher taxes to help preserve the environment. They indicate that they would contribute to organizations that address sustainability and participate in activities related to sustainability. They show that they would reduce the amount of waste, reduce the use of energy at home, recycle everything they possibly can, and buy environmentally friendly products. ANOVA results indicate that younger generations are more active in supporting environmental sustainability.
12 The Chinese middle class is also concerned about the regulation on environmental protection. About one third (33 percent) of them emphasize that anti-pollution laws should be enforced more strongly. It is interesting to note that people with lower income would like to see more law enforcement on environmental protection than those with higher

income. Further, females recommend more law protection on the environment than males.

13 Overall, females are more active in pro-environmental behaviors than men. Chinese middle class with more education and younger age are also found to be proactive in environmental protection. People in younger generations would like to see more regulations to control the environmental degradation.

Future Research Directions and Conclusion

This is the first study to survey the Chinese middle class on their attitude toward sustainability. The majority of the items in the questionnaire are adopted from previous research and most analyses are descriptive in nature. An interesting follow-up for the data collected for this research would be a regression analysis between participants' demographic variables and their attitude variables toward sustainability. Results could be used to identify the target groups to enhance environmental quality in China. A comprehensive study could be conducted to compare how factors related to Chinese middle class' attitudes toward sustainability are changing over time.

Future research could also be directed toward theoretical development and research: (1) develop theoretical constructs related to Chinese middle class and sustainability, (2) develop measures for the constructs, and (3) explore the inter-relationships among these constructs. For example, future research could be conducted to identify the antecedents and consequences of Chinese middle class' attitudes toward sustainability. Cross-national studies could be used to investigate the differences between middle class in China and developed countries on the attitude toward sustainability and important factors affecting environmental sustainability. Finally, this study measured the middle class based purely on income. Further research could be conducted to incorporate other dimensions such as social and ethical behaviors to define the middle class.

The rapid growth of the middle class in China will dramatically lead the economic, political, and cultural changes in the nation as well as in the world. However, this is only the beginning of the effect of middle-class expansion. By 2030, the middle class in emerging markets such as China and India will more than double in size (Barton, Chen, and Jin 54–60). The study shows that the Chinese middle class is becoming more concerned about the sustainable development of both the national and the world's economy. They are willing to pay more to purchase environmentally friendly products and in pressing the government to enforce anti-pollution laws. It can be seen that more and more Chinese middle class will be active in supporting environment protection and resource conservation.

Works Cited

Barkmann, Jan, Jiong Yan, Anne-Kathrin Zschiegner, and Rainer Marggraf. "The Dao of the sceptic and the spiritual: attitudinal and cultural influences on preferences for sustainable tourism services in the domestic Chinese tourism market." *International Journal of Services Technology and Management* 13.3/4 (2010): 281–304. Print.

Barton, Dominic, Yougang Chen, and Amy Jin. "Mapping China's Middle Class." *McKinsey Quarterly* 3 (2013): 54–60. Print.

Bask, Anu, Merja Halme, Markku Kallio, and Markku Kuula. "Consumer Preferences for Sustainability and Their Impact on Supply Chain Management: The Case of Mobile Phones." *International Journal of Physical Distribution & Logistics Management* 43.5/6 (2013): 380–406. Print.

Chan, Ricky Y.K. "Environmental Attitudes and Behavior of Consumers in China: Survey Findings and Implications." *Journal of International Consumer Marketing* 11.4 (1999): 25–52. Print.

Chikweche, Tendai, and Richard Fletcher. "Rise of the Middle of the Pyramid in Africa: Theoretical and Practical Realities for Understanding Middle Class Consumer Purchase Decision Making." Journal of Consumer Marketing 31.1 (2014): 27–38. Print.

Choi, Hwan-Suk Chris, and Ercan Sirakaya. "Measuring Residents' Attitude Toward Sustainable Tourism: Development of Sustainable Tourism Attitude Scale." *Journal of Travel Research* 43.4 (2005): 380–394. Print.

Crabb, Mary W. "Governing the Middle-Class Family in Urban China: Educational Reform and Questions of Choice." *Economy & Society* 39.3 (2010): 385–402. Print.

Cui, Allison, and Kheehong Song. "Understanding China's Middle Class." *China Business Review* 36.1 (2009): 38–42. Print.

Dias-Sardinha, I, L Reijnders L, and P Antunes. "From Environmental Performance Evaluation to Eco-Efficiency and Sustainability Balanced Scorecards: A Study of Organisations Operating in Portugal." *Environmental Quality Management* 12.2 (2002): 51–64. Print.

Epstein, M.J., and P.S. Wisner. "Using a Balanced Scorecard to Implement Sustainability." *Environmental Quality Management* 11.2 (2001): 1–10. Print.

Hedlund, Therese. "The Impact of Values, Environmental Concern, and Willingness to Accept Economic Sacrifices to Protect the Environment on Tourists' Intentions to Buy Ecologically Sustainable Tourism Alternatives." *Tourism and Hospitality Research* 11.4 (2011): 278–288. Print.

Horrigan, Michael W., and Steven E. Haugen. "The Declining Middle-Class Thesis: A Sensitivity Analysis." *Monthly Labor Review* 111.5 (1988): 3–13. Print.

Hubacek, K., D. Guan, J. Barrett, and T. Wiedmann. "Environmental Implications of Urbanization and Lifestyle Change in China: Ecological and Water Footprints." *Journal of Cleaner Production* 17.14 (2009): 1241–1248. Print.

Kilbourne, William E., and Michael J. Polonsky. "Environmental Attitudes and Their Relation to the Dominant Social Paradigm Among University Students in New Zealand and Australia." *Australasian Marketing Journal* 13.2 (2005): 37–48. Print.

Lee, Kaman. "Opportunities for Green Marketing: Young Consumers." *Marketing Intelligence & Planning* 26.6 (2008): 573–586. Print.

Lee, Kaman. "The Green Purchase Behavior of Hong Kong Young Consumers: The Role of Peer Influence, Local Environmental Involvement, and Concrete Environmental Knowledge." *Journal of International Consumer Marketing* 23.1 (2011): 21–44. Print.

Munasinghe, M. "Is Environmental Degradation an Inevitable Consequence of Economic Growth: Tunneling Through the Environmental Kuznets Curve." *Ecological Economics* 29.1 (1999): 89–109. Print.

Nkamnebe, Anayo D. "Sustainability Marketing in the Emerging Markets: Imperatives, Challenges, and Agenda Setting." *International Journal of Emerging Markets* 6.3 (2011): 217–232. Print.

Pressman, Steven. "The Middle Class Throughout the World in the Mid-2000s." *Journal of Economic Issues* 41.1 (2010): 243–262. Print.

Radjou, Navi, and Jaideep Prabhu. "Mobilizing for Growth in Emerging Markets." *Sloan Management Review* 53.3 (2012): 81–88. Print.

Ravallion, Martin. "The Developing World's Bulging (but Vulnerable) Middle Class." *World Development* 38.4 (2010): 445–454. Print.

Shen, J., and T. Saijo. "Reexamining the Relations between Socio-Demographic Characteristics and Individual Environmental Concern: Evidence from Shanghai Data." *Journal of Environment Psychology* 28.1 (2008): 42–50. Print.

Sheth, Jagdish N., Nirmal K. Sethia, and Shanthi Srinivas. "Mindful Consumption: A Customer-Centric Approach to Sustainability." *Journal of the Academy of Marketing Science* 39.1 (2011): 21–39. Print.

7 Understanding the Characteristics and Entrepreneurial Activities of Middle-Class Consumers in Emerging Markets

The Case of India

Rajshekhar (Raj) G. Javalgi and David A. Grossman

Introduction

In the era of globalization, coupled with economic transformations of nations, the "middle class" segment of the global population has become a force of great economic importance in consumer markets around the world. Since the mid-1990s, many emerging markets have experienced technological, sociological, and economic transformations. This has enabled many low-income households to climb to the status of middle class. This segment of the population has shown the world a new-found appetite for goods and services. Middle-class consumers in emerging markets are spending over $10 trillion a year (Homi and Gertz 2). This figure is expected to increase as more middle-class consumers in emerging markets spend their money to improve their lifestyles. This segment is creating a voracious market power characterized by growth in numbers and a need for goods and services.

Researchers and practitioners alike are trying to better understand this important segment of middle-class consumers. The purpose of this essay is to better understand the demographic characteristics, attitudes and behavior, entrepreneurial activities, materialism and global connectivity of middle-class consumers in India. Using India as an example of emerging markets, this study attempts to address the following research questions. Who are middle-class consumers in India, and what are their demographic characteristics? Do middle-income consumers in India display favorable attitudes toward materialism, openness to foreign culture, global connectivity, value consciousness and entrepreneurial activities? What factors influence their attitude toward global connectivity, entrepreneurial activity and their purchase behavior toward foreign products?

The chapter is organized as follows: A brief discussion of the importance and definitions of middle-class consumers is provided, followed by the related literature review. Next, the collection and analysis of data and results is presented. Lastly, implications, limitations and directions for future research are discussed.

The Emergence of Middle-Class Consumers: Importance and Definitions

The growth of a "new generation of consumers" called the middle-class consumers is driven by rising incomes, exposure to international life styles and media, access to information and telecommunication technologies and willingness to try foreign products and services. Learning about the tendencies of the middle class in a market economy provides a wealth of knowledge about economic growth (Easterly, 332), consumer demand (Murphy, Shleifer, and Vishny, 1024), entrepreneurial development (Acemoglu and Zilibotti, 716), and long-term investments (Doepke and Zilibotti, 29). In a market-driven economy the middle-class consumer is considered "the backbone of both the market economy and of democracy in most advanced societies" (Birdsall, Graham, and Pettinato, 1; Lopez-Calva, L. F., Rigolini, J., and Torche, F., 2). As the middle class of emerging markets continues to grow, the classification of what defines the middle class remains dynamic. To date there is no commonly accepted, standard definition of the middle class, nor is there a definition that economists and organizations seem willing to adopt (Birdsall; Pressman, 244). Though it is accepted that the middle class is not a homogeneous group, the term often applies to a group of people to emphasize their collective identity in relation to other classes (Mathur, 218). Weber (282) suggests that the middle class is the source of economic values that focus on savings and accumulation of human capital, thus promoting economic growth. Today's educated middle class emphasizes ideologies such as social position, public influence and Western-style education (Mathur, 220).

While generalizations based on research of the middle class are not disputed, the common measures and characteristics of what constitutes middle class vary. The difficulty in classifying the middle class is also due to the susceptibility of economic changes impacting their income levels and values (Torche and Lopez Calva, 424). Existing evidence (Birdsall; World Bank) suggests a $10 per capita per day (at 2005 PPP) minimum for being India's middle class in today's global economy. Cashell (6) notes that problems occur if income quintiles are used to define the middle class, because of the fluid economic status of the people in this group.

India's Middle Class

The world's current middle class size of 2 billion people is expected to be close to 5 billion people by 2030 with the majority of the growth coming from the Asia-Pacific region (Rohde). As this growth occurs India is expected to be the world's largest middle-class consumer market by 2030, surpassing not only China, but also the total population of the developed West. Between now and 2039, India is projected to add over 1 billion people to the global middle class creating the world's fifth-largest consumer market (Dobbs). Over the last decade, the growth of India's middle class has been a subject of much scrutiny with estimates between 5 million and 300 million people (World Bank). India's middle class saw its largest growth during the early 1990s when economic reforms led to integration into global markets. As Western countries were experiencing economic contraction, India's economy continued to grow above 5 percent (KAS International Reports).

The definition of India's middle class is also disputed because of the rapidly changing environment. We draw from the 2007 India National Council of Applied Economic Research (NCAER) published definition that identified India's middle class as comprising two sub-groups: 1) Seekers: annual household income between Rs. 200,000 and Rs. 500,000, and 2) Strivers: annual household income between Rs. 500,000 and Rs. 1 million. Using 2001/2002 prices these numbers would be about $8 to $20 per capita per day for seekers, and $20 to $40 per capita per day for strivers (Birdsall and Meyer). According to the McKinsey Global Institute (MGI), in the next two decades from 2005–2025, Indian household income would grow an average of 5.3 percent annually. MGI defines India's middle class as a household income segment between US $4,930 and US $24,651. The number of middle class today is between 50 million to 100 million. MGI points out that this number will grow to 583 million by 2025. Birdsall and Meyer research concludes that if being middle class means reasonable security in material terms, then India's middle class constitutes less than 100 million people and is crowded into the top docile along with the much smaller number of "rich" households. In that sense, India does not yet look much like the middle-class "societies" of Latin America, let alone of the mature Western democracies.

Literature Review and Hypothesis Development

The following is a review of the existing evidence and theory regarding middle class consumers and entrepreneurial characteristics in developing countries. We have identified six factors that are important in understanding India's middle class consumers. The six factors are openness to foreign culture, global connectivity, materialism, value consciousness, consumer nationalism, and entrepreneurial activity.

Openness to Foreign Culture

As globalization in emerging markets progresses, materialistic consumers embrace a more open, global cultural identity (Sharma, 287). Openness reflects a consumer's empathy for and interest in other cultures (Skrbis, Kendall, and Woodward, 117) and represents a willingness to explore and learn from alternative systems of meaning held by others (Levy et al., 233). Indian consumers have become much more open minded and experimental in their perspective. According to Ahmed, the "open mind" of India's society can be attributed to the numerous foreign influences. While Indians' demand for foreign goods is limited, they do not seem to have an 'open mind' greater than what is observed in other countries.

Kosterman and Feshbach (271) discuss openness to foreign culture in their discussion of internationalism, where internationalism reflects positive impressions of other counties. Sharma, Shimp and Shin (35) found that the "cultural openness" was negatively related to consumers' ethnocentric tendencies. In contrast, internationalism takes a more active stance focusing on "international sharing and welfare, and reflects an empathy for the peoples of other countries" (Kosterman and Feshbach, 271). Consumers that are more open to foreign culture are more likely to find it acceptable to buy imported products as a means of supporting globalization and the people of other nations (Balabanis, et al, 169).

Global Connectivity

Technological advances such as the Internet and telecommunications form a pillar of globalization. As developing and emerging markets have improved their infrastructure, including Internet access, consumers in these markets have improved their connectivity and awareness (Javalgi, 178). While connectivity is improving, it is only available to those who can afford it, and thus connectivity is becoming more common for those in the middle and upper classes. As the middle class improves their financial well-being, they are more inclined to access the Internet to conduct business and for personal interest (Cleveland & Laroche, 246).

Consumers desire to learn, emulate and purchase products from other cultures as well as interact with those from other countries (Thompson & Tambyah, 226). Furthermore, consumers that admire foreign lifestyles do so to help them feel more connected. Consumption of foreign products is highly desirable for consumers seeking a more cosmopolitan outlook and lifestyle.

Age has a negative influence on connectivity. Those who are younger are more world-minded because they are avid patrons of the Internet where they access the media that enhances their knowledge (Cleveland & Laroche, 246). Younger people are more flexible and trusting in different viewpoints when compared to the older generations (D Mooij), and they are more trusting when it comes to accessing information online. Additionally, people with higher levels of education typically display more global behavior, are less likely to succumb to local cultural forces and are quicker to accept the accessibility of global connectivity (Cleveland & Laroche, 241).

Materialism

Recent definitions of materialism include Belk (265) who states that materialism is "the importance a consumer attaches to worldly possessions." Rassuli and Hollander (5) describe materialism as "a mind-set … an interest in getting and spending." Sahlins (291) refers to materialism as "a cultural system in which material interests are not made subservient to other social goals" and material self-interest is preeminent. Richins and Dawson (303) define materialism as the importance attributed to the ownership and acquisition of goods in attaining life goals or desired states.

In both developed and emerging markets materialism is related to an individual's overall happiness (Rindfleisch, Burroughs, & Wong, 14). As the number of consumers in the emerging markets grows, their behavior becomes materialistic and indicative of a becoming global consumer (Belk et al., 266). Other work has demonstrated that global segments of consumers have stronger materialistic values and more positive attitudes toward global brands (Riefler, 32), as well as greater acculturation to a global consumer culture (Cleveland & Laroche, 257). Individuals who are engaged in global consumer culture can pursue a more affluent and materialistic lifestyle (Strizhakova and Coulter, 79). Global culture has clearly been connected to increasing materialism (Cleveland and Laroche, 257).

Cleveland et al. wrote about materialism among Indian consumers and discussed the relationship that materialism has with cultural loyalty as well as materialism's impact on various purchase behaviors such as purchasing frequency of luxury products, and so on. Cleveland et al. (257) also studied the relationship between materialism and various demographic variables like age, income, gender and educational qualification for the Indian sample, but they did not establish significant results with these relationships (Gupta, 265).

Value Consciousness

Value consciousness refers to uncertainty when paying low prices based on quality constraint (Ailawadi, Neslin, & Gedenk, 71). Value-conscious consumers are concerned about low prices and product quality, and they compare the prices of different brands in order to get the best value. Brouthers & Xu (670) indicate that consumers in emerging markets are more value conscious and price sensitive because of their lower purchasing power, higher price elasticity of demand and greater tendency to spend savings rather than buy on credit. Price also has a greater influence on emerging market consumer purchase decisions when compared to product quality or brand image (Sharma, 300). Thus, consumers in emerging markets may perceive imported products as more favorably, but may not necessarily buy them.

Consumer Nationalism

Wang defines consumer nationalism as the "invocation of individuals' collective national identities in the process of consumption to favor or reject products from other countries." We accept Wang's definition of products when it comes to measuring consumer nationalism, where products refer to finished goods and services and exclude products that are used for making other products. Balabanis, et al. (166) explain how consumer nationalism is part of the attitudes reflected in economic nationalism. In addition to consumer nationalism, the impact of trade protection and restriction of foreign investment are included in this measurement. Several studies have found that consumers indicate a preference in purchasing domestic products over imported foreign products (Peterson and Jolibert, 894). A consumer with a nationalistic mentality is likely to purchase domestic products to support local industry and/or protest the purchasing of imported products to avoid dependence on foreign products.

Entrepreneurial Activity

Entrepreneurship is about individuals creating opportunities where others do not and attempting to exploit those opportunities through various modes of organizing, without regard to resources currently controlled (Stevenson & Jarillo, 25). It can involve individuals or teams creating products and services for other persons in a marketplace (Mitchell, 93). Countries that inspire entrepreneurial spirit have a greater chance of attaining economic growth, which can also lead toward a path of industrialization (Mali).

Entrepreneurial abilities have been identified as a group of competencies relevant to success. Researchers in the field of entrepreneurship distinguish between managerial and entrepreneurial competencies (Lerner and Almor, 122). Entrepreneurial abilities are needed to start a business, managerial skills are needed to grow the business, and successful entrepreneurship requires competencies in both areas (Man, Lau and Chan, 138). An understanding of the nature and role of such competencies can have important consequences for practice (Mitchelmore and Rowley, 109).

India's entrepreneurial spirit is fueled and growing. Debroy and Bhandari found that 52 percent of the workforce in India is self-employed. Indian entrepreneurship is helping to create new sources of income for even the poorest members of society. "India's backyard inventors are coming up with creations that their backers hope will make it big, solve a few of the world's problems, boost India's exports and continue cutting the country's dismal poverty rate." (Goering)

Empirical studies indicate that entrepreneurs in India score rather low on risk-taking propensity measures (Rutten). However, Gupta, Surie and Macmillan (256) conclude that risk-taking propensity is a culturally specific entrepreneurial trait and not culturally universal (Gupta, 53). McClelland identified a need for achievement as key to entrepreneurship and noted that high achievers are motivated by an enduring desire to succeed and "to exploit opportunities, to take advantage of favorable trade conditions; in short, to shape his own destiny." (37) Early empirical studies indicated that Indian entrepreneurs have low levels of achievement motivation (McClelland & Winter). However, more recent studies show high levels of achievement motivation among Indian entrepreneurs (Shivani, Mukherjee, and Sharan, 11). Kairos Future reports that Indians between sixteen and twenty-nine years old are the happiest in the world, and these youth have a high level of optimism about the future for themselves and for India. In addition, the working mentality comes as a top priority for Indian youth, followed by a good career and high status; these priorities exemplify values of both endurance and entrepreneurship (Gupta, 53).

Consumer Demographics and Purchase Behavior Foreign Products

Singh (57) refers to the additive components of education, income and occupation as consumer sophistication. Mager and Hulpke (82) found that demographics (income, education, occupation and family background) substantially determine buying behavior of foreign goods. Demographic factors (education, age and income) are also found to be highly correlated to information search and product knowledge. To satisfy the segmentation criteria, four of the most common demographic variables employed in domestic and international segmentation include age, gender, income and education (Wedel and Kamakura). More educated consumers have been found to be more adventurous, less likely to harbor ethnic prejudice, less nationalistic and rate foreign products more favorably than domestic products (Ray, 189; Watson & Johnson; Rose, 94; Wall & Heslop, 34). Xin (45) reveals that middle-class families spend more effort and money on their children's education than rural and low-income families.

As people's incomes increase, they tend to travel abroad and try different products that may result in greater acceptance or openness to foreign products (Sharma, Shimp and Shin, 25). Research in country image has supported the positive correlation between higher income and the tendency to evaluate foreign products more favorably (Wall & Heslop, 34; Wang). Chan and Lin (47) also have found that there is a strong correlation between income and product familiarity. Younger consumers have less restrictions and limitation as to choice of products (Lundstrom, 1998). Bannister and Saunders (568) found that older consumers favor domestic products more, tend to be more conservative and that younger consumers favor imported products more (Lundstrom, 25).

The types of goods and services sought by individuals change as people age and go through various lifecycle stages. Compared to their older counterparts, younger individuals are less committed to defined patterns and are more open to new perspectives and products (De Mooij), particularly those involving advanced technology. Income also strongly affects product choice, as higher-income consumers are better able to purchase expensive, status-enhancing items, such as household appliances, consumer electronics, and luxury products (De Mooij). Higher education levels expose individuals to different cultural perspectives and make them less likely to follow local behavioral norms and more likely to be global consumers (Keillor, D'Amico and Horton, 17). The differential effect of gender is among the most robust findings in the literature. Males and females differ on many aspects of consumer behavior including shopping patterns, information processing, judgment, responses to advertising and the products they tend to buy (Cleveland et al., 256).

Based on the literature noted earlier, all of the characteristics described individually had influence on India's middle class. When these characteristics are combined together their interrelationship is expected to have an additional influence on a set dependent variable. Materialism, global connectedness and buying foreign products have similarities that may appeal to India's growing middle class. As middle-class consumers become more globally connected, their desire to own foreign goods may increase. Openness to foreign culture, global connectedness, value consciousness and demographics have similarities that influence middle-class consumers in a similar manner. As middle-class demographics change and members of the middle class become more globally connected, they may seek value from the foreign goods that they desire. Likewise as India's middle-class consumers become connected to the world using their technological skills, they are more likely to appreciate goods that are locally made as well as foreign made. Thus, based on the above discussion, we propose the following hypotheses.

H: Indian middle-class consumers' demographics (age, education, employment status) are significantly related to the likelihood of purchasing foreign products.

H1: Indian middle-class consumers' openness to foreign culture is positively related to a) materialism, b) global connectedness and c) the likelihood of buying foreign products.

H2: Indian middle-class consumers' a) openness to foreign culture, b) global connectedness, c) value consciousness, and d) demographics (age, education, employment status) are significantly related to materialism.

H3: Indian middle-class consumers' a) openness to foreign culture, b) consumer nationalism, c) global connectedness, d) technological savvy, and e) demographics are significantly related to the likelihood of purchasing foreign products (appliance, electronics, and vehicles).

H4: Indian middle-class consumers' a) demographics, b) technological savvy, and c) creativity and innovation are significantly related to entrepreneurial activity.

Research Methodology

We developed a survey and asked middle-class consumers of India to reflect on their individual views on topics ranging from consumer behavior and lifestyle orientation to global connectedness and entrepreneurial activity. Table 7.1 lists key constructs used in the study. In addition, we asked several demographic questions. A total of 125 questions were asked with a majority of the questions in this study using a seven-point Likert scale (Colman, Morris, and Preston, 356). There were 115 viable surveys. The survey was administered online over a period of two months using a web-based tool, where a link to the survey was emailed to willing participants who would then click on the link and answer the questions. Participants were contacted using word-of-mouth beginning with those participants familiar with the researchers.

The sample of this survey includes middle-class consumers who currently live in India with a preference given for those that have started a business. Respondents for this survey live in one of two cities in India: Rajkot or Chennai. Rajkot and Chennai are both large cities in India that have an increasing middle class and are showing signs of economic growth. Following the existing literature (Birdsall and Meyer; Mukherjee, et al. 484; Gupta, 253), we consider a respondent "middle class" if they have an annual household income between RS 199,999 and RS 1,000,000.

Measurement and Data Analysis

Descriptive statistics of the demographics are listed in Table 7.1. The scales for the constructs materialism, value consciousness, global connectedness, openness to foreign culture, entrepreneurial activities, and technological savvy are obtained from the existing literature. A seven-point Likert scale was used to obtain the information on each item corresponding to the constructs. Sample items, factor loadings, and reliabilities are presented in Table 7.2.

The analysis had three phases. Phase 1 consisted of a frequency analysis of the demographic questions. Phase 2 involved a confirmatory factor analysis of the statements related to materialism, global connectedness, consumer nationalism, openness to foreign culture and entrepreneurial activities in order to determine whether or not a stable and reliable set of factors existed consistent with the literature. To test the reliability of the resulting factors, Cronbach alpha coefficient was computed on each construct (see Table 7.2). Phase 3 consisted of testing the hypotheses using multiple regression analysis.

Table 7.1 Demographic Profile of Sample

What is your level of education?	
Completed undergraduate degree	51%
Some graduate work	11%
Completed masters, doctorate or professional degrees	38%

What class do you think your family belongs to?	
Lower-middle class	3%
Middle class	13%
Upper-middle class	84%
What class do you think your family belongs to?	
Lower-middle class	2%
Middle class	12%
Upper-middle class	86%
Have you been educated abroad?	
Yes	21%
No	79%
Do you own a house?	
Yes	66%
No	34%
Have you started your own business?	
Yes	20%
No	80%
Marital status	
Single	21%
Married	79%
Gender	
Male	85%
Female	15%
Employment status	
Employed full time	90%
Retired or work part time	10%
Do you have any relatives living or working abroad?	
Yes	63%
No	37%

Table 7.2 Research Constructs, Sample Items, and Reliability Coefficients

Constructs (sources)	*Number of Items*	*Sample Items*	*Factor Loadings (range)*	*Cronbach's Alpha*
Materialism (Richins and Dawson (1992))	7	• I admire people who own expensive homes, cars, and clothes. • Some of the most important achievements in life include acquiring material possessions. • The things I own say a lot about how well I'm doing in life. • I like to own things that impress people.	.80–.90	.87

(*Continued*)

Constructs (sources)	*Number of Items*	*Sample Items*	*Factor Loadings (range)*	*Cronbach's Alpha*
Value Consciousness (Sharma, 2011)	4	• When shopping, I compare the prices of different brands to be sure I get the best value for the money. • When I buy products, I like to be sure that I am getting my money's worth.	.91–.97	.95
Global Connectedness (Strizhakova and Coulter (2012); Steenkamp and de Jon (2010))	7	• Thinking about my identity, I view myself as a global citizen. • I feel connected to the global world • Feeling like a citizen of the world is important to me. • I have a strong attachment to the global world.	.87–.93	.86
Openness to Foreign Culture	4	• I am interested in foreign cultures. • I like to keep up with international affairs. • I enjoy foreign films and televisions programs.	.67–.90	.89
Technologically Savvy	4	• I always interact with my friends using social media. • I frequently buy products online.	.76–.84	.75
Entrepreneurial Activity (Kuratko, Honsby, Naffziger (1997); Perri and Chu (2012)).	8	• I started my own business so I will always have job security. • I started my own business to be my own boss. • I started my own business to increase my annual income. • I started my own business to maintain personal freedom.	.77–.88	.89

Results: *Demographic Analysis*

The average age of the respondents is 37.5 years. While 51 percent of the respondents indicate completing an undergraduate degree, the remaining 49 percent noted completing masters' and/or professional degrees. The majority of the respondents are employed full-time. Twenty-one percent of the respondents noted that they have received education abroad. Most respondents (over 95 percent) noted that they belong to middle class or upper middle class. As per the qualifying requirement, all respondents also noted that their current household incomes are between Rs.200,000–Rs 1,000,000.

To test the hypotheses, we performed several multiple regression analyses. For H1, the dependent variable used was materialism. The levels of education, employment status, and age (the younger middle class) were related to materialism. Openness to foreign culture and global connectedness are positively related to materialism, thus providing support for H1 (see Table 7.3). However, value consciousness was not related to materialism. To test H2, the dependent variable used was global connectedness, and the independent variables used were demographics, openness to foreign culture, consumer nationalism and technological savvy. As shown in Table 7.4, all these variables are significantly related to global connectedness. These findings support H2. In terms of the direction, the younger members of the middle class tend to be more globally connected, and consumer nationalism was negatively related.

To test hypothesis H3, the construct entrepreneurial activity was used as a dependent variable, and the independent variables were demographics, technological savvy and creativity/innovation. As shown in Table 7.5, all the variables were significant, supporting H3. Again, in terms of demographics, younger, employed, and more educated consumers tend to be more entrepreneurially active. Finally, to test H4, the dependent variable used was the likelihood of purchasing foreign products (appliances, televisions, and vehicles). As shown in Table 7.6, demographics (age, education and employment status) and global connectedness are significantly related to likelihood of purchasing appliances, televisions and vehicles. Openness to foreign culture influences the purchase of televisions and vehicles. While younger middle-class consumers are more likely to purchase televisions and vehicles, their older counterparts are more likely to purchase foreign-made appliances. These findings support H4.

Table 7.3 Factors Influencing Materialism

Variables	*Standardized Coefficients*
Age	–.34**
Value consciousness	.05
Openness to foreign culture	.37***
Employment status	.21*
Level of education	.24*
Gender	.27**
Global connectedness	.20**

R^2 Adjusted = .32
F = 9.84 **
N = 114
*p < .01; ** p < .001; p < .0001

Table 7.4 Factors Influencing Global Connectedness of Middle Income Consumers

Variables	*Standardized Coefficients*
Openness to foreign culture	.68***
Consumer nationalism	–.26***
Age	–.16**

(*Continued*)

Variables	*Standardized Coefficients*
Gender	.23**
Education level	.24**
Employment status	.15*
Technologically savvy	.17*
An employee of a foreign company	.03
Relatives working or living abroad	.05

R^2 Adjusted = .61
N = 114; F = 13.1

Table 7.5 Factors Influencing Entrepreneurial Activity of Middle Income Consumers

Variables	*Standardized Coefficients*
Creativity and innovation	.30*
Age	–.16**
Education level	.17*
Employment status	.14*
Technological savvy	.19*

R^2 Adjusted = .63
N = 22; F = 12.3

Table 7.6 Factors Influencing the Likelihood of Purchasing Foreign Products

	Appliances	*Televisions*	*Vehicles*
Variables	*Standardized Coefficients*	*Standardized Coefficients*	*Standardized Coefficients*
Openness to foreign culture	.03	.26**	.23*
Consumer nationalism	–.07	–.09	–.03
Global connectedness	.19*	.27*	.36*
Age	.40***	–.20*	–.23*
Gender	.091	.11	.09
Education level	.20*	.16*	.17*
Employment status	.65***	.19*	.15*
Technological savvy	.06	.27***	.10
An employee of a foreign company	.20***	.09	.18*
Relatives working or living abroad	.06	.25**	.20*

Appliances: R^2 Adjusted = .66;
Televisions: R^2 Adjusted = .19
Vehicle: R^2 Adjusted = 21
N = 114
*P < .05; **P < .01; ***P < .001

Discussion and Implications

With a population of nearly 1.2 billion, India is the largest democracy in the world. Since economic reform in the 1990s, the Indian middle class has been celebrated for its economic transformation in the new global economy. The middle class has become an important economic, historical and sociological category in modern India. This new, affluent population is showing a greater need for foreign made products and services. As this segment of the population grows and continues to increase the demand for goods and services, the economy will also experience growth. The educated, skilled members of this class are comparable to the rest in the world today in terms of their individual achievements and capabilities to excel in the "new" economy.

The middle class also needs to be better understood in terms of its role in relation to economic power, target market opportunities and global cultural identity. This study provides several implications relating to the middle-class consumers. Demographic profiles show that those belonging to the middle class have a higher participation in lucrative service industries like banking, finance, information technology, engineering and health care services.

As the study findings suggest, Indians, especially the middle class, are getting more materialistic. Several factors support this, including their openness to foreign culture, age, gender, education and employment. Ger and Belk (74) found that higher levels of materialism are associated with countries undergoing rapid social and cultural change. Belk, Ger and Askegaard (348) uncover further evidence that supports a global diffusion of materialistic consumer culture. Educated, younger consumers are likely to be less susceptible to local conformity pressures, while holding a greater desire and economic ability to purchase foreign, status-enhancing products (Cleveland, Laroche, and Papadopoulos, 144). Richins and Dawson did not find any relationship between educational attainment and materialism. Although higher levels of income are naturally associated with the ability to purchase status-enhancing items, most research (e.g., Ger and Belk, 74; Richins and Dawson) has established no relationship between materialism and affluence. One explanation is that income is confounded by age, given the general finding that older people tend to be less materialistic than their younger counterparts despite higher earning power in general.

This study is also helpful in identifying middle-class consumers' purchase behavior. Multinational companies entering the Indian market need to understand India's middle-class consumers' purchasing decisions since they are influenced by demographic and socio-psychological variables. Appliances such as foreign-made refrigerators and washing machines are sought out by the older middle class compared to foreign-made televisions that are sought out by the younger generation. Other variables that influence the middle class' decision to purchase foreign-made appliances include employment status, education, global connectivity and employment with a foreign company. Foreign-made televisions are being purchased by those who are younger, but also by those who are more open to foreign culture, global connectivity, technological savvy, relatives working abroad, and who are educated and employed. This emphasizes to organizations that are offering their products to India's middle class that knowing your target market is important. Knowing if your market prefers foreign-made compared to locally made products will have an impact on sale.

Indians are more motivated than ever by personal ambition and a desire for personal success, satisfaction and freedom. Our findings also indicate that middle-class consumers' entrepreneurial activity is influenced by creativity and innovation. To develop a new business and be persistent with one's ideas, a person must have an innovative and creative mindset. Drucker supports this by stating that innovation is the tool of entrepreneurship. Both innovation and entrepreneurship demand creativity. Wyckoff (310) defines creativity as new and useful and is the act of "seeing things that everyone around us sees while making connections that no one else has made." Our research also indicates that demographic variables such as age, education, employment status and technological savvy also have an impact on the middle-classes entrepreneurial ability. This is an important finding for policymakers and provides evidence that they should provide more opportunities and incentives for creating businesses. Entrepreneurs are coming from good schools, but they can also be found in areas where creativity is rampant. Developing and supporting programs to incentivize entrepreneurial activity will aid in supporting the growth of the middle class.

Conclusions, Limitations and Directions for Future Research

Though the present survey provides useful insight into Indian middle-class consumers' attitudes and behavior, the sample size is small. This study differentiates between middle and lower-middle class by income. Since India is not a homogenous market, a larger sample will help capture more variations in middle- and lower-middle-class consumers such as attitudinal and behavioral differences. Future work should include a study with a larger sample of the same group using the same two cities, or using cities identical in composition. In addition, future work should include an investigation of the low income/poverty class of India in these cities so that a comparison can be made regarding the differences between the middle class and poverty class. This would provide a clear image about global connectivity and the differences between the classes. Finally, using the same survey utilized in this study it is suggested that there be an investigation of the middle class in other emerging economies. This would also be helpful in identifying trends that are common in emerging economies as this pertains to global connectivity as well as entrepreneurial spirit.

Indian FDI policy was liberalized in January 2012, therefore it is likely to facilitate the entry of more foreign brands and to impact India's middle-class consumers' attitudes and purchase behavior of foreign products. Hence, future research needs to be conducted to better understand the attitudinal and behavioral difference of middle- and lower-middle-class consumers. While this research is cross sectional, longitudinal research helps to track the attitudinal changes related to materialism, openness to foreign culture and entrepreneurial activities.

In conclusion, with the liberalization of the economy in the 1990s, there has been not only an increase in income but also a change in the demographic profile of consumers. Educational qualifications have increased and women have started entering the workforce. More and more consumers are becoming more materialistic and open to foreign culture. There is also increased interest in foreign-made products prompted by the liberalization of the media and access to international travel and global connections. All factors contributed to the rise of middle-class consumers, who are playing a key role in determining the market power of the Indian economy.

Works Cited

Acemoglu, Daron, and Fabrizio Zilibotti. "Was Prometheus unbound by chance? Risk, diversification, and growth." *Journal of Political Economy* 105(4) (1997): 709–751.

Ahmed, Kishwar. "A Study of the Closed Mind in Relation to Authoritarianism, Conservatism and Rigidity and Familial Antecedents within the Indian Context." *Unpublished Doctoral Thesis, Department of Psychology, Panjab University* (1979).

Ailawadi, Kusum L., Scott A. Neslin, and Karen Gedenk. "Pursuing the value-conscious consumer: store brands versus national brand promotions." *Journal of Marketing* 65(1) (2001): 71–89.

Balabanis, George, et al. "The impact of nationalism, patriotism and internationalism on consumer ethnocentric tendencies." *Journal of International Business Studies* (2001): 157–175.

Bannister, Jim P., and John A. Saunders. "UK consumers' attitudes towards imports: The measurement of national stereotype image." *European Journal of Marketing* 12(8) (1978): 562–570.

Baron, Robert A. "Cognitive mechanisms in entrepreneurship: Why and when entrepreneurs think differently than other people." *Journal of Business venturing* 13(4) (1998): 275–294.

Belk, Russell W. "Materialism: Trait aspects of living in the material world." *Journal of Consumer Research* (1985): 265–280.

Birdsall, Nancy. "The (indispensable) middle class in developing countries; or, the rich and the rest, not the poor and the rest." *Equity In A Globalizing World, Ravi Kanbur and Michael Spence, eds., World Bank, Forthcoming* (2010).

Birdsall, Nancy, Carol Graham, and Stefano Pettinato. "Stuck in tunnel: Is globalization muddling the middle?" (2000).

Birdsall, Nancy and Christian Meyer. "New estimates of India's middle class." *CGD Note, Center for Global Development, Washington, DC* (2012).

Brouthers, Lance Eliot, and Kefeng Xu. "Product stereotypes, strategy and performance satisfaction: The case of Chinese exporters." *Journal of International Business Studies* (2002): 657–677.

Burke, Timothy. "Lifebuoy men, Lux women." *Commodification, consumption, and cleanliness in modern Zimbabwe* (1996).

Cashell, Brian W. "Who Are the "Middle Class?" (2008).

Chan, T. S., and Gong-shi Lin. "An empirical analysis of consumer decision processes in the People's Republic of China." *Journal of International Consumer Marketing* 4(4) (1992): 33–48.

Cleveland, Mark, et al. "Information search patterns for gift purchases: a cross-national examination of gender differences." *Journal of Consumer Behaviour* 3(1) (2003): 20–47.

Cleveland, Mark, and Michel Laroche. "Acculturation to the global consumer culture: Scale development and research paradigm." *Journal of Business Research* 60(3) (2007): 249–259.

Cleveland, Mark, Nicolas Papadopoulos, and Michel Laroche. "Identity, demographics, and consumer behaviors: International market segmentation across product categories." *International Marketing Review* 28(3) (2011): 244–266.

Cleveland, Mark, Michel Laroche, and Nicolas Papadopoulos. "Cosmopolitanism, consumer ethnocentrism, and materialism: An eight-country study of antecedents and outcomes." *Journal of International Marketing* 17.1 (2009): 116–146.

Colman, Andrew M., Claire E. Morris, and Carolyn C. Preston. "Comparing rating scales of different lengths: Equivalence of scores from 5-point and 7-point scales." *Psychological Reports* 80(2) (1997): 355–362.

Das, Sanjay Kanti. "Entrepreneurship through Micro Finance in North East India: A Comprehensive Review of Existing Literature." *Information Management & Business Review* 4(4) (2012).

Debroy B & Bhandari L (2007). Exclusive growth-inclusive inequality. Working Paper, Centrefor Policy Research, Delhi. 2007.

De Mooij, Marieke. *Consumer behavior and culture: Consequences for global marketing and advertising*. Sage, 2010.

Doepke, Matthias, and Fabrizio Zilibotti. *Occupational choice and the spirit of capitalism*. No. w12917. National Bureau of Economic Research. 2007.

Dobbs, Richard, et al. *Urban world: Cities and the rise of the consuming class*. McKinsey Global Institute. 2012.

Drucker, P.F. Innovation and Entrepreneurship: Practice and Principles, Heinemann, London. 1985.

Durfee, Mary, and James N. Rosenau. "Playing catch-up: International relations theory and poverty." *Millennium-Journal of International Studies* 25(3) (1996): 521–545.

Easterly, William. "The middle class consensus and economic development." *Journal of Economic Growth* 6(4) (2001): 317–335.

Ger, Güliz, and Russell W. Belk. "Cross-cultural differences in materialism." *Journal of economic psychology* 17.1 (1996): 55–77.

Goering, L. "India nurturing homegrown ideas." *The Chicago Tribune*. 2007.

Gong, Wen. "Chinese consumer behavior: a cultural framework and implications." *Journal of American Academy of Business* 3.1/2 (2003): 373–380.

Gupta, Nitin. "Globalization does lead to change in consumer behavior: an empirical evidence of impact of globalization on changing materialistic values in Indian consumers and its aftereffects." *Asia Pacific Journal of Marketing and Logistics* 23.3 (2011): 251–269.

Gupta, Vipin, Ian C. MacMillan, and Gita Surie. "Entrepreneurial leadership: developing and measuring a cross-cultural construct." *Journal of Business Venturing* 19.2 (2004): 241–260.

Gupta, Vipin. "An inquiry into the characteristics of entrepreneurship in India." *Journal of International Business Research* 7(1) (2008): 53.

Haughton, Jonathan Henry, and Shahidur R. Khandker. *Handbook on poverty and inequality*. World Bank Publications. 2009.

Helson, Ravenna, and Jennifer L. Pals. "Creative potential, creative achievement, and personal growth." *Journal of Personality* 68(1) (2000): 1–27.

Hu, Xiaoling, et al. "The effects of country-of-origin on Chinese consumers' wine purchasing behaviour." *Journal of Technology Management in China* 3(3) (2008): 292–306.

Indian Middle Class: KAS International Reports 12. 2011.

Javalgi, Rajshekhar (Raj) G., et al. "Assessing competitive advantage of emerging markets in knowledge intensive business services." *Journal of Business & Industrial Marketing* 26(3) (2011): 171–180.

Kharas, Homi, and Geoffrey Gertz. "The new global middle class: a cross-over from West to East." China's emerging middle class: beyond economic transformation, Brookings Institution Press, Washington, DC (2010): 2.

Keillor, Bruce D., Michael D'Amico, and Veronica Horton. "Global consumer tendencies." *Psychology & Marketing* 18.1 (2001): 1–19.

Kinra, Neelam. "The effect of country-of-origin on foreign brand names in the Indian market." *Marketing Intelligence & Planning* 24(1) (2006): 15–30.

Klonoski, Robert. "How Important Is Creativity? The Impact Of Age, Occupation And Cultural Background On The Assessment Of Ideas." *Journal of Applied Business Research* 28(3)(2012): 411–426.

Knight, Frank H. *Risk, uncertainty and profit*. Courier Corporation. 2012.

Kosterman, Rick, and Seymour Feshbach. "Toward a measure of patriotic and nationalistic attitudes." *Political Psychology* (1989): 257–274.

Kotkin, Joel. "In Pictures: The Next Decade's Fastest-Growing Cities." *Forbes*. 2010.

Lange, F. A. *History of materialism and criticism of its present importance* (Vol. 1). K. Paul, Trench, Trübner. 1980.

Lerner, Miri, and Tamar Almor. "Relationships among strategic capabilities and the performance of women-owned small ventures." *Journal of Small Business Management* 40(2) (2002): 109–125.

Levy, Orly, et al. "What we talk about when we talk about 'global mindset': Managerial cognition in multinational corporations." *Journal of International Business Studies* 38(2) (2007): 231–258.

Leavy, Brian. "A leader's guide to creating an innovation culture." *Strategy & Leadership* 33(4) (2005): 38–45.

Levy, Orly, et al. "What we talk about when we talk about 'global mindset': Managerial cognition in multinational corporations." *Journal of International Business Studies* 38(2)(2007): 231–258.

Lopez-Calva, Luis F., Jamele Rigolini, and Florencia Torche. *Is There Such a Thing As Middle Class Values?* Working Paper 286. Washington DC: Center. 2012.

Lundstrom, William J., Oscar W. Lee, and D. Steven White. "Factors influencing Taiwanese consumer preference for foreign-made white goods: USA versus Japan." *Asia Pacific Journal of Marketing and Logistics* 10(3) (1998): 5–29.

Mager, John, and John F. Hulpke. "Social Class in a Classless Society: Marketing Implications for China." *Journal of International Consumer Marketing* 2.4 (1990): 57–88.

Mali, D. D. "Entrepreneurship Development in North East." *Indian Institute of Entrepreneurship, Guwahati*. 2000.

Man, Thomas WY, Theresa Lau, and K. F. Chan. "The competitiveness of small and medium enterprises: A conceptualization with focus on entrepreneurial competencies." *Journal of Business Venturing* 17(2) (2002): 123–142.

Manrai, Lalita A., et al. "A cross-cultural comparison of style in Eastern European emerging markets." *International Marketing Review* 18(3) (2001): 270–285.

Mathur, Nita. "Shopping malls, credit cards and global brands consumer culture and lifestyle of India's new middle class." *South Asia Research* 30(3) (2010): 211–231.

McClelland, David C. *Achieving society*. Simon and Schuster. 1961. 36–62.

Mills, Colleen. "Enterprise orientations: a framework for making sense of fashion sector start-up." *International Journal of Entrepreneurial Behavior & Research* 17(3) (2011): 245–271.

Mill, John Stuart. *Principles of Political Economy With Some of Their Applications to Social Philosophy. 1857*. New Edition introduced by Sir WJ Ashley. London. 1848.

Mitchell, Ronald K., et al. "Toward a theory of entrepreneurial cognition: Rethinking the people side of entrepreneurship research." *Entrepreneurship Theory and Practice* 27(2) (2002): 93–104.

Mitchelmore, Siwan, and Jennifer Rowley. "Entrepreneurial competencies: a literature review and development agenda." *International Journal of Entrepreneurial Behavior & Research* 16(2) (2010): 92–111.

Mittelman, James H., and Ashwini Tambe. "Reconceptualizing global poverty: globalization, marginalization, and gender." *Principled World Politics*. 2000. 166–180.

Mukherjee, Arpita, et al. "Are Indian consumers brand conscious? Insights for global retailers." *Asia Pacific Journal of Marketing and Logistics* 24(3) (2012): 482–499.

Murphy, Kevin M., Andrei Shleifer, and Robert W. Vishny. "Industrialization and the big push." 1988.

Nuruzzaman, Mohammed. "Economic liberalization and poverty in the developing countries." *Journal of Contemporary Asia* 35(1) (2005): 109–127.

Park, Gregory, David Lubinski, and Camilla P. Benbow. "Ability differences among people who have commensurate degrees matter for scientific creativity." *Psychological Science* 19(10) (2008): 957–961.

Peterson, Robert A., and Alain JP Jolibert. "A meta-analysis of country-of-origin effects." *Journal of International Business Studies* (1995): 883–900.

Pressman, Steven. "The middle class throughout the world in the mid-2000s." *Journal of Economic Issues* 44(1) (2010): 243–262.

Rai, Shailendra Kumar. "Indian entrepreneurs: an empirical investigation of entrepreneur's age and firm entry, type of ownership and risk behavior." *Journal of Services Research* 8(1) (2008).

Rassuli, Kathleen M., and Stanley C. Hollander. "Desire-induced, innate, insatiable?" *Journal of Macromarketing* 6(2) (1986): 4–24.

Ray, John J. "Racism, conservatism and social class in Australia: with German, Californian and South African comparisons." *Personality and Individual differences* 11.2 (1990): 187–189.

Richins, Marsha L., and Scott Dawson. "A consumer values orientation for materialism and its measurement: Scale development and validation." *Journal of Consumer Research* (1992). 303–16.

Riefler, Petra. "Why consumers do (not) like global brands: The role of globalization attitude, GCO and global brand origin." *International Journal of Research in Marketing* 29(1) (2012): 25–34.

Rindfleisch, Aric, James E. Burroughs, and Nancy Wong. "The safety of objects: Materialism, existential insecurity, and brand connection." *Journal of Consumer Research*. 36(1) (2009): 1–16.

Rohde, David. "The swelling middle. Reuters." (2012).

Rose, Richard. "National pride in cross-national perspective." *International Social Science Journal* 37.1 (1985): 85–96.

Ross, Catherine E., and John Mirowsky. "Sex differences in the effect of education on depression: resource multiplication or resource substitution?" *Social Science & Medicine* 63(5) (2006): 1400–1413.

Rutten, M. "The Study of entrepreneurship in India: In need of a comparative Perspective." *The Oxford India Companion to Sociology and Social Anthropology, eds. Veena Das*. 2006.

Sahlins, Marshall. *Culture and practical reason*. University of Chicago Press, 2013. 291.

Say, J. B. "Treatise on Political Economy: On the Production." *Distribution and Consumption of Wealth* (translation 1964) New York: Kelley (1803).

Shultz, Clifford, Anthony Pecotich, and Khai Le. "Changes in marketing activity and consumption in the Socialist Republic of Vietnam." *Research in Consumer Behavior: Consumption in Marketizing Economies* 7 (1994): 225–57.

Sharma, Piyush. "Country of origin effects in developed and emerging markets: Exploring the contrasting roles of materialism and value consciousness." *Journal of International Business Studies* 42(2) (2011): 285–306.

Sharma, Subhash, Terence A. Shimp, and Jeongshin Shin. "Consumer ethnocentrism: a test of antecedents and moderators." *Journal of the Academy of Marketing Science* 23(1) (1995): 26–37.

Shivani, Shradha, S. K. Mukherjee, and Raka Sharan. "Socio-cultural influences on Indian entrepreneurs: The need for appropriate structural interventions." *Journal of Asian Economics* 17(1) (2006): 5–13.

Simon, Mark, Susan M. Houghton, and Karl Aquino. "Cognitive biases, risk perception, and venture formation: How individuals decide to start companies." *Journal of Business Venturing* 15(2) (2000): 113–134.

Singh, Jagdip. "A typology of consumer dissatisfaction response styles." *Journal of Retailing*. 1990.

Sklair, Leslie. "The culture-ideology of consumerism in urban China: Some findings from a survey in Shanghai." *Research in Consumer Behavior* 7(2) (1994): 259–92.

Skrbis, Zlatko, Gavin Kendall, and Ian Woodward. "Locating cosmopolitanism between humanist ideal and grounded social category." *Theory, Culture & Society* 21(6) (2004): 115–136.

Stevenson, T. H. C. "The vital statistics of wealth and poverty." *Journal of the Royal Statistical Society* (1928): 207–230.

Stevenson, T. H. C. "The social distribution of mortality from different causes in England and Wales, 1910–12." *Biometrika* (1923): 382–400.

Stevenson, T. H. C. "Suggested lines of advance in English vital statistics." *Journal of the Royal Statistical Society* (1910): 685–713.

Stevenson, Howard H., and J. Carlos Jarillo. "A paradigm of entrepreneurship: Entrepreneurial management." *Strategic Management Journal* 11.5 (1990): 17–27.

Strizhakova, Yuliya, and Robin A. Coulter. "The "green" side of materialism in emerging BRIC and developed markets: The moderating role of global cultural identity." *International Journal of Research in Marketing* 30(1) (2013): 69–82.

Sumner, Andy. "Where do the poor live?" *World Development* 40(5) (2012): 865–877.

Thompson, Craig J., and Siok Kuan Tambyah. "Trying to be cosmopolitan." *Journal of Consumer Research* 26(3) (1999): 214–241.

Torche, Florencia, and Luis F. Lopez-Calva. "Stability and vulnerability of the Latin American middle class." *Oxford Development Studies* 41(4) (2013): 409–435.

Usher, Abbott Payson. *A History of Mechanical Inventions: Revised Edition*. Courier Corporation, 2013.

Usunier, Jean-Claude. "Social status and country-of-origin preferences." *Journal of Marketing Management* 10(8) (1994): 765–782.

Uygun, Ramazan, and Ali Akdemir. "Entrepreneurial Behaviors of Turkish Entrepreneurs: A Research about Perception and Seize of Opportunities of Turkish Entrepreneurs." *International Journal of Business and Social Science* 3(15) (2012): 78–91.

Wall, Marjorie, and Louise A. Heslop. "Consumer attitudes toward Canadian-made versus imported products." *Journal of the Academy of Marketing Science* 14(2) (1986): 27–36.

Wang, Chih-Kang. "The effect of foreign economic, political and cultural environment on consumers' willingness to buy foreign products." PhD. Dissertation. Texas A&M.1978.

Watson, Goodwin Barbour, and David W. Johnson. *Social psychology: Issues and insights*. Philadelphia: Lippincott. 1972.

Weber, Max. *The Protestant Ethic and the Spirit of Capitalism: and other writings*. Penguin, 2002. 282.

Wedel, Michel. *Market segmentation: Conceptual and methodological foundations*. Springer Science & Business Media. 2000.

World Bank. "Economic Mobility and the Rise of the Latin American Middle Class. Regional Flagship 2012", Office of the Chief Economist for the Latin America and the Caribbean Region. 2012.

Wyckoff, Paul Gary. "The elusive flypaper effect." *Journal of Urban Economics* 30.3 (1991): 310–328.

Xin, Wang. "Desperately Seeking Status: Political, Social and Cultural Attributes of China's Rising Middle Class." *Modern China Studies* 20(1) (2013).

Zhou, Lianxi, and Michael K. Hui. "Symbolic value of foreign products in the People's Republic of China." *Journal of International Marketing* 11(2) (2003): 36–58.

Section III

Politics and Ideology

8 Meanings of Money Among Middle-Class Hindu Families in India

Altaf Merchant, Gregory M. Rose and Mohit Gour[1]

Introduction

> *"It is you who bestow both worldly enjoyment and spiritual liberation*
> *Be gracious, O Lovely One."*
> Hymn invoking Lakshmi
> (the Hindu Goddess of wealth)
> (Rhodes 173–174)

> *"The wife alone, whate'er await*
> *Must share on earth her husband's fate."*
> Sita's (wife of Rama) speech in The Ramayana of Valmiki, Canto XXVII, Book 2 (Griffith)

> *"This duty first and paramount,*
> *That sons, obedient, aye fulfill*
> *Their honoured fathers' word and will."*
> Rama's (son of Dasharatha) promise in The Ramayana of Valmiki, Canto XIX, Book 2 (Griffith)

Lakshmi, Sita and Rama illustrate the predominant role of meanings of money, family and duty in Hindu society. Lakshmi, the goddess of wealth, is "one of the most popular and widely venerated deities of the Hindu pantheon" (Kinsley 32), while (Hindu Gods) Sita and Rama emphasize the culturally prescribed familial role of women and men. The meanings of money are socially constructed, pervasive, and enacted within a cultural context within different income levels (rich, middle class and poor). Families perpetuate and reflect cultural values (Rose), and represent a primary social group. This research project examines the meanings of money and the enactment of these meanings within middle-class Hindu Indian families.

The Middle Class in India

India is an emerging nation. Decades of socialism have given way to more market driven policies (Virmani). India's growing middle class (estimated at 28.4 million households or 153 million people; [Shukla]) is projected to emerge as the world's largest economy within the next forty years (Rowley).

This growth has led to a corresponding change in lifestyle reflected in the ownership of goods. For example, 76.7 percent, 9.7 percent, 82 percent of urban households had a TV, car and telephone respectively in 2011 compared to 64.3 percent, 5.6 percent and 23 percent in 2001 (Haub). Education is the pathway to more skilled, higher paying, aspirational jobs and improved incomes. The growing middle class is now the key beneficiary of an increasing array of products and services marketed in India (Zachariah).

Middle-class families in India strive to enhance their status by acquiring branded products and services. The purchase of these products is driven by novelty value, vanity and pride (Srivastava). Indian consumers' market-habits, lifestyles, tastes and preferences are also evolving. Retail malls and multiplexes have transformed shopping habits, along with increased urbanization. While the majority of the population in India is rural, the urban population is growing much faster, with 28 percent now living in urban areas and growing at 31.2 percent as compared to the rural population which is growing at 17.9 percent (Ministry of Urban Affairs of the Government of India). Migration contributes to about 24 percent of the increase in India's urban population, and reflects and precipitates rising aspirations and consumption (Banerji). Indian family dynamics are also evolving and transitioning from a joint-extended family to a nuclear family structure. Middle-class aspirations are accompanied by anxieties and insecurities that are associated with changing lifestyles that challenge traditional beliefs and class (and caste) systems. This evolution echoes previous treatise on the struggles and challenges experienced by emerging middle class around the world in embracing a Western lifestyle (Lopez and Weinstein 5).

Urbanization, economic development and increased aspirations are interpreted through the lens of traditional values and teachings, which profoundly influences consumers' attitudes toward and use of money in India. Understanding money meanings provides a means of and gateway to better comprehending how people spend and save money and how money practices are enacted within and adapted to specific economic and family circumstances.

Religious teachings provide an important means of understanding money meanings and consumption in India. Hindus account for 80.5 percent of the country's population (827 million people; Census of India). They have a rich set of prescriptive cultural beliefs that provide an interesting contrast to previous North American research on attitudes toward money (Rose and Orr; Yamauchi and Templer; Goldberg and Lewis). Keeping in mind these economic, social and cultural dynamics, we examine the attitudes of Hindu Indian consumers toward money.

Literature Review

In this section extant research on money and Hinduism will be reviewed. Two research questions will also be presented.

Meanings of Money

Money motivates a variety of consumer behaviors. "Money is probably the most emotionally meaningful object in contemporary life; only food and sex are its close competitors as common carriers of such strong and diverse feelings, significances, and strivings" (Krueger 3). Cultural attitudes toward money are complex. In the United States, the protestant ethic has a traditional pervasive influence on consumers. It involves hard work, self-sacrifice and conscientiousness. Earning money through hard work reflects God's blessings, but too much money and money acquired easily are decried as sinful (Belk and Wallendorf; Goldberg and Lewis). Past research reveals that people often perceive money as if it were a drug, which possesses an abundance of motivational and rewarding properties (Lea and Webley). Recently, Rose and Orr found four motivational dimensions of the symbolic meanings of money in the United States (status, achievement, worry, and security) and called for further research in different cultures. This study responds to this call by investigating the following research question:

RQ1: What are the meanings of money among middle-class Hindu families in India?

Hinduism

Hinduism consists of diverse traditions, has no single founder, and provides a variety of prescriptive duties and beliefs for daily morality based on *dharma*, *karma*, and societal norms (Radhakrishnan). *Dharma* refers to one's duties, relative to one's position and situation in life (Creel). Doing one's dharma is believed to support the universe and contribute to a sense of *rita* or cosmic order (Young 29). *Karma* is another important feature of Hinduism, where each person is responsible for his/her actions and he/she alone has to bear the consequences of these actions in this and any future lives (due to reincarnation) (King). The idea of *moksha* (salvation or liberation from the continual cycle of birth and rebirth) reinforces the social system by providing a motive for fidelity to *dharma*: only by dutifully maintaining the social order through *dharma* could one be properly prepared to attain *moksha*. What results is a society of *dharma* for the many and *moksha* for the few, with *dharma* and *karma* being instrumental to attain *moksha* (Creel). This search for spiritual liberation (*moksha*) through doing ones duty (*dharma*) motivates the attitudes and actions of Hindus including attitudes toward money. To comprehend the complex meanings of money from the Hindu perspective it is crucial to appreciate the context of Hindu Gods. Hindus believe in the *Trimurti* (the trinity of Gods). Brahma is the creator, Vishnu is the protector, and Siva is the destroyer. Siva and Vishnu are worshipped through many of their *avatars* (incarnations). Krishna (promoting proper actions and the fulfillment of duty in his discourse the *Bhagvad Gita*) and Rama (idealized son and King of the epic the *Ramayana*) are the most widely worshipped *avatars* of Vishnu (Brockington 120). Sita and Lakshmi are two of the most popular Hindu goddesses. They are Vishnu's consorts in different *avatars*. Sita presents a feminine *avatar* of devotion, while Lakshmi represents wealth, prosperity and wellbeing (Kinsley 20).

As per Hindu tradition, a man goes through successive life stages. The first stage is that of a student (a period of celibate study); followed by a householder (married with children), a forest dweller (withdrawn from society) and lastly a renouncer (a wandering ascetic). In reality, most people never go beyond the householder stage, which is described as the most important and celebrated stage (Young).The ancient Hindu text *Manu Smriti* (*Laws of Manu*) links the material (acquired by working appropriately) to familial and spiritual happiness (Saunders). It states: "Just as all living creatures depend on air in order to live, so do members of the other stages of life subsist by depending on householders. Since people in the other three stages of life are supported every day by the knowledge and the food of the householder, the householder stage of life is venerated. It must be carried out with zeal by the man who wants to win an incorruptible heaven (after death) and endless happiness here on earth ..." (50). These philosophies encompass all classes including the middle class; however, synthesizing modernity with the fulfillment of duty, as laid out by tradition, are particularly important to understanding the emerging middle class, because this group represents the vanguard of the effort to adapt traditional beliefs to an emerging consumer culture, marked by an evolving trend (although far from universal) toward dual income nuclear families. Both tradition and modern beliefs are reflected in how the middle class view money and its role in the subsequent fulfilment of the duties of the householder.

The Hindu Household

To get a detailed understanding of the role of money in the lives of Hindus in India, it is crucial to examine the dynamics of the Hindu household. In Hindu families, traditionally family goals and unity are primary, while personal considerations are secondary. About 90 percent of Indian marriages are arranged (Toledo). The role of the wife is outlined in ancient Hindu texts like the *Manu Smriti* or *Laws of Manu* (The Laws of Manu). It states that: "A virtuous woman should constantly serve her husband like a God, even if he behaves badly, freely indulges his lust, and is devoid of any good qualities" (115). The wife is the center of the household: "children, the fulfillment of duties, obedience, and ultimate sexual pleasure depend upon the wife, and so does heaven for oneself and one's ancestors" (200).

Family relationships in India and other nations, including the United States, are dynamic and slowly moving in an egalitarian direction (Commuri and Gentry). Indian women today are increasingly becoming co-providers (Andrade, Postma, and Abraham), with 29 percent of all women participating in the labor force (outside of the home) (*India: Why is Women's Labour Force Participation Dropping?*). As women increasingly work out of the home, their new financial status endows them with a voice on household matters, including how money is spent and saved. The increased labor force participation of women has also precipitated changes in the family structure. More specifically, the traditional joint family system in India (with several generations living, eating and praying in the same household; Singh) is giving way to a nuclear family system. This evolution, combined with career roles and increased income for women, has enhanced their role in financial management (Venkatesh). Spousal roles are influenced by the proportion of income accounted for by the husband and wife but are also influenced by the presence of elderly parents and relatives in close physical proximity, and the family's adherence or non-adherence to traditional norms of behavior.

Thus, in spite of the increasing role of the wife as a co-provider, a decrease in family size and an evolving shift toward a nuclear family structure (Niranjan et al.), the influence of the extended family and its traditions continues (Belk; Carson and Chowdhury). Keeping these traditional beliefs and the evolving role of the Indian husband and wife in mind, we investigate the following research question:

RQ2: How is money management negotiated within middle-class Hindu families in India?

Methodology

Twenty-four semi-structured audio-taped interviews (of twelve Hindu married couples) were conducted in 2012 across three Indian cities – Delhi, Hyderabad and Bhubaneshwar. These three cities were chosen because they encompass different regions and likely vary in their degree of cosmopolitanism, traditionalism and attitudes. The population of Delhi, Hyderabad and Bhubaneshwar are 11, 6.8, and 0.84 million, respectively (India Census). Delhi is located in the northern region and is the second most populous metropolis in India. Hyderabad is the capital of the southern state of Andhra Pradesh and is an emerging information technology hub. Bhubaneshwar, which is often referred to as the temple city of India, is the capital of the eastern state of Odisha. One of the authors traveled to India to conduct the interviews along with a local marketing research firm. Spouses were interviewed separately so that their thoughts could be ascertained without any domination from either spouse. Three socio-economic[2] groups were sampled based on income, education and occupation. Different family structures (six joint/six nuclear) and income statuses (seven dual/five single) were sampled. Three families were upper middle class, three were middle class, and six belonged to middle to lower-middle class. All described Hinduism as their religion. Respondent profiles are presented in Table 8.1 (with the names changed).

Table 8.1 Respondent Profile

Respondent Number	*Husband's Name (Age) and Wife's Name (Age)*	*Socio-Economic Classification*	*Income Single/ Dual*	*Occupation*		*Family Type*	*Annual Family Income (Rs.; $)*
				Husband	*Wife*	*Joint/ Nuclear*	
	DELHI						
C1	Suraj (36 years) and Meena (34 years) Gupta	B2	Single	Clerk	Housewife	Joint	400,000; *6,600*
C2	Vijay (38 years) and Alka (36 years) Bambani	A1	Dual	Owns a small business	Fashion coordinator	Nuclear	1,200,000; *20,000*
C3	Anand (49 years) and Yashi (46 years) Pushp	B2	Single	Junior officer	Housewife	Nuclear	450,000; *7,500*
C4	Arman(35 years) and Ankita (32 years) Lulla	A2	Dual	Senior manager	Executive	Joint	650,000; *10,800*
	HYDERABAD						
C5	Natraja (41 years) and Prabha (36 years) Ravindran	B1	Dual	Real estate agent	Small jewelry business	Joint	300,000; *5,000*
C6	Rajesh (28 years) and Mallika (28 years) Reddy	A2	Single	Engineer	Housewife	Nuclear	500,000; *8,300*
C7	Kishor (54 years) and Smita (45 years) Gouda	A1	Dual	Business	Small business	Joint	850,000; *14,100*
C8	Manoj (48 years) and Padmini (38 years) Nagarajan	B2	Dual	Business	Teacher	Nuclear	300,000; *5,000*
	BHUBANESHWAR						
C9	Mahadev (37 years) and Madhuri (35 years) Sahoo	B1	Single	Supervisor in a hospital	Housewife	Joint	300,000; *5,000*
C10	Chitran (38 years) and Anjali (36 years) Pradhan	A2	Dual	Lawyer	Teacher	Nuclear	550,000; *9,100*
C11	Jayesh (48 years) and Reena (46 years) Biswal	B1	Single	Teacher	Housewife	Nuclear	300,000; *5,000*
C12	Nikhil (27 years) and Tinu (25 years) Mohapatra	A1	Dual	Lawyer	Teacher	Joint	700,000; *11,600*

We started with broad questions about money and then moved to questions about married life and money management within the household. The interviews yielded 220 pages of single-spaced verbatim transcripts. Analysis of the transcripts was initially done by two of the authors and an external consultant (Thompson et al.). All three members of the interpretive group were of Indian origin and qualitative researchers. They read each transcript for the husband and wife separately and then as a couple, iteratively discussed and re-read each transcript, and revised and re-examined their interpretation until an internal structure was derived for a couple. Then, attention was turned to the next couple, the process was repeated, points of similarity and differences from the previous interview(s) were noted, and a pattern of thematic relationships common to all participants was noted in a themes notebook (Thompson et al.). Thus, we moved from an emic view (focusing on the informant's point of view) to an etic framework (examining broader/cultural meanings and patterns).

The interpretive group analyzed the transcripts over a four-month period and regularly returned back to the transcripts to facilitate discussion and identify themes (Thompson et al.). One of the three authors was held out to provide an external audit to the interpretive groups' themes and interpretations. He went through each transcript and developed his own set of themes. Differences in interpretations were resolved through depth discussions (Wallendorf and Belk). The authors also contacted four of the twelve couples and discussed emerging themes as a respondent check. All respondents confirmed the resonance of these themes with their own experience.

Results

The findings from the twenty-four interviews will be presented in this section. Emerging themes around multiple meanings of money, fickle nature of prosperity, limitations of money, saving, consumer culture, and domestic money management will be discussed in detail.

Multiple Meanings and the Pervasive Role of Money

All respondents emphasized the importance of money. They emphasized that money was needed to live and buy necessities, such as food, medicine and housing. The need for money has become amplified with economic development and exposure to the consumer culture. Many respondents said that without money nothing is possible. For example, Ankita (female; a thirty-two-year-old married executive from Delhi; C4) stressed the essential nature of money and cited a popular hymn in praise of Lakshmi (the Goddess of wealth):

> "It (money) is very necessary. In the puja (hymn) of Lakshmiji (Goddess of wealth)it also says that Tum Bin Koi Kaam Sambhav Nahin Hai (without you, Lakshmi, it is not possible to do anything). And if money is not there a person feels scared."

Respondents often referred to mythological and religious stories to make sense of their desire for money. For example, Vijay (male; a thirty-eight-year-old business man from Delhi; C2) cites a story from the ancient Hindu text *Ramayana* where the God Rama was exiled at the request of his step mother Kaikayi; who wanted her biological son Bharat to be King of Ayodhya instead of Rama (who was the rightful heir). Vijay explains that it is alright for humans to desire money since the Gods are greedy as well, trying to come to terms with his desire for money. Traditionally thrift and austerity are often emphasized in India (Osella and Osella 1001). As economic opportunities emerge and incomes grow many individuals are strained by the conflict between the conflicting values of austerity and consumption (Osella and Osella).

> "If you have money, you can enjoy everything in your life. Honey is sweet and the money brings that sweetness in your life. Kaikayi wanted her son to be the King so that he can get all the benefits which Rama would have got. We are human beings and they were Gods and even they were greedy. Money is so important."

According to respondents, money is also associated with security, social legitimacy and respect. For example, according to Ankita (C4, wife), a man without money is almost not a man. She stated,

> "Money makes a man. Without money you cannot get a wife, and the family thinks of you as a social wreck."

The need to display one's status and "*keep up with the neighbors*" was commonly discussed. This finding is in line with previous work of Batra and colleagues who found that Indian consumers often choose brands and products to reflect social upward mobility and differential status among friends and families (86). This is more pronounced since India has always been a "very hierarchy and status-conscious society" (Batra et al. 86). Fulfilling socially expected norms in one's use of money was also related to festival seasons. For example, Anjali (a thirty-six-year-old woman from Bhubaneshwar) emphasized the need for money to celebrate festivals and extended family marriages:

> "I think in India we spend a lot of money during festivals and weddings. As you know, in our culture there are many festivals in comparison to other cultures. We also have many relatives and have to attend their marriages in which we have to spend money because of our culture. This is something that I sometimes do not like but what can I do; we all have to do it because it is in our culture." (C10, wife)

This finding echoes past research on the importance of festivals in India. Some studies have estimated that almost 15 percent of the household budget is spent toward festivals (Rao 72). Spending on food, clothes, gifts and entertaining family and friends during festivals signals the social stature of the family (Rao). Similarly weddings are big events in India. Many families spend up to six times their annual income on weddings (Bloch et al. 675). These decisions are based on how the family will be viewed by others, hence Bloch et al. state "Clearly, wedding celebrations have a lot to do with social status and prestige" (677).

The Fickle Nature of Prosperity and Fortune

Respondents also frequently discussed the transient nature of money by relating stories of popular Bollywood actors, such as Amitabh Bachchan and Chiranjeevi, who respondents perceived to be risk taking, hardworking, and glamorous. Implicit in these descriptions was the notion that hard work was associated with earning and enjoying money. Also implicit in these articulations was the transient nature of prosperity and life:

> "Money can be like Amitabh Bachhan. He has seen so many ups and downs in his life as we've heard them. He was an unknown actor earlier on in life, he struggled, and then everything changed. So the role of money was very big in his life." (C2, husband)

This theme was reinforced when respondents described money by calling it Goddess Lakshmi (the Goddess of prosperity and wealth). She embodies prosperity and wellbeing but is also fickle and transient. She does not stay at one place for long. Since she is desired by everyone she may be with a person on one day and soon move to another (Bhalla 68):

> "So important is Lakshmi that even a visit to the mighty God Jagganath's (the God of all material creations) temple is incomplete without praying first to Lakshmi (the Goddess of wealth) (C10, husband).
>
> "Lakshmi by nature is Chanchal (fickle minded), wants to run away, wants to escape, but she is loyal if you treat her well with respect and look after her." (C4, wife)

Limitations and Dangers of Excessive Material Desire

Another interesting finding in our interviews echoes the findings of Dutta-Bergman and Doyle's (2001). They argue that British literary texts emphasize safeguarding and accumulating money, while Indian texts emphasize earning and using money as well as its limitations. Several of our respondents stressed both the utility and limitations of money. They stressed that it cannot buy affection or love, and that too much money comes with its own problems, including negatively affecting relationships and changing those who possess it. These views were summarized by Arman from Delhi (C4) who called it the electricity of life:

> "I tell you money is just like electricity; it is a very bad master but an excellent servant. Electricity is a fantastic servant but if it owns you, if you get electrocuted then you are dead. Similarly for money, if money becomes your master; you are only after money and it can make you do anything, then it is a bad master but if you use it well, it is a fantastic servant"

This caution was also connected to an excessive desire for money. For example, Smita (C7, wife) discussed the sacred nature of money and the repercussions of desiring too much. Citing a mythological story she explains how money (personified by Lakshmi, the Goddess of wealth) belongs to the Gods, and they get angry when you desire too much of it:

> "Lakshmiji is the wife of Vishnuji (the Protector of the world). So if someone calls Lakshmiji many times then Vishnuji will get angry. So, why call her too many times and disturb her? She is like a lady who shouldn't be disturbed. She keeps roaming from one place to another. She doesn't have stability, she cannot stay at any one place. If you give her due respect she stays with you. Otherwise she doesn't stay with anyone."

Need to Save

In the previous section we discussed respondents' articulation of the transient and fickle nature of money. Given this transience, respondents also emphasized the need to save. Saving is a major priority for middle-class families, with estimated savings rates of between 10 and 33 percent of income (Economic Research Service), as compared to a savings rate of 3.8 percent in the United States (Bureau of Economic Analysis). Indians save for a variety of reasons, as per the life cycle model proposed by Athukorala and Sen; retirement is one of the key reasons. Other reasons include hedging against inflation, for children's education, weddings, medical expenses, among others. As a developing country there is also no state safety net, in terms of education, health care, or retirement, hence Indians need to create their own safety net through savings (Anand).

Mahadev (C9, husband) called money a flowing stream, "money flows like water, if you don't save, it will flow away." Respondents also stressed the need to save money for security and to weather of bad times and future problems.

> "If we start collecting it now, then only we can have it as the older people say that "BOOND – BOOND SE BHARTA HAI SAGAR" (drop by drop fills the lake), then we can have money." (C2, wife)

> "Money is very important. If you have money, you can do anything you want to do ... My attitude is always to save money so that in bad times it will help us. Basically I always believe in saving." (C10, wife)

Children were a major motivation for saving. Respondents repeatedly emphasized the need to sacrifice to provide a better future for their children.

> "I need to save for my children's studies and for their health and marriage. Because, we have faced many problems in our lives, our children should not face problems in the same way." (C5, husband)
>
> "Life is very uncertain, anything can happen to me at any moment. I save in LIC (life insurance endowment policy) for my children. At least they can get some money and it will be very helpful to them. They will not have to depend on anyone and can also get good education." (C11, husband)

In terms of the saving options, investing in gold and bank deposits were the most preferred. Indian households control $600–800 billion of gold, mostly in women's jewelry. Gold is associated with good fortune, culturally ingrained practices of gift given, considered "stree dhan" (a woman's asset), and linked with family honor and support during tough times (McCarthy).

> "Before my son was born I used to spend a lot of money. I never thought before shopping but now I think twice. I did not have any responsibilities but now I have to keep something for my son. That is why I invest in gold." (C2, wife)
>
> "I prefer gold, mostly gold biscuits. My wife does not say it but she is also crazy about gold. She likes to buy gold ornaments." (C6, husband)

A few couples also discussed other forms of investments. Some respondents, especially husbands, discussed investments like shares and stocks.

> "She invests in gold, and I also found it good but now the government has increased the interest on bank fixed deposits; so we keep some money in banks as well. ... I also invest in the share market. ... I take risks. I bought Jet Airways shares three days ago ..." (C2, husband)

As early as 1500 BC Indo-Aryans stressed marriage and procreation (Netting). A girl's father would find her a suitable husband, provide a dowry, and continue to send gifts to her new family after marriage. Dowry is a payment of cash or gifts from the bride's family to the bridegroom's family upon marriage. It may include cash, jewelry, electrical appliances, furniture, bedding, crockery, utensils and other household items that help the newlyweds set up their home. Dowry has been a prevalent practice in India's modern era. There are variations on dowry prevalence based on geography and class. States in the north are more likely to participate in the dowry system among all classes, and dowry is more likely to be in the form of material and movable goods. In the south, the bride price system is more prevalent and is more often in the form of land or other inheritance goods. This system is tied to the social structure of marriage, which keeps marriage inside or close to family relations (Dalmia and Lawrence 74). Even though there are laws against dowry, the practice continues.

Several of our respondents mentioned saving money for the dowry of their daughter(s). For example,

> "My daughter is still small but I have to save money for her dowry. Today we need Rs. 5 lacs (half a million rupees; $8,300), and in the future I will need around 15–20 lacs (1.5–2 million rupees; $25,000-$33,300) for her dowry." (C1, husband)

The couples embraced education as the ticket to a better life for subsequent generations and saving for the children's education in order to lessen their future financial burdens. The rising cost of primary and higher education is prompting parents to start saving early for their children's education. While the cost of private education has always been high, education in government-run institutions has also increased sharply (Dhawan). There was a time when parents hardly planned in advance about how to meet the costs of their children's education, but saved some money for their wedding. Now financial planners advise new parents to start accumulating funds for meeting their children's education right from their primary school years (Sinha). The rising cost of education, has become a major cause of worry for parents. Some estimates indicate 65 percent of parents spend more than half their take-home pay on their children's education, extra co-curricular activities placing significant burden on their family budget (Dhawan). For example,

> "For my daughter I keep aside some money in the bank. Similarly, for my son I keep aside some money. I save for their education. I want to give the best education they can get." (C7, wife)

A Developing Consumer Culture and Burgeoning Consumption

Economic development has led to a growing culture of consumption. As people move from villages to cities, they simultaneously increase their income and desire to spend money on new products. According to the Household Consumer Expenditure Survey, rural India's average monthly per capita expenditure stood at Rs.1,278 ($21) in 2012, while that of urban India was Rs. 2,399 ($40), depicting a rural-urban divergence of approximately 87.6 percent (Ting Hin). Several of our respondents compared their new life with the village lifestyle they left behind. They recognize increased expenditures and a concomitant desire to earn money. For example,

> "In towns there is a culture to go to our friends and relatives house and they come to our house as well, so money is spent in their entertainment. In towns there is some expenditure which we are bound to do, but in village there is no such opportunity to spend money. If you want to have a lunch or dinner in a restaurant you will not find a good restaurant there. So even if you have money you cannot spend it." (C10, husband)

Enhanced consumption has come with its own difficulties. Owning a car and having a mobile phone have become an essential part of urban life. Respondents discussed social influences on consumption and an increasing preference for branded and high-quality products and services. For example,

> "Nowadays everyone has their own vehicle, and so do we. We only travel in our car. You already know how expensive petrol has become at present and so is maintenance. And mobile has also become an integral part of our lives. We cannot live without the mobile phones anymore." (C10, wife)
>
> "Earlier, money was required only for food and clothes for the family but today our needs have grown. Today you want a television, an air conditioner and electronic gadgets. Moreover if your neighbors have things which you don't have, then you will feel really low and inferior. People will also mock you." (C3, husband)
>
> "Now we buy only branded and good quality items. ... We buy branded clothes now, buy good mobile phones which costs more than Rs. 50,000 ($830), we go to PVR (a premium cinema hall) to watch movies, go out to dine. Life style has totally changed." (C4, wife)

This desire for goods and services has also resulted in consumers beginning to use credit cards. The penetration of credit cards in India still remains low at 2 percent (about 23 million) (Deloitte and Assocham India). About 30 percent of credit card spending is online, where transactions have seen a compounded annual growth of 19 percent in the period 2009–2013 (Shinde). In our interviews, we found substantial variability in attitudes toward credit cards. Some couples were still learning about credit cards while others were more comfortable using them. There were several instances where credit cards were used by the husband but not the wife (e.g., C9). Some (e.g., C4, husband) used their credit card to make purchases and were open to keeping an outstanding balance and paying interest. Most respondents, however, were skeptical about paying interest and the potential risks of credit mismanagement. Some reported having returned their credit cards and going back to paying cash.

> "No, I do not use any credit card because we can't pay that much interest. If we have credit card we have to face trouble because we will like to use it more and spend more. ... I won't use any credit card; I just pay by cash only." (C8, husband)
>
> "He had many credit cards from HDFC bank, HSBC bank. ... Now, only Citi Bank credit card is with him. He was spending too much, so I took away all the other credit cards." (C4, wife)

Increased consumption appears particularly pronounced in dual income, educated families with professional occupations. All couples strive to provide for and educate their children; however, professional, dual-income families appear particularly concerned with owning products and brands reflecting their lifestyle and status. They also frequently discussed the difficulty and expense of maintain an urban, consumption-oriented lifestyle. The next section discusses the impact of family structure.

Domestic Money Management

The variability of money management strategies between single and dual income families, in nuclear and joint families, is explicated here.

Single Income Families

In situations where the wife did not work outside of the home, she was primarily involved in running the house, doing domestic chores, and taking care of the children. Women in these families appeared to define their identity by their role as a mother, nurturer and caretaker. They often consulted their husband on home expenses, were provided a household budget, stressed the importance of spending wisely and attempted to save some money to treat themselves, and their families.

> "A husband should keep his wife and a wife should also support her husband in ups and downs of life. A wife should understand when to make demands in front of their husband or when not. My husband makes all decisions regarding big amounts and I take care of household activities. My husband always advises me on what is important." (C9, wife)

Single income families were more traditional, particularly when they live in joint/extended families. Mothers or fathers (in law) often controlled the expenses in extended families. In these cases the husband gave his share of home expenses to the elders and his wife participated in daily chores. Meena (a thirty-four-year-old housewife from Delhi) and her husband represent such a case:

> "My mother-in-law looks after household expenses. She looks after all the expenses and we both sisters (in laws) work together to manage

household chores. My mother-in-law is the head of the family. My husband gives money to my mother-in-law every month for household expenses. However, we don't give her the complete salary; we keep aside some money to spend on ourselves." (C1, wife)

Single income nuclear families reported more egalitarian money management than single income joint/extended families. In these families wives expressed their views since they did not fear any inhibition from parents in law. An interesting example is a single income nuclear family from Hyderabad. Though the husband is the sole earner in the family, he and his wife reported frequent discussions about money and valued each other's opinions, despite apparent traditional patriarchal patterns:

> "I just tell him my opinion on how to spend money, but I don't tell him that you have to listen to it for sure. ... Sometimes he considers it and sometimes he doesn't." (C6, wife – nuclear family)
>
> "I involve my wife in 90 percent of all the issues. For the rest, I make decisions on my own. I keep telling her how to handle things and she immediately understands. Now she has more knowledge and often gives me suggestions. Recently, while buying a refrigerator I felt unsure whether we could afford it and if I should buy it or not. At that time she gave me advice and said that she will reduce the household expenditure next month to pay for the refrigerator." (C6, husband)

Dual Income Families

Wives in dual income families stressed the financial benefits of working outside the home. Their work provided a source of confidence and identity, and they frequently used words like "*confidence*", "*status*" and "*refreshing*" with respect to their employment:

> "Working and earning money makes me have my own status." (C5, wife)
>
> "I work but my job is only for refreshment so that I don't get bored at home. Basically I work to utilize my education." (C12, wife)

These working women were also confident about saving and investing money and spending on their own needs (clothes, jewelry, etc.), on their children, and on household expenses. For instance, C5 (wife) paid for her children's school fees, decorations for the house and also saved some money by buying gold. Women working outside the home generally had a larger say in how the money was managed and spent. In some instances the husband managed the wife's earnings, and the wife was comfortable with this arrangement. For example, while Anjali and Chitran (C10) maintained individual bank accounts, Chitran controlled and managed both these accounts. He felt that his wife did not have much experience in money management and that he was better placed to handle these responsibilities. Thus, he would give his wife a fixed amount of money every month for routine home expenses; Anjali appeared comfortable with this arrangement as she felt that this was what was expected out of her as a wife. On the other hand, there were other instances where the couple kept and individually managed their own accounts. A case in point is the Bambani family (C2; Alka and Vijay). They both maintained and operated separate bank accounts, even though they had nominated each other as beneficiaries of their respective accounts, each drew from their separate accounts to spend on their particular needs.

In some nuclear family homes, the wife had an equal or dominant say in how money was spent. For instance, Alka (C2, wife) said that she would not hesitate to confront her husband on family expenses she felt were necessary. However, she did emphasize compromise and not needing to win all debates: "sometimes he wins and sometimes I do." Similarly, even though Anjali's husband (C10) controlled the bank accounts, she had substantial control over the home expenses.

Wives in dual income couples that lived in joint, extended families, however, were more circumspect in their influence and money management. For example, in the case of Smita (C7, a small business owner from Hyderabad), her in-laws played a more dominant role. In her family all earning members gave their earnings to the father-in-law. Every month the women of the house would give him a list of items they needed and he would disburse the money accordingly. On high value items, like buying a TV or refrigerator, the wives would tell their husband who in turn would tell the father (in-law), who would go to the store and buy the product of his choice. This process was more democratic in the Ravindran family (C5). Here, all family members, including the father/mother (in-law), would discuss the product to be purchased, with the final decision made by consensus. This process of negotiation was not always smooth. Tinu (C12, wife) reported some conflicts with her husband about her mother-in-law. Although she cedes control of her money to her in laws, this often annoys her. Sometimes this leads to conflict with her mother-in-law, and she also sometimes privately gives her husband a piece of her mind. She claimed that in the end the family manages to arrive at compromise solutions: "But both of us adjust."

Discussion

Money is regarded as the fuel of life. There is a desire for money because of its material and symbolic benefits associated with possessions, social status and security. However, the desire for money is generally tempered with caution; money is viewed as transient and hence needs to be saved, especially for children and their future. Rapid economic development has heralded an emerging consumer culture. Indian consumers often relate religious texts and mythological stories to the meanings and uses of money in their life. The Goddess Lakshmi is inherently linked to Hindu interpretations of money. She is one of the most widely venerated and popular deities in the Hindu pantheon (Kinsley 19) and frequently invoked to bring wealth and prosperity despite her fickleness. Several myths describe Lakshmi as being the consort to several Gods. She is described as leaving one God for another, leaving each rejected God lusterless and powerless. Her notorious fleetingness earned her a reputation for transience and inconstancy. However, when Lakshmi marries God Vishnu, whose main role is to maintain 'Dharmic' order, she embraces his human followers, bestowing her power and prosperity upon them so that they can effectively perform their dharma (duty) (23). This represents a wedding of Dharma (duty) and Lakshmi (prosperity). The point of this association is to explicate the concomitance between money and dharma, by performing dharma one obtains prosperity, upward mobility and success. This suggests that Hindus in India believe, doing their 'dharma,' as articulated in ancient religious texts, facilitates economic progress in modern times.

Hindus follow a utilitarian, usage-centered approach to money. The family man (in the householder stage), for example, seeks money for his family's prosperity. Not only do all family members reap the rewards of the householder's labor but by doing his *dharma* (providing for his dependents), the householder himself will earn rewards in this life as well as in the next life (The Laws of Manu 41). Thus, the Hindu view of money is at its core practical but has metaphysical layers and dimensions as well. Money facilitates the householder in doing his *dharma* (duty) toward family and society, which allows for the possibility of attaining *moksha* (spiritual release from the cycle of repeated death and rebirth).

Comparing the impact of dharma on Hindu attitudes toward money to previous descriptions of Western money attitudes impacted by the Protestant Ethic (Weber) provides an interesting contrast. The Protestant Ethic focuses on hard work and frugality. Prosperity through diligent work marks one's predestination to salvation in Calvinist philosophy (Weber 98). The Hindu notion of money and prosperity is in one sense similar to this conception in that both philosophies approve of material gain provided that it is tied to other constructive activities (specifically, hard work and dharmatic duty in the Protestant Ethic and Hindu philosophy, respectively). Hinduism, however, contains fewer admonishments toward spending. Dutta-Bergman and Doyle (2001) argued that British discourse highlights a love-hate relationship with money and wealth, which is consistent with Christian thought, where the love of money promotes evil (206). Weber summarizes the Protestant Ethic as containing three central components: (a) asceticism (living a modest life and abstaining from spending your earnings on unnecessary material objects) (149); (b) treating work as a Biblical 'calling' (85); and (c) saving wealth achieved as a gift from God (172). Hindu philosophy, in contrast, focuses on dharmatic duty, which in some respects is similar to treating one's work as a calling, but contains no specific call for living a modest life or explicit moral judgment about spending.

Spending money and social signals associated with spending are valued. Respect and status are important for Indians, which reflects the vertical-collectivist nature of Indian society (Triandis and Gelfand). Thus, spending to maintain relationships and even to delineate and maintain one's status was frequently discussed. This acceptance of status-oriented spending, contrasts sharply with the Christian premise of humility and the Protestant notion of frugality. Interestingly, both the Protestant Ethic and Hindu philosophy embrace material gain, which arguably promotes economic growth. Although differences exist in their treatment of spending, both embrace duty and purpose beyond oneself.

Dharmatic duty is at the core of Hindu teachings; it impacts money attitudes, in that money is seen as a tool for facilitating and marking family success (with particular attention paid to education and promoting the success of one's children). Dharma also pervades and impacts family interactions. Doing one's duty to contribute to the success of the family is paramount within the householder stage (potentially leads to Moksha) and provides the foundation for spousal interactions and the enactment of the husband and wife role within the family.

Our investigation did, however, find variability in the wife's involvement in the management and control of domestic money. Wives working outside the home generally reported greater participation in financial decisions than those not working outside the home. This finding is consistent with the theory of resources (Dahl 409), which holds that "the greater one's resources, the greater one's power." However, past research also highlights the limitations of this theory, including its failure to capture cultural factors that inhibit the use of power (Xu and Lai).

Family structure and traditional Hindu values play a role in our study. The Indian family ethos venerates women as the *grihani* (nurturer and homemaker). Devotion to the family is idealized, and historically a women's identity is defined by her role as a mother, wife and daughter. An Indian woman's identity after marriage is often rooted in her relationship with her family; her "self" concept is embedded in a maze of relationships and duties, which include the entire extended family and not just her husband (Bharat).

Our findings do, however, differ from Bharat's (2002) discussion of Indian family dynamics. She concluded over ten years ago that even though wives enjoy more power when they work, the "power sharing is restricted to routine and seemingly less significant areas" (163). We, in contrast find that some working wives in India (especially in nuclear families) have a considerable voice in how the family manages and spends its money. Increasing female urban literacy rates (from 72.9 percent in 2001 to 79.9 percent in 2011), and their rising employment in industry and the services sector (from 21.7 percent in 2001 to 29.2 percent 2011) (India Census) reflect the escalating status of working wives in India. The evolving family dynamics found in this study further reflect these trends and are precipitated by the increased presence of women in the workforce, along (speculatively) with the influence of Western-style egalitarianism fueled by an economic boom.

The complex and dynamic interaction between traditional and evolving, modern developments likely occurs in many societies but is particularly pronounced and prevalent in rapidly developing traditional nations. The dualistic presence in India of growing middle-class aspirations and associated anxieties fueled by economic development, along with long-standing traditions and teaching, which are adapted, synthesized and incorporated to interpret modern reality, reflects the struggles of the middle class all over the world (Heiman et al.; Lopez and Weinstein). India provides a prototypical example of a traditional nation with strong, established, prescriptive cultural practices and beliefs, which are presently being synthesized, incorporated and juxtaposed against a rapidly evolving economy, increased urbanization, and an evolving consumer ethos. Other nations, such as China, Russia, Brazil, and South Africa, are likely experiencing similar developments.

In sum, this study examines the symbolic meanings of money and consumption practices of middle-class Hindu couples. Money provides a means of doing one's duty, fulfilling one's dharma. Spousal interactions adapt and incorporate the concept of dharma to the specific circumstances of the family. Dual income, nuclear families tend to exhibit more egalitarian roles and provide women with greater power within the family. Increased income and education appear to magnify the importance of status and lifestyle oriented consumption; however, all families sampled focused on obligations, required familial consumption (related to attending festivals and weddings), and utilizing money and saving to facilitate the success of one's children. Although spending money is expected and accepted, particularly in the service of doing one's dharma, prosperity (represented by the goddess Lakshmi) is fickle, which provides an important motivation toward saving. In short, dharma pervades the symbolic money meaning and family money management practices of the couples sampled in our study, who are in the householder stage of their lives.

Suggestions for Future Research

Future research could examine money attitudes among couples in other life stages and in other nations. Examining additional nations will enhance our understanding of the historical and cultural forces that impact the meanings of money, money management and family dynamics. Additional research among other subcultures (e.g., Muslims in India) and research that more comprehensively examines differences among social classes (using larger samples) is warranted.

Notes

1. The authors would like to thank the Milgard School of Business (University of Washington - Tacoma) for providing financial assistance for this project; and Nilesh Patel (Issues and Answers Research Network) for helping with data analysis.

2. Socio-Economic groups: A1: upper-middle class [annual household income Rs. 700,000 ($11,600) and higher; graduate; white collar/business], A2: middle class [Rs. 500,000 ($8,300)-700,000 ($11,600); graduate/white collar], B1/B2: middle to lower-middle class [less than Rs. 500,000 ($8,300); some university; white/blue collar]). This description is comparable to recent economic definitions by Meyer and Birdsall (2012), who use a range of $10-$50 per capita per day pegged at 2005 PPP (corresponding annual income of Rs. 200,000 ($3,300) – 900,000 ($15,000)).

Works Cited

Anand, Shefali. "Indians Are Better Off Than Americans." *Times of India*. 2 July 2010. Web. 13 Feb. 2015.

Andrade, Chittaranjan, Kirstine Postma, and K. Abraham. "Influence of Women's Work Status on the Well-Being of Indian Couples." *Journal of Language and Social Psychology* 45.1 (1991): 65–75. Print.

Athukorala, Prem-Chandra, and Kunal Sen. "The Determinants of Private Saving in India." *World Development* 32.3 (2004): 491–503. Print.

Banjeri, Devika. "Stop Blaming Rural Migration for Urban Ills: Study." *The Economic Times*. 30 Nov. 2011. Web. 15 May 2014.

Belk, Russell. "Sharing." *Journal of Consumer Research*. 36. February. 2010. 715–734. Print.

Belk, Russell W., and Melanie Wallendorf. "The Sacred Meaning of Money." *Journal of Economic Psychology* 11.1. 1990. 35–67. Print.

Bhalla, Prem P. *Hindu Gods and Goddesses*. Delhi, India: Pustak Mahal, 2007.

Bharat, Shalini. "Women, Work and Family in Urban India." *Psychology in Human and Social Development*. Eds. John W. Berry, R.C. Mishra and R. C. Tripathi. New Delhi, India: Sage, 2002. 155–169. Print.

Bloch, Francis, Vijayendra Rao, and Sonalde Desai. "Wedding Celebrations as Conspicuous Consumption." *Journal of Human Resources* 39. 3. 2004. 675–695.

Brockington, John. "The Sanskrit Epics." *Blackwell Companion to Hinduism*. Ed. Gavin Flood. Maden MA: Blackwell, 2003. 116–128. Print.

Bureau of Economic Analysis. *Personal Income and Outlays, March 2014*. U.S. Department of Commerce. May 2014. Web. 14 May 2014.

Carson, David K., and Aparajita Chowdhury. "Family Therapy in India: A New Profession in an Ancient Land?" *Contemporary Family Therapy* 22.4. 2000. 387–406. Print.

Census of India. *The Census of India 2011*. Web. 15 August 2013.

Commuri, Suraj, and James W. Gentry. "Resource Allocation in Households with Women Chief Wage Earners." *Journal of Consumer Research* 32. September. 2005. 185–195. Print.

Creel, Austin B. "Dharma as an Ethical Category Relating to Freedom and Responsibility." *Philosophy East and West* 22.2. 1972. 155–168. Print.

Dahl, Robert A. "Power." *International Encyclopedia of Social Sciences* 12. 1968. 405–415. Print.

Dalmia, Sonia, and Pareena G. Lawrence. "The Institution of Dowry in India: Why It Continues to Prevail." *Journal of Developing Areas* 38.2. 2005. 71–93. Print.

Deloitte and Assocham India. *Mobile Payments in India: New Frontiers of Growth*. 20 June 2014 Web. 14 Feb. 2015.

Dhawan, Himanshu. "Rising Cost of Education Worries Parents, Survey Shows." *Times of India*. 9 Jan. 2013. Web. 13 Feb. 2015.

Doyle, Kenneth O. *The Social Meanings of Money and Property: In Search of a Talisman*. Thousand Oaks: Sage, 1999. Print.

Dutta-Bergman, Mohan J., and Kenneth O. Doyle. "Money and Meaning in India and Great Britain: Tales of Similarities and Differences." *American Behavioral Scientist*, 45.2. 2001. 205–222. Print.

Economic Research Service. *Growth and Equity Effects of Agricultural Marketing Efficiency Gains in India/ERR89*. United States Department of Agriculture. December 2009. Web. 14 May 2014.

Goldberg, Herb, and Robert T. Lewis. *Money Madness: The Psychology of Saving, Spending, Loving and Hating Money*. New York: William Morrow and Company, 1978. Print.

Griffith, Ralph T.H. *The Ramayana of Valmiki: Translated into English Verse*. London: Tribuner and Co, 1874. Print.

Haub, Carl. "2011 Census Shows How 1.3 Billion People in India Live." *Population Reference Bureau* March 2012. Web. 12 Feb. 2015.

Heiman, Rachel, Carla Freeman, and Mark Leichty. *The Global Middle Classes: Theorizing Through Ethnography*. Santa Fe: SAR Press, 2012. Print.

International Labor Organization. *India: Why is Women's Labour Force Participation Dropping?* 13 Feb. 2013. Web. 24 Apr. 2013.

King, Richard. *Indian Philosophy*. Washington, DC: Georgetown University Press, 1999. Print.

Kinsley, David. *Hindu Goddesses*. Berkeley: University of California Press, 1986. Print.

Krueger, David W. "Money, Success, and Success Phobia." *The Last Taboo: Money as Symbol and Reality in Psychotherapy and Psychoanalysis*. Ed. David W. Krueger. New York, NY: Brunner/Mazel. 1986. 3–16. Print.

Lea, Stephen E. G., and Paul Webley. "Money as Tool, Money as Drug: The Biological Psychology of a Strong Incentive." *Behavioral and Brain Sciences* 29.2. 2006. 161–209. Print.

Lopez, A. Ricardo, and Barbara Weinstein. *The Making of the Middle Class: Towards a Transnational History*. Durham and London: Duke University Press, 2012. Print.

McCarthy, Julie. "A Gold Obsession Pays Dividends For Indian Women." *NPR Morning Edition*. NPR, New Delhi. 14 Apr. 2014. Web. 20 May 2014.

Meyer, Christian, and Nancy Birdsall. "New Estimates of India's Middle Class." *GCD Note* (2012). Center for Global Development, Washington DC.

Ministry of Urban Development. *Level of Urbanisation*. Government of India. 3 Dec. 2013. Web. 15 May 2014.

Niranjan, S., Saritha Nair, and T.K. Roy. "A Socio-Demographic Analysis of the Size and Structure of the Family in India." *Journal of Comparative Family Studies* 36.4. 2005. 623–651. Print.

Netting, Nancy S. "Marital Ideoscapes in 21st Century India: Creative Combinations of Love and Responsibility." *Journal of Family Issues* 31.6. 2010. 707–726. Print.

Osella, Filippo, and Carolline Osella. "From Transience to Immanence: Consumption, Life-Cycle and Social Mobility in Kerala, South India." Modern Asian Studies 33.4. 1999. 989–1020. Print.

Radhakrishnan, S. "The Heart of Hinduism." *Cultural and Religious Heritage of India: Hinduism*. Eds. Suresh K. Sharma and Usha Sharma. New Delhi, India: Mittal Publications, 2004. 243–260. Print.

Ramu, G.N. "Indian Husbands: Their Role Perceptions and Performance in Single-and Dual-Earner families." *Journal of Marriage and the Family* 49. November 1987. 903–915. Print.

Rao, Vijayendra. "Celebrations as Social Investments: Festival Expenditures, Unit Price Variation and Social Status in Rural India." *Journal of Development Studies* 38.1. 2001. 71–97. Print.

Rose, Gregory M. "Consumer Socialization, Parental Style, and Developmental Timetables in the U.S. and Japan." *Journal of Marketing* 63.3.1999. 105–119. Print.

Rose, Gregory M., and Linda M. Orr . "Measuring and Exploring Symbolic Money Meanings." *Psychology and Marketing* 24.9. 2007. 743–761. Print.

Rowley, Emma. "India Will become World's Biggest Economy in less than 40 years." *Telegraph*. 30 Sep. 2012. Print.

Saunders, Jennifer B. "Dharma, Discourse and Diaspora: When Work and Family Demands Overlap." Working paper of the Emory Center for Myth and Ritual in American Life, GA 30306. 2002.

Shinde, Shivani. "Credit card base to reach 19 mn by FY13 end." *Business Standard*. 26 February 2013. Web. 14 May 2014.

Shukla, Rajesh. *How India earns, Spends and Saves-Unmasking the Real India*. New Delhi: Sage and NCAER-CMCR, 2010. Print.

Singh, Shalini. "Family Matters." *Hindustan Times*. 14 Apr. 2012. Web. 15 May 2014.

Sinha, Partha. "Start Saving for Child's Education Early." *Times of India*. 4 Nov. 2014 Web. 13 Feb. 2015.

Srivastava, Samar. "Despite Slowdown, Aspirations Propel Luxe in India." *Forbes India*. 14 Oct. 2013. Web. 20 May 2014.

The Laws of Manu. Translated by Wendy Doniger O'Flaherty and Brian K. Smith. New Delhi: Penguin Books, 1991. Print.

Thompson, Craig J., William B. Locander, and Howard R. Pollio. "Putting Consumer Experience Back into Consumer Research: The Philosophy and Method of Existential-Phenomenology." *Journal of Consumer Research* 16.September. 1989. 133–146. Print.

Ting Hin, Yan. "Diverse Consumption Behaviour Between Rural and Urban India." *CEIC*. 15 Apr. 2014. Web. 15 May 2014.

Myrna Toledo. "First Comes Marriage, Then Comes Love" *ABC World News*, 30 Jan. 2009. Web. 28 May 2014.

Triandis, Harry C., and Michele J. Gelfand. "Converging Measurement of Horizontal and Vertical Individualism and Collectivism." *Journal of Personality and Social Psychology* 74.1.1998. 118–128. Print.

Venkatesh, Alladi. "India's Changing Consumer Economy: a Cultural Perspective." *Advances in Consumer Research* 21. 1994. 323–328. Print.

Virmani, Arvind. "The God That Failed: Nehru-Indira Socialist Model Placed India In Precipitous Decline Relative To The World." *Times of India,* 21 Nov. 2013. Web. 12 Feb. 2015.

Wallendorf, Melanie, and Russell W. Belk. "Assessing Trustworthiness in Naturalistic Consumer Research." *SV - Interpretive Consumer Research*. Ed. Elizabeth C. Hirschman. Provo: Association for Consumer Research, 1989. 69–84. Print.

Weber, Max . *The Protestant Ethic and the Spirit of Capitalism*. London: George, Allen and Unwin Ltd, 1930. Print.

Webster, Cynthia. "Is Spousal Decision Making a Culturally Situated Phenomenon?" *Psychology and Marketing* 17.12. 2000. 1035–1058. Print.

Xu, Xiaohe, and Shu-Chuan Lai. "Resources, Gender Ideologies, and Marital Power." *Journal of Family Issues* 23.2. 2002. 209–245. Print.

Yamauchi, Kent T., and Donald I. Templer. "The Development of a Money Attitude Scale." *Journal of Personality Assessment* 46.5. 1982. 522–528. Print.

Young, Serinity. *Hinduism*. New York: Marshall Cavendish Benchmark, 2001. Print.

Zachariah, Binu. "The Great Indian Consumer Market – A close up view from an insider's perspective." *On Device Research*. 18 Sep. 2012. Web. 14 May 2014.

9 Middle Class and Higher Education in the MENA Region

Mourad Dakhli and Ihsen Ketata

Introduction

The rise of the middle class in emerging markets is creating many opportunities and challenges. As incomes rise and disposable incomes become more readily available, the nature of the demand for basic and non-basic goods and services changes. Similarly, the nature of the challenges of meeting these ever-evolving demands also undergoes transformations. For instance, the "Arab Spring" has raised the hopes of millions in the Middle East and North Africa region (MENA) for a better future (Arab World Competitiveness 7). At the same time, the popular uprisings across the region have also exposed many of the underlying grievances and challenges that the region faces. Unemployment, especially among highly educated youth has been identified as one of the most pressing issues, and as one with significant political and social implications (O'Sullivan, Rey and Mendez 1). Many have called for urgent educational reforms as a means to tackle youth unemployment and other social malaise. For example, Farouk El-Baz, in his discussion of educational reforms, states: "Today, we live in the information age and Arab countries could be left behind once again if they do not modernize their education system" (42). In general, many governments in the MENA region agree on the need for reforms and have been experimenting with new strategies and initiatives to ensure that education can respond to the growing and changing needs of the job market.

In this study we focus on higher education as one of the most important areas of savings and expenditures in the Middle East North Africa (MENA) region. We build on existing research and use in-depth interviews to explore how MENA middle-class respondents perceive current higher education offerings as well as what options are at their disposal to fund higher education plans. In this study, we focus on the middle class in the MENA region and explore attitudes and perceptions of various stakeholders in the middle class toward higher education. We focus on education as an important driver of economic development and overall well-being (Dakhli and De Clercq 109). To that end, we interview three types of stakeholders: students, parents and employers, and complete an exploratory study that aims to shed light into the changing nature of demand for higher education in the MENA region. We argue that as incomes rise and middle-class aspirations for better living standards increase, we would expect a stronger emphasis on education and consideration of wider educational options as the means to ensure upward mobility or to sustain more comfortable living standards. Our research identifies a number of trends associated with middle-class perception of higher education beyond its role as a means to secure better paying jobs and move up the socio-economic strata. We conclude our study by first discussing the implications and limitations of our exploratory research before we end by offering directions for future research in this important area.

The MENA Region: Definition and Key Facts

The term MENA is an acronym that is often used for "Middle East and North Africa." In general, MENA has been synonymous with Arab World, though many non-Arab countries, such as Iran and Turkey, have traditionally been understood as belonging to the MENA region. This region's economy is highly diverse and includes mainly two groups of countries. The first is a high-income group where the economy tends to be based on oil extraction and exports, and a second, lower-income group, where the economy tends to be more diversified. For example, rich oil countries such as Qatar have the absolute highest GDP per capita in the world of about $100,000. At the other end of the spectrum, Yemen, one of the poorest in the region, has a GDP per capita of about $2,500, forty times smaller than that of Qatar. Tunisia's per capita income is at $10,000 and that of Kuwait is about $42,000 (International Monetary Fund). These data highlight the great disparity in wealth and subsequently overall wellbeing within the MENA region.

The Middle Class in the MENA Region

The definition of the middle class is not consistent and differs from one study to another. booz&co address this point and point out that defining middle classiness has been problematic (4). In addition, accurate and consistent information regarding the middle class in particular is lacking. Some research defines the middle class by using descriptive parameters arguing that a middle-class group is one that lives comfortably. This group should have stable jobs, the ability to own homes and have access to healthcare, education, entertainment and travel options (Middle Class in America 8). Other research uses quantitative measures based on income and/or consumption patterns (booz&co 4). Other studies use both quantitative and qualitative indicators to define middle class. For example, Saif uses consumption and income levels as well as several other indicators including education, type of work, family size, type of housing, and the level of engagement in civil society organizations (1).

Although the middle class is considered to be more of a social designation than an economic categorization, most research defines middle class based on the levels of income, consumption patterns, and/or the availability of disposable income (Kharas and Gertz 3). The choice between the quantitative and qualitative schools of thoughts on middle class often depends on the purpose of any given study.

In this study, we use a definition of the middle class as proposed by the World Bank, which conceives of the middle class as synonymous with middle income. Since average income levels and the availability of disposable income are important variables in the choice among various education alternatives, we thus use the World Bank's conceptualization of middle class as the population in the middle income bracket, which includes both lower and upper-middle income categories.

Table 9.1 shows the percentage of the middle class in several Arab countries. In this region, Qatar and Saudi Arabia have the highest percentage

Table 9.1 The Arab Middle Class

Country Population	*Top of Pyramid*	*Middle Class*	*Bottom of Pyramid*
Algeria 36 million	17%	55%	28%
Bahrain 1.1 million	7%	60%	33%
Egypt 80.4 million	13%	34%	53%
Jordan 6.3 million	20%	41%	39%
Kuwait 3.7 million	22%	57%	21%
Lebanon 4 million	10%	60%	30%
Libya 6.5 million	15%	35%	50%
Mauritania 3.5 million	3%	30%	67%
Morocco 32.2 million	13%	32%	55%
Oman 3.1 million	6%	63%	31%
Qatar 1.8 million	8%	70%	22%
Saudi Arabia 28.2 million	13%	65%	22%
Sudan 32.7 million	8%	46%	46%
Syria 20.8 million	3%	57%	40%
Tunisia 10.7 million	22%	52%	26%
UAE 5.4 million	11%	60%	29%
Yemen 25.1 million	4%	60%	36%

Middle Class Definition: Household income in U.S. dollars, adjusted for purchasing power parity (PPP), of 75 percent to 150 percent of the median for each country.
Source: Harvard Business Review 2013

of middle-class citizens. The table also shows how a number of countries with scarce resources, such as Lebanon and Syria have a middle class that represents over 50 percent of the population, though recent turmoil in Syria is having a disastrous effect on the Syrian middle class, many of whom are now refugees in neighboring countries. Table 9.1 is particularly insightful as it highlights the significant structural differences in MENA societies as seen through the large disparities in the percentage of people that constitute the middle class. However, the data need to be interpreted with caution due to the large differences in per capita income across these countries. As such, someone classified in the bottom of the pyramid in Qatar, for instance, would be classified at the top of the pyramid category in Egypt. Cross-country comparison thus becomes more difficult but not impossible.

Literature Review

In the following section, we review seminal work that explores challenges related to higher education in the MENA region. More specifically, we address the perceived mismatch between higher education and the job market, and the growing need for alternative education and capacity development options that may be driving the privatization and deregulation in the education space in both Tunisia and Kuwait.

Unemployment and Education in the Mena Region

Job creation has become a top priority in the region especially after the Arab Spring. Unemployment rates in countries like Tunisia, Morocco and Egypt have remained high for the last ten years (O'Sullivan et *al.*, 2). The unemployment rate among university graduates in Tunisia, for example, has reached 23.2 percent at the national level, and is much higher in the underdeveloped regions of the south and the interior (Gafsa, 47.5 percent and Tozeur, 42.8 percent) (Haddar 1). According to O'Sullivan et al. (2), unemployment rates remain low among countries that are rich in oil such as Kuwait, the United Arab Emirates and Saudi Arabia. Nonetheless, many point to the high youth and university graduates unemployment or under-employment, upwards of 35 percent, even in rich, oil-based economies.

To tackle the chronic unemployment problems, policymakers in the region have focused on education reforms with the goal to improve the link between education and the needs of the job market (O'Sullivan et al. 2). Education is in fact seen as an effective means to promote economic growth at the country level and increase incomes at the household level. According to the World Bank, the region has been investing heavily in education for the last forty years allocating an average of 5 percent of GDP and 20 percent of government budgets to investment in education. Progress has been made in many areas. For example, today, nearly all children benefit from mandatory schooling, and a large percentage has greater access to higher education. Nonetheless, when compared to other regions in South America and Asia, it becomes obvious that the MENA region has performed poorly, especially in the area of international standardized assessments. Illiteracy rates are still high and the number of graduates in the humanities is larger than the number of graduates in the sciences. In addition, the unemployment rate among graduates remains high and a significant percentage of the educated labor work for the government. Finally, the educational systems in the MENA region are not completely ready to generate skilled graduates with the necessary expertise to compete worldwide (The Road Not Traveled 7). As investment in education grows, educational options expand. As a result, MENA's middle-class expenditures on education grow significantly, and education becomes a top priority and a basic need in the region. For MENA's middle class, the largest expenses are allocated to food and housing with education occupying the third place with 7 to 8 percent of total spending (booz&co 12).

Focus on Tunisia and Kuwait

As stated earlier, we focus on Tunisia and Kuwait to represent the MENA region. Our choice of these two countries is based on the fact that Tunisia is a good representative of the low-income, high unemployment group of MENA countries, while Kuwait is a good representative of the oil-rich, high-income, and low-unemployment group. These two countries share quite a bit on the cultural side, but are quite different on the economic side. Arabic is the official language and Islam is the main religion of both countries. French is the language of Business in Tunisia, a legacy of the French colonial years, and English is the main language of Business in Kuwait, again a legacy of its colonial past as a British protectorate. Kuwait, as a major labor importing country, counts a large number of expatriates, most of whom come in search of better paying jobs. Tunisia, on the other hand, is a labor exporting country and many Tunisians travel to Europe or the Middle East (including Kuwait) in search of better job opportunities (Labor Migration-ILO). Recent data shows Kuwait's per capita GDP of around $40,000 as four times that of Tunisia. The historical colonial heritage of both countries as well as economic realities are important factors in shaping middle-class perception of higher education.

Because of lower per capita income in Tunisia, Tunisians tend to spend a larger percentage of their earnings on education, about 6.1 percent of total expenditures in 2011, as compared to 3.5 percent for Kuwaitis. However, growth of spending on education in Tunisia is much higher than that of Kuwait (Euromonitor International). We suggest two reasons behind these trends. First, many Tunisians need to leave home and move to the larger education centers of Tunis, Sousse or Sfax to pursue tertiary education. This usually involves additional financial burdens. Kuwait is a city state, and students can remain at home while being enrolled at any university in the country. Second, on a purchasing power parity basis, private education can be prohibitively expensive for many, and it can represent a significant portion of any disposable income.

We believe that this is due to the growth in private higher education options resulting from the deregulation and the privatization of higher education. As for enrollment in tertiary education, research shows that the proportion of high-school graduates in Tunisia enrolling in higher education is larger than that in Kuwait, and is also growing at a faster rate (Euromonitor International).

Having outlined some of the main characteristics of middle-class education consumption facts and trends in our two MENA representative countries, we now proceed to our survey of middle-class perceptions and attitudes toward education as well as the strategies people in the middle class plan to fund higher education for themselves and their children. Our results, discussed later, point to a number of similarities as well as important differences. Higher education is seen as an important driver of social mobility for middle classes in the region. However, mainly due to economic differences, the drivers for seeking education abroad and the value of a "Western" degree differs.

Methodology

In order to assess the changing perceptions of education of MENA's middle class, we conduct in-depth interviews using open-ended questions. We identify potential respondents through our university contacts in both Tunisia and Kuwait. We collect qualitative data based on a total of twenty interviewees from eight universities, with students coming from undergraduate business and engineering majors at advanced stages of their studies. All the interviewees were in their early to mid-twenties, and half were male and the other female. In addition, we interview six parents and six employers split equally between the two countries. Employers represent two sectors: financial services and information technology. We identify respondents by seeking the assistance of in-country contacts that facilitated the interview process. In-country contacts also ensured that students, parents and employers were 'middle-class' nationals who do not come from the same family. Kuwaiti student respondents came from two universities on Kuwait City, one public and one private. Tunisian student participants came from a public University in Tunis and another one in the central industrial city of Sfax. The method of conducting a small number of in-depth interviews is justified by a desire to deepen the understanding of the issues and possibly find out some aspects, dimensions, or variables associated with middle class's attitudes and possibly changing perceptions of higher education in the MENA region that cannot be explored through quantitative statistical methods. While the number of interviewees is small, we resort to triangulation whereby we diversify the sources of information by seeking responses from three different stakeholders that we identify as important actors in the higher education domain, namely, students, parents, and employers (Wacheux 89).

The questions included in the interviews focus on the perception of the importance of higher education, plans to finance higher education, preferences for public versus private institutions, preferences for in-country versus out of country educations, the short- and long-term goals from seeking higher education, as well as general comments regarding the overall quality of higher education. We also ask respondents to add any comments and provide non-structured feedback regarding their view and perceptions of higher education. One advantage of the interview data collection method is that follow-up probing is possible. So whenever answers were vague, or an interesting comments that warranted follow-up was made, it was possible for us to reach out to interviewees for clarification or additional insight. We do not collect biographical data from parents and employers.

We slightly modified our questions based on the category of interviewee. For example, only students and parents were asked about plans for funding higher education for themselves or their children. Employers were asked to assess the quality and readiness for the workplace of public versus private university graduates.

As stated earlier, Kuwaitis are generally better off financially than Tunisians, and as a result they enjoy higher disposable incomes. We use the survey data as a way to identify any possible changes in respondents' answers that may be driven by income differences. Considering the exploratory nature of this study, our preliminary findings may open up opportunities for future research on the changing perceptions of higher education for the middle classes as incomes rise. While in-depth interviews with a limited number of stakeholders constituted an important part of this exploratory study, we complement our findings with external sources as applicable. Thus, providing added support for our methods and interpretations.

Analysis and Discussion

Our initial results point to the importance of education for students, parents and employers in both countries. Each of these stakeholders believe that it is imperative that people in the region seek higher education, though the reasons or the importance of any given reason may vary depending on the stakeholder in question, and the country where the interviews were conducted.

1. Students' Perspectives

While both Kuwaiti and Tunisian students see education as very important their goals and reasons behind perusing higher education are different:

Reasons Behind Perusing Higher Education

For Kuwaiti students, higher education is strongly related to personal and professional development. As one student pointed out: "Higher education enhances many aspects in any person. Higher education enhances many skills including public speaking, group work, communication and critical thinking." While personal growth and enhancement of skills are first mentioned by our Kuwaiti respondents, securing jobs seems to be the main drivers behind seeking higher education for Tunisian students. Notwithstanding, students in both countries mention personal, professional and future employment potential as goals that are best attained through higher education. We believe the difference is mostly related to availability of employment opportunities. Unemployment rates, especially unemployment for graduates is much higher in Tunisia than it is in Kuwait. Economic needs and necessities affect one's perception of the importance of higher education. More specifically, securing stable and well-paying jobs seems to be the most important priority for students in Tunisia. Students in Kuwait, on the other hand, while still seeking high-paying jobs, worry less as employment is essentially guaranteed by the government. Graduates in Kuwait who are on the job market receive a government subsidy while they are searching for employment and can be placed on a waiting list for jobs in the public sector. Those who secure jobs in the private sector, receive a government subsidy as part of the private sector promotion program (El-Enezi 7).

Funding Education

There appear to be differences related to options for funding higher education between the two countries. Most Kuwaiti students see government scholarships as a viable and a readily available alternative. This, we argue, is a result of the perceived generous nature of educational scholarships available in Kuwait. As a high-income country, Kuwait has developed a robust welfare system. Students who meet good academic standards are usually accepted at a public institution of higher education where education is free of charge. Alternatively, students can enroll in an accredited private institution where fees are for the most part covered by the government (Private Universities Council). In contrast, higher education scholarships are much harder to obtain in Tunisia and only those very few with superior academic performance may qualify for one (Ministere de l'Education Tunisie).

Public/Private Education

It is also somewhat apparent from the interviews that public education is generally preferred, not only because it is free as a few point out, but also because it is perceived as providing better quality education. This is in line with existing research that highlights the limitations of private education in the MENA region (The Road Not Traveled 105). In both countries, students who are not accepted into public institutions often enroll in private ones. This means that higher education is much more accessible for Kuwaiti students as they can still receive government subsidies to enroll in private universities should they fail to access public institutions. On the other hand, for many Tunisians, the inability to access public institutions of higher education is often the end of the education-seeking road and is consequently a major reason behind the high rate of youth unemployment (Stampini & Verdier-Chouchane 10). Therefore, while youth in both countries strive to secure a place at a public institution, the stakes are much higher for Tunisians. This point finds support in the booz&co's, 2011 study, on MENA middle class that points to greater levels of satisfaction with government support for education and other domains in oil-based economies (9).

In Country/Out of the Country Studying

Interestingly, both male and female respondents show preference and a desire for higher education outside the country. At least two respondents clarify that it may be a good option to complete the undergraduate degree at home and then seek more advanced degrees at institutions in foreign countries. Our follow-up discussions with interviewees on this point highlight a number of interesting variables. First, many in the region associate higher education at leading Western institutions with greater professional and financial achievement. International rankings of universities, which are readily available on the Internet, show a clear gap between leading institutions of higher education in North America and Europe and their counterparts in the region (Selmi 80). Students in the region have access to and follow these rankings and cite them as evidence of better higher education in Europe or North America. Another factor that may be at play here is the prevalence of role models who have received Western education. Political and business leaders in both countries have predominantly pursued Western higher education. These 'role models' may play an indirect, but important role in reinforcing the perceptions that higher education at leading Western universities is a key to personal and financial success. For example, Bourguiba, the longest-serving president of Tunisia, attended the University of Paris where he studied law and political science, while the children of the Kuwaiti royal family and other royal families in the region traditionally complete higher education or at least advanced training in political or military affairs in the United Kingdom (Gifty & Krcmaricz 1). Despite recent trends and movements against Western political, economic, and cultural presence or dominance in the MENA region, it seems that education remains an area where favorable views of the West still hold strong.

Education and Personal Liberty

Interestingly, studying in a foreign country, especially in North America or Europe, may be seen as an opportunity to gain additional freedoms for students who are raised in a relatively more conservative environment. This seems to be the case for both female and male interviewees. However, parents generally express reservations toward allowing their children to travel to Western countries to pursue higher education. While anecdotal in nature, our observations point to a wider tension between conservatism and modernity in the region, and perhaps education is an area where this tension is best seen. The younger, more Western-oriented students not only seek higher education in Europe and North America, but also aspire for a lifestyle that allows for more personal freedoms away from family and societal control.

Education and Colonial Legacies

For Tunisian students, France, the former colonial power, is mentioned as the destinations of choice. Kuwaiti students list the United States and the United Kingdom, the former colonial power, as the countries of choice for college education. This is in agreement with current data on students studying abroad, whereby the absolute majority of Tunisians peruse higher education in France, while Kuwaitis study abroad primarily in the United Kingdom and the United States (UNESCO). A number of factors are involved here. One is language. As a francophone country, where French is still the language of business and many education areas, it is easier for Tunisian students to think first of France as a destination of choice for education. In Kuwait, however, English is widely spoken. Therefore, the U.K. and the U.S. may seem to be more suitable choices. French for Tunisia and other North African countries, and English for Kuwait and other Middle Eastern countries are important lasting legacies from the colonial heritage for MENA region countries. What we see through these few interviews provides support for Ziltener and Künzler's discussion of education as a tool to extend colonial dominance beyond the stages of formal political independence (304). For our student interviewees, the issues concern educational and career attainment, and the opportunity to live beyond the full reach of strict parental and societal control. One, however, cannot be oblivious to the historical and cultural contexts that shape young people's educational aspirations.

One additional and notable difference in the answers provided by the Tunisian and Kuwaiti students is that Tunisians see higher education in France or French-speaking Canada as a means to relocate and secure jobs in these countries. Kuwaiti students on the other hand, see study abroad as a way to earn a more prestigious degree that could secure an equally prestigious job at home. We see this as fundamentally driven by economic realities. As we mention earlier, unemployment rates are much higher in Tunisia than they are in Kuwait. In addition, average per capita income and wages in Kuwait is almost ten times that of Tunisia and is on par with that of leading Western nations. Consequently, job scarcity may drive Tunisian students to see France as a destination for both higher education and jobs, hence the high number of Tunisian University graduates who end up working and living in France. High salaries, coupled with generous welfare system are important factors in the preference for working at home for Kuwaitis and other oil-rich country nationals (Global Flow of Tertiary-Level Students).

Limited Options at Home

When addressing the questions regarding perceived limitations of higher education and possible recommendations, students in both countries were generally critical. They view higher education options in the country as limited and are unsatisfied with the private education options available, though some mention the growing partnerships with international universities as a potential draw. One respondent from Tunisia notes: "The agreements with international universities all over the world can help me succeed, allows me to have a good degree, improves my study skills, and allows me to have a successful professional life." The growing presence of foreign, mostly Western, universities in the MENA region is changing the higher education landscape. A number of researchers have looked at the globalization of higher education, and the effects this phenomenon is having in various regions including China and Latin America. For the MENA region, the presence of leading Western universities such as New York University, Carnegie Mellon, Sorbonne, L'Institut des Hautes Etudes Commerciales (IHEC) and others made it possible for students in the region to have access to top-notch education without traveling abroad. This trend is somewhat in line with what is taking place elsewhere. For example, recent studies on the proliferation of educational partnerships involving Western universities in China, have identified the benefits of acquiring a global education at home as one of the most important consequences (Higher Education Global Trends and Emerging Opportunities to 2020). In addition, given the more conservative nature of the MENA societies, females stand to benefit to a greater degree, as they are now able to pursue higher education at leading Western universities without the need to travel outside the country. Female university participation rates have increased significantly over the last few decades, and in some cases, surpass that of males (The Road not Traveled 92). However, because of cultural norms, females are less likely than their male counterparts to travel outside the country and enroll at a foreign university (Global Flow of Tertiary-Level Students). Therefore, the presence of foreign universities in MENA countries may have an equalizer effect, allowing more women to attend leading foreign institutions.

2. Parents' Perspectives

We also collect feedback from parents of high-school or college-age students. These were identified by our two in-country contacts. Interview questions were shared ahead of time, and follow-up phone interviews were completed to clarify any issues or to delve into any areas that was deemed as warranting further exploration. As is the case for the previous group, Tunisian interviewees were from two major cities: Tunis and Sfax, and Kuwaiti interviewees were Kuwaiti nationals residing in Kuwait City. We did not collect biographical data for these participants. We see parents as important stakeholders who play a significant role in decision making regarding education. Parents in the region see higher education as an absolute necessity. While parents in both countries prefer that their children seek education at public institutions, they are saving money to ensure their children's education at private schools, if needed. Tunisian and Kuwaiti parents confirmed that securing high-paying jobs is the main goal for attaining higher education, thus reinforcing the idea that education is key to personal success.

A clear difference between parents in Kuwait and those in Tunisia is that Kuwaiti parents favor education at local universities, and express a preference for "keeping children close by." Tunisian parents, on the other hand, express a preference for education abroad and are more critical of the educational options available at home. As explained earlier, these differences may be related to higher job scarcity in Tunisia, and as such, a higher need for a more 'valuable' university degree to secure employment in a tight labor market. Interestingly, proximity is an important factor for both parents. Kuwaiti parents prefer the U.K., and Tunisian parents list France as the country of choice for study abroad. For both groups, the U.S. and Canada are seen as too distant and are perceived as 'unsafe.' Some of these preferences are probably explained by the collectivist nature of MENA societies, where proximity and closeness are highly valued, and children are expected to stay and live with parents or at least close by even after marriage (Hofstede 273).

3. Employers' Perspectives

To provide varied perspectives in our study of middle-class perception and attitudes about higher education, we include four employers in our interviews—two from a large financial and technology firm in Tunisia and two from large financial institutions in Kuwait. All four are major employers of university graduates. We believe that our interviews with the employers can provide important insight to this study because of the familiarity of the employers with the various types of graduates, and the large number of graduates they employ every year. In general, interviewees indicated that they are reasonably satisfied with graduates of select local institutions, and they list very few public institutions, as providing reasonably rigorous education. Interestingly, one employer notes that his firm hired a number of graduates of local private universities, and that his managers are quite satisfied with their performance over time. This may be reflective of an emerging trend in the region where small private universities are making significant strides in improving the quality of education, and by transferring and localizing 'best practices' often through seeking and securing international accreditation for their various programs (Dakhli & El Zohairy 47).

Both Kuwaiti and Tunisian employers note a general lack of match between the qualifications of local university graduates and the firms' needs. This is in line with recent research on higher education that identified a lack of fit between higher education and the labor market in the MENA region as a major shortcoming (The Road Not Traveled 86). Another limitation noted by two interviewees was the lack of English language proficiency. This could simply be associated with the fact that the interviewed employers represent firms with significant international business linkages. One of the Tunisian managers mentioned that his firm now conducts more business with North America and other non-francophone countries than ever before. Consequently, he expects the need for English-language proficient graduates to increase over the next few years. While our sample size does not allow us to draw firm conclusions here, we expect this to be a growing trend across the board as local firms engage in more cross-border transactions.

While employers in both countries are somewhat unsure about the quality of private education, they seem upbeat about its future. They do acknowledge the role of private education in filling the gap in certain fields including English-based communication skills and a few other practicum-oriented fields. As private universities in the region mature and shift their focus from survival to educational quality, we expect them to increasingly provide a better fit between education and labor market needs. The flexibility that these newer institutions enjoy would allow them to respond faster to the changing educational needs of a growing middle class. The two interviewed employers in Tunisia also perceive graduates of foreign institutions as generally better qualified than local ones. However, they do caution against the blanket assumption that all foreign universities are solid and express a greater need to scrutinize foreign university graduates' qualifications. They also note that they prefer to see investment in improving local education rather than sending the best minds outside the country. Employers in Kuwait are even more cautious and express mixed views on the merits of a foreign-earned degree. One participant argued that a graduate might be better qualified only if he or she receives a degree from a well-established, highly ranked foreign institution. Interestingly, the same employer notes that pursuing a degree outside the country may work against a future job applicant. He explains that social networks are very important, and that many students are hired as a mean to build and expand the firm's network of ties with the business community. Students who travel and study abroad may find it harder to build extensive business network upon their return. Given the highly collectivist and relational nature of the society, foreign university graduates may 'miss out' on the opportunity to build and sustain valuable in-country professional relationships. Consequently, employers suggest to the students who seek higher education abroad to be mindful of the potential drawbacks associated with a few years of absence from their country.

Conclusion

Our aim in this study is to provide insight into how higher education is perceived by the rising middle class in the MENA region. Higher education seems to be seen as paramount in the construction of a modern, advanced society. While many acknowledge the shortcomings of local education offerings, we see interest and clear desire to foster a home-grown model that is more embedded in the local socio-cultural context, but still allow for the transfer and adoption of 'best' practices from other nations, mainly from Europe and North America. Perhaps for MENA, higher education is a space where the conflict between modernity and conservatism is best seen. We see strong evidence of aspirations for a more modern and successful education system. Nonetheless, regional cultural values and norms will probably continue to drive the adaptation of Western educational models as to fit the local context (The Making of the Middle Class). In this study, we focus on Tunisia and Kuwait that share strong cultural and historical communalities but offer maximally different economic contexts. Public education is in general the first alternative for students and parents. However, better quality private options are expanding in the region, and students in both countries now have other options. An interesting finding is the difference between how students and parents perceive education outside the country. All the students we interview express a clear preference for joining foreign universities, mostly in the West. Parents on the other hand while acknowledging the value of a foreign degree, express reservations, and in general prefer that children remain close by. The increasing presence of foreign, well-established universities in the MENA region would probably offer a reasonable compromise, and would lessen the need to travel abroad to seek higher education. Furthermore, local private universities may see an opportunity to play a more aggressive and entrepreneurial role in the higher education field. They are probably best positioned to develop unique programs that are more responsive to the needs of local employers and to reduce the gap between graduates qualifications and the needs of the labor market. It would be informative to investigate how middle-class preferences and attitudes about public versus private, and local versus foreign higher education evolve over time, and what factors affect changes in these attitudes and preferences, especially in light of the major global trends affecting higher education. Our study is exploratory in nature, though a number of interesting comparisons come to light. We believe the rise of the middle class and the changing perceptions and attitudes are areas that warrant more extensive research. We focus on education as an important area, on which the rising middle class spends a significant and a growing share of its disposable income. Our sample of interviewees is small and as such the results should be seen as exploratory in nature, and as potential means for identifying venues for further inquiry. For example, we only include employers from two industries, financial services and information technology. Business and engineering are among the most sought-after fields of study, and as such, enrollment at public institutions may be highly competitive. This may create higher need for private institutions to fill the gap (The Road Not Traveled 4). In short, the views of students, parents and employers may be significantly different for other programs such as medicine and liberal arts. Expanding future research to include a wider array of majors and specializations can provide added insight.

Most of the studies that focus on the middle class in the MENA region do not dissociate between the two distinctly different regions: scarce resource-countries and oil rich countries (Lange, Saavedra and Romano 1; Anderson 771; Bornemann 11; El-Baz 43). Dissociating between the two regions is very important at the global, regional and local levels, as the two areas exhibit significant economic differences. Our findings with respect to perceptions and attitudes provide support for the need to take these differences into account and develop a more refined consideration of the MENA region. Therefore, while we reference two countries to make inferences about the middle class and education in the MENA region, we must remain cognizant of the country-by-country variations that could be driven by different political, institutional, and economic realities. Recent studies that focus on educational achievements note that some countries such as Jordan and Qatar have fared better than others in this area due to sound directives from policy makers. To what degree are policies in place responding to middle-class aspirations for better higher education is an area that warrants further investigation. Furthermore, as a number of countries in the region continue to experience instability and turmoil, how do the these challenges change students and parents attitudes about higher educations is an area that warrants further consideration. Preliminary research identifies greater accountability as one effect of the Arab Spring movement on policy making in the area of higher education (Hamdan 1). We argue that development in higher education cannot be disassociated from the major political and economic trends that are shaping the region and the world.

Works Cited

Al-Enezi, Awadh Khalaf. "Kuwait's Employment Policy: Its Formulation, Implications, And Challenges." International Journal of Public Administration (2002): 885–900. Print.

Anderson, Lisa. "Fertile Ground: The Future of Higher Education in the Arab World." Social Research 79(3) (2012): 771–84. Print.

"Arab World Competitiveness Report 2013." *World Economic Forum* May 2013. Print.

Bornemann, Erin. "MENA: Big Growth in Education." Information Today 29.8 (2012): 11. Print.

Dakhli, Mourad, and Dirk De Clercq. "Human Capital, Social Capital, and Innovation: a Multi-Country Study." Entrepreneurship & Regional Development, (2004): 107–128. Print.

Dakhli, Mourad, and Dina El-Zohairy. "Emerging Trends in Higher Education in the GCC – A Critical Assessment." Innovation in Business Education in Emerging Markets. Ed. I. Alon, V. Jones, and J.R. McIntyre. 2013. Pp. 43–63. Print.

ElBaz, Farouk. "Reform in Arab Countries: The Role of Education." Journal of Education 188.3 (2007): 41–49. Print.

Euromonitor International. Web. 20 May 2015.

Gift, Thomas, and Daniel Krcmaric. "Who Democratizes? Western-Educated Leaders and Regime Transitions" Paper accepted for publication at the Journal of Conflict Resolution. Web. 20 May 2015.

"Global Flow of Tertiary-Level Students." UNESCO. Web. 20 May 2015.

Haddar, Mohamed. "La Transition économique En Tunisie Démocratique" Business News. 29 Mar. 2011. Web. 18 Nov. 2013.

Hamdan, Sara. "Arab Spring Inspires Academics to Improve Quality of Higher Education; Forum Examines Ways Raise Global Profiles and Create Partnerships." International New York Times 7 Nov. 2011: 11. Print.

"Higher Education Global Trends and Emerging Opportunities to 2020." British Council. Web. 20 May 2015.

Hofstede, Geert. "Culture and Organizations: Software of the Mind." 2010. Print.

International Monetary Fund. www.imf.org.

Kharas, Homi., and Geoffrey Gertz. "The New Global Middle Class: A Cross-Over from West to East." Defining the Middle Class: An Absolute Approach. Ed. C. Li. Washington, DC: Brookings Institution, 2010. 1–14. Print.

Labor Migration-ILO, International Labor Organization. Web. 20 May 2015.

Lange, Lis, Mauricio Saavedra, and Jeanine Romano. Institutional Research in Emerging Countries of Southern Africa, Latin America, and the Middle East and North Africa: Global Frameworks and Local Practices. 157th ed. New Directions for Institutional Research, 2013. 23–38. Print.

"Middle Class in America." *U.S. Department Of Commerce-Middle Class Task Force* Jan. 2010. Print.

Ministere de l'education, Tunisie. W.eb. 18 May 2015.

O'Sulivan, Anthony, Marie-Estelle Rey, and Jorg Galvez Mendez. "Opportunities and Challenges in the MENA Region." *OECD* Jan. 2011. Print.

Private Universities Council, State of Kuwait, h.ttp://puc.edu.kw/en/

Saif, Ibrahim. "THE MIDDLE CLASS AND TRANSFORMATIONS IN THE ARAB WORLD." The Cairo Review of Global Affairs. 2 Nov. 2011. Web. 20 May 2015.

Salmi, Jamil. "The Challenge of Establishing World Class Universities."World Bank. 2009. Print.

Stampini, Marco, and Audrey Verdier-Chouchane. "Labor Market Dynamics in Tunisia: The Issue of Youth Unemployment." African Development Bank, Working Paper Series. 2011. Print.

Shediac, Richard, Samer Bohsali, and Hatem Samman. "The Bedrock of Society Understanding and Growing the MENA Region's Middle Class." Booz&co (2012): 1–40. Print.

"The Making of the Middle Class: Toward a Transnational History." Web. 20 May 2015.

"The Road Not Traveled: Education Reform in the Middle East and North Africa. MENA Development Report." World Bank. Jan. 2008. Web. 20 May 2015.

Wacheux, Frédéric. "Méthodes qualitatives de recherches en gestion." Paris Dauphine University, 1996. Print.

Ziltener, Patrick, and Daniel Künzler. "Impacts of Colonialism – A Research Survey1" Journal of World-Systems Research, (2013): 290–311. Print.

10 Not in My Backyard

Middle Class Protests in Contemporary China

Andrew Wedeman

Introduction

In 1966, in his seminal analysis of the emergence of democracy, Barrington Moore wrote the iconic sentence "No bourgeoisie, no democracy," arguing that democracy emerged after the creation of a commercial middle class strong enough to force the king and lords to share political power with those who had economic power (Moore, 418). Since then, it has become conventional wisdom that when the middle class reaches a certain size and per capita income rises above a certain threshold, pressures will mount on authoritarian rulers to either allow for increased democratic participation or face "peoples' revolutions" in which the normally conservative middle class defects to join anti-regime protesters, thereby stripping the regime of its basis of power and casting it on the dustbin of history. When, why and how the ultimate democratic transition unfolds has become the focus on much debate. Nevertheless, it is widely assumed, as Moore implied, that emergence of a large middle class presages transitions to democracy.

Over the past generation, a sizable Chinese middle class has emerged. Nonexistent in the 1980s when the Chinese Communist Party began to adopt piecemeal market reforms, it numbered approximately 150–180 million as of 2012 and is anticipated to double to about 300 million, with 29 million projected to be in the upper class by 2022, 193 million in the upper middle class, and 78 million in the lower-middle class (Barton, Chen, and Jin; Haras and Gertz; and Li). If these estimates are correct, in a decade, almost one in four Chinese would be members of the middle and upper classes. Within urban China, however, McKinsey projects that the middle and upper classes will outnumber the urban poor four to one.[1]

Assuming the slowing growth does not retard the growth of the Chinese middle class, does that suggest increasing pressures on the Chinese Communist Party (CCP) to adopt political reforms that would move China toward democracy? Will, in other words, the rising middle class demand greater openness, transparency, freedom of expression, and, ultimately, the right for the people to pick their rulers? Prior to the emergence of a sizable middle class in the later 1990s, most pressure for political change came from intellectuals and university students, small but elite groups. Both groups were, however, largely cowed by the suppression of anti-government demonstrations in June 1989 and the crackdown that continued into 1993. Student political activism, in fact, all but ceased as students turned their attention for pursuing the new Chinese Dream of prosperity and wealth (i.e., membership in the new middle class).[2] Individual dissidents and fluid groups of rights defenders continue to skirmish with the authorities, but thus far demands for political reforms remain muted and lack mass support. When the Chinese middle class first began to emerge, many in the west assumed it would begin to chafe under the strictures of the CCP authoritarian rule and begin pushing for political liberalization. China's emerging capitalists were also assumed to be pro-democratic and unwilling to accept a political system in which they as tax payers and property owners had no effective means of political representation or leverage.

Public opinion polls conducted by Chen and Dickson (Dickson, 2003 and Chen, J and Dickson 2010), however, called the validity of these assumptions into question. Rather than finding high levels of discontent with the existing system, poll after poll revealed that not only were Chinese generally much more optimistic about the future and the likelihood that their incomes would rise in the future than citizens in other countries, but also a majority had a positive view of the existing political system and rather than rejecting the CCP, and many actually aspired to become party members (Chen, A 2002; Chen, J 2003 and 2013; Chen, J and Dickson 2008 and 2010, Chen, J and Lu 2011; and Dickson 2003 and 2008). Business owners and managers in particular proved to have high levels of support for the party and regime (Dickson 2010). Although perplexing to some, the results were not illogical, as Wright and others have concluded, because not only could the CCP claim to have dramatically raised living standards and put the economy into high gear, those in the business sector and the members of the middle class were in fact among the major beneficiaries of economic reform (Wright 2010 and Zhou and Qin 2010). Moreover, many in the middle class seem to fear that democracy would empower the unwashed masses of workers and farmers, who would fall victim to the slippery and silver tongues of demagogues and populists who would incite them to use their power in numbers to expropriate the wealth and property of their "betters" (Unger 2006).

Although the Chinese middle class may continue to accept the political status quo, it has not been quiescent. Chen and Lu, for example, have shown that a majority of middle-class Chinese are interested in politics and believe that grassroots resident's committees should be directly elected (Chen, J and Lu 2006; Ming 2011, and Ming, Woods, and Zhao 2009). Despite fearing to confront the state, Cai and Reed found that middle-class homeowners were willing to organize against perceived threats to their property and community rights (Cai 205 and Reed 2003). Middle-class "netizens" have also proven increasingly willing to speak out, as evidenced to the very strong online reaction to official's attempts to cover up the high-speed rail accident in Wenzhou that killed over three dozen and injured almost 200 in July 2011, as well as joining with other to create "viral" outpourings of angst over official corruption and misconduct (Weber, 2011 and Wu 2012).[3]

In fact, the propensity of the Chinese middle class to take to the streets in defense of its rights appears to have increased significantly in recent years. Urban residents have turned out in the tens of thousands to protest against the construction of "nuisances" such as power plants, incinerators, trash dumps and refineries. Thousands turned out in Guangzhou after a political figure remarked that Cantonese should no longer be used as a broadcast language and that it should be replaced with state-standardized Putonghua. Fear of the magnetic waves from the Maglev high-speed train triggered a series of protests in Shanghai, as did noise from high-speed rail in Beijing. In Beijing, condominium residents took to the streets after management announced they would have to buy the parking spaces in building's underground garage. Citizens in Nanjing rallied against the cutting down some of the city's iconic "wutong" (parasol) trees to make way for a new subway stop. Pollution and industrial accidents have also triggered demonstrations. The middle class is not, of course, alone. Between 1993 and 2010, the number of "mass incidents," which are general defined as any unlawful gathering of ten or more individuals, has reportedly skyrocketed from 9,000 to 180,000. If the latter figure is correct, it implies that China now witnesses on average upward of 500 illegal assemblies, protests, demonstration, and riots a day.

The upsurge in street protests raises a series of questions. First, how widespread are protests involving members of China's emerging middle class? Second, what brings members of the urban middle class into the streets? Third, how does the state respond to middle-class protest movements? Fourth, how politically salient are middle-class protests and are they a harbinger of increasing middle-class political militancy?

Answering these questions is complicated by the highly imperfect nature of the available data. There are no systematic data on mass incidents. Most of the information on these protests comes from the news media, including Chinese language websites based outside the "Great Firewall" of China. Although some of the media have staff reporters on the ground, many rely on freelance "stringers" and social media for reports on developments, particularly for the vast majority of the country that lies outside the major cities along China's eastern coast.[4] At best, the available volume of reported demonstration is a tiny fraction of the total and most mass incidents go unreported. The veracity of some reports is also hard to gauge. And yet, data on upwards of 4,000 of these incidents exists. We have data, but only on the tip of the iceberg, this "tip" is, however, perhaps the most politically salient part of the "iceberg" because it is the part that is not only visible to outside observers but it is also the part that is most likely to be seen by members of the Chinese middle class and hence the part that is most likely to shape their perceptions of the extent and nature of protest.

Not only is the small sliver of data available an issue, bias is also a major issue. Events deep in China's countryside are much less likely to be picked up by the news media than events in the major cities. Protests organized by people with technical knowledge; access to social media and the Internet, including access to Virtual Private Networks (VPNs) that enable them to sidestep around the Great Firewall; and some knowledge of different media organizations are also much more likely to come to the attention of reporters and bloggers. In combination, these biases likely mean that urban middle-class protests are much more likely to be reported in the media than other forms of protests, with the possible exception of rural protests in Guangdong where proximity to Hong Kong means that reporters are more likely to receive reports of protests than in other parts of the county, including reports channeled through Hong Kong residents with relatives living in Guangdong. Coverage of middle-class protests, which by definition will be urban-based, likely skews somewhat toward more extensive coverage of protests in affluent cities such as Beijing, Shanghai, and Guangzhou, most of which are located on China's eastern seaboard and away from mid-sized and smaller inland cities. China's middle class is, however, concentrated in the major east coast cities, with the result that the severity of geographic bias may be limited.

The key to understanding middle-class protests is not simply a matter of looking for patterns in reports of protests and what brings the Chinese middle class out into the streets. The real key lies in understanding the broader political significance of these protests. Most middle-class protests involve what is known in the west as "not in my backyard" (NIMBY) issues.[5] In broad, terms NIMBY protests center on opposition to local "nuisances" or "public bads" by members of a community. In and of themselves, NIMBY protests are thus reactive, conservative, and localized. As argued in the following sections, the politics and political salience of NIMBY-driven protests can be much more complicated and their linkage to broader political pressures indirect and subtle. Studies of NIMBY movements in fact suggest that although often narrowly focused on a particular perceived threat to a local community, participants may develop a new sense of citizen empowerment and their perceived ability to successfully confront state authority. As such, even though the objective of NIMBY involvement by members of the Chinese middle class may be superficially apolitical and many members of the middle class may have high levels of political efficacy, the growth in NIMBY-type protests may provide a precursor for future politically motivated protests. NIMBY protests can also serve as a way for activists to begin to form connections that span multiple communities and thereby link locally oriented protests into larger, issue-driven movements. In fact, China's pubic security apparatus reported believes that the formation of such networks may already be underway and that these networks are partly responsible for a spate of large NIMBY protests in the recent years. Sources in China report that activists with ties to a loose "citizen's rights" campaign detained during the summer of 2013 were interrogated about what the police called "behind-the-scenes organizers" and hidden "sources of funding" (Li, X 2013).

Not in My Back Yard

NIMBY protest movements are a form of collective action that emerge from intense local opposition to the siting of some sort of "nuisance facility" such as hazardous waste storage facilities, nuclear power plants, incinerators, garbage dumps, coal-fired power plants, prisons, drug rehabilitation clinics, low-income housing developments, transportation facilities, and so on (see Welsh 1993; Walsh, Warland, and Smith, 1993; Takahashi and Dear 1997; Rasmussen 1992; Peterson, Kowalewski, and Porter 1993; Mitchell and Carson 1986; Groothuis and Miller 1994; and Fischel 2001). In the view of many commentators, NIMBY protests are driven by a combination of emotion and fear, which leads residents to believe that the siting of such facilities near to their homes will not only put them in physical danger but will also sharply decrease the value of their real property and degrade their daily lives. The unwanted facility, in other words, will "ruin" their lives and communities. Historically, NIMBY protests have been linked to the rise of the urban middle class and hence have tended to be associated with Europe and the North America. But NIMBY protests are not a uniquely "Western" phenomenon. The Japanese middle class, for example, also has a history of resistance to nuisance facilities (McKean).

The literature posits that NIMBY protests stand out among other forms of collective action because the perceived costs of the object of protest are relatively concentrated and those groups that will likely bear those costs are often pre-existing communities (Hermansson 2007 and Kraft and Clary 1991). Overcoming collective action problems and mobilizing protests are hence easier than in contexts where costs are more diffuse and groups less connected, thus exacerbating the free rider problem. NIMBY protesters, in fact, are assumed to grossly overestimate the costs associated with the proposed facility.[6] The degree of preexisting community solidarity matters, of course, but the ability of activists to quickly and easily frame the threat to the community can compensate for lack of strong community spirit at the onset of protest mobilization. NIMBY threats can, in fact, create community solidarity where it may have been largely absent or relatively weak.

In many cases, the subjective risks of protest are also assumed to be low. NIMBY protesters often cast their grievances in abstract "technical terms" and focus on whether those seeking to site a nuisance facility have adequately and appropriately weighed the wisdom of siting it in that particular community. Protesters seek to claim the high moral ground rather than focusing on what outsiders might deem egoistic, selfish interests. Thus, for example, residents may turn out to protest the construction of a power plant in their neighborhood on the grounds that its proponents have not taken adequate steps to insure public safety when in reality they fear it will drive down home prices and hurt them financially. Because NIMBY protests are presumed to be easy to mobilize and do not directly challenge political authorities, they are also presumed to have a high probability of success. In part, this assumed high probability of success stems from protesters' belief that their demands are reasonable and that if the siting authority can be held up to public scrutiny they will realize the error of their decision. A high probability of success is also associated with the fact that the siting authority can simply relocate the nuisance facility in an area where either the residents see it as a benefit (e.g., source of employment) or offer less fierce resistance. Thus, compared to other forms of popular collective actions in which diffuse costs and limited gains created significant free rider problems, NIMBY movements are assumed to have much lower mobilization thresholds and are hence more likely to emerge and gain significant momentum.

Although normally cast by their supporters as defenses of the quality of community life, NIMBY protests have been characterized by others as selfish and even irrational because in many cases the protests would prefer to have the proposed facility built, but in somebody else's backyard.[7] In other cases, it has been argued that NIMBY protests may involve an element of racism or prejudice, because while the target may be overtly a facility, in reality the goal is to keep those who would use the facility out of the community (Wolsink 2006 and Hubbard 2006). Affluent communities, for example, have resisted homeless shelters and substance abuse facilities out of fear of the "sorts of people" who they will bring into their neighborhoods (Takahashi and Dear 1997). In Britain residents of Nottingham blocked the construction of a facility for asylum seekers, citing environmental and aesthetic grounds, when in reality their opposition stemmed from fear the shelter would bring in "aliens" (Hubbard 2005). In the wake of Hurricane Katrina, residents of communities in the New Orleans area and further afield often fought bitterly to prevent the construction of trailer parks for those displaced by the storm because the parks would, they claimed, bring in the "wrong element" and "destroy" their communities (Aldrich and Cook 2008).

Whether for good community-based reasons or selfish reasons, the NIMBY response to the siting of nuisance facilities is generally driven by the desire of local residents to defend their property and to preserve its value, both monetary and subjective. The link between property and NIMBY protests means that NIMBY-ism is more likely among the property-owning middle classes. When faced with a proposed nuisance facility, renters can, if they can afford it, "vote with their feet" and move. Middle-class homeowners are apt to be considerably less mobile, because in order to relocate they first need to sell their homes, homes that often represent the bulk of their financial assets. The announcement that a nuisance facility will be located in their community, however, is likely to drive housing prices down and thus put homeowners in a position where they would have to sell their property at a loss and then incur the additional cost of purchasing property in another community. Middle-class homeowners, therefore, often have to choose between suffering considerable financial losses and fighting back.

NIMBY-ism in China emerged out of housing reforms begun in the 1980s. Prior to reform, employers (aka "units" or *danwei*) generally provided housing at nominal rents and most workers lived in compounds co-located or close to their workplace (Man 2010 and Tomba 2010). Other urban residents living in housing that had been expropriated from private owners in the 1950s and converted into public housing, with the residents paying rents to the community housing authority (Zhao and Bourassa 2003; Huque 2005; Lee 2000; Gu 2002; Hui and Wong 1999, and Zhang 1997). A smaller number of residents continued to reside in privately owned homes. Many of this latter group had, however, been forced to hand over parts of their home to community housing authorities, which allocated the space to other families.[8] At the time, siting locations were controlled by the state, and urban residents had little say in where nuisance facilities were located. Moreover, because they had no ownership rights and little discretion over where they lived, urban residents had few reasons to actively resist siting decisions made by local authorities. In the 1980s, local government began to experiment with a number of reforms that included construction of new private housing and the sale of preexisting public housing.

Housing reform and the construction of new residential communities, often in emerging suburban areas, had three major effects. First, housing reform created a new and large class of homeowners. Today, upwards of 80 percent of urban families own their homes (Gaulard 2013). Second, it created a much greater degree of mobility and choice. Urban residents were now able to decide where they wanted to live – subject, of course, to affordability. Third, it led to community differentiation, with lower-income families either forced to remain in older, lower-cost housing or to relocate to subsidized, "affordable" housing while families with better and rising incomes were able to move to newly built communities (Li, Z and Wu 2006 and Wu 2002). New middle-class communities, many of which had much greater green space and other amenities than older communities, thus came into existence and came to be highly valued by would-be buyers (Shen and Wu 2009 and Wang and Li 2004). Fourth, rapidly rising housing prices meant that a greater share of family wealth came to exist in the form of housing assets (Gaulard 4). Many middle-class families, in fact, see real estate as a key mechanism for creating greater wealth and, where possible, individuals are quick to buy multiple properties based on the belief that housing prices will rise substantially over the long term and hence enable those who buy now to get rich later.[9]

Housing reform not only created new middle-class communities in suburban areas, urban redevelopment led to the displacement of many other urban residents (He 2012). In many cities, residential areas located in the urban core have been slated for either commercial development or the replacement of often dilapidated low-rise housing with new high-rise condominiums. In the process, lower-income families have been forcibly evicted from their homes, without "fair" compensation in many cases. Resistance to forced evictions has in fact emerged as a major source of urban unrest among working residents.

Among the urban middle class, by contrast, resistance to nuisance facilities has increased significantly in recent years. As documented in the following section, China's growing middle class, while supporting the government at what many may see as anomalously high levels, have been willing to take to the streets to fight for what they see as their community rights. NIMBY protests have, in some cases, mobilized large numbers of urban residents to fight against unwanted facilities. Other issues, including opposition to perceived threats to local culture, have also sparked large scale protests. Nationalism, primarily in the form of anti-Japanese protests, has also emerged as a source of mass mobilization, particularly among younger urban residents.

Middle-Class Protests in China

Anecdotal evidence of NIMBY protests in China is not hard to come by. On the contrary, there has been extensive reporting of such protests in both the international press and the state-controlled official Chinese press. Systematic data are, however, lacking. In the past, the Chinese government issued statistics on "mass incidents." In recent years, the government has stopped issuing even crude aggregate data. These data were never broken down into categories that would allow analysts to focus in on middle-class protests.

In order to get a better picture of the scope of middle-class protests, I have compiled anecdotal reports published in the press, into a database. The database includes data on some 4,200 "mass incidents" between 1990 and 2012.[10] During the early years, the extent of reporting was limited. The spread of the Internet and social media, along with the proliferation of video and camera equipped cellphones, has led to a tremendous increase in the volume of reporting in more recent years. Despite the best efforts of China's "Great Firewall" to suppress politically sensitive news, it is clear that reports quickly leak out and are picked up by websites and activist groups located outside of China and then re-broadcast. Sites such as *Boxun*, *Want China Times*, Radio Free Asia, *Kan Zhongguo*, and the Hong Kong Information Center for Human Rights and Democracy actively collect and published reports of unrest, as do a variety of Tibetan, Uyghur and Mongol groups. The international press regularly reports on incidents of mass unrest. The official Chinese press, including *Xinhua, China Daily, Global Times, Renmin Ribao* and other news sources, also regularly carry reports of unrest. The official Chinese news agency *Xinhua*, in fact, often proves to be the original source of reports carried in the international press and on advocacy websites. The reliability of reports is hard to gage. Reports in the mainstream news media are likely properly fact checked. Reports published by activist groups, including Falun Gong, are more likely "spun" and hence less reliable. Reports originating with "local stringers" or from social media, while frequently accompanied by photos and video, are of uneven quality and uncertain reliability. Despite these issues, experience shows that reports that appear on activist websites are often carried by multiple agencies. In the end, the data are what they are: less than pristine, but they are what we have to work with and, as argued earlier, the data provide important insights into the extent and nature of social protest.

Detailed demographic data on those involved in mass incidents are often lacking. Protesters are apt to be identified in general terms such as "farmers," "villagers" "workers," and so on. By and large, protesters in urban areas are categorized as simply as "residents." In some cases, urban protesters are identified as member of specific demographics such as "retirees," "demobilized soldiers," "teachers," "students" or "petitioners." The latter refers to individuals seeking to take advantage of the government and party's "letters and visits" system to seek redress and justice. Not all petitioners are urban residents and they are often villagers or members of the lower classes. I have thus focused on protests involving "urban residents."

Of the 4,167 incidents of collective action I was able to document between 1990 and December 2012, 71 percent occurred in urban areas.[11] Work-related incidents such as strikes, protests over working conditions, or demonstrations sparked by unpaid wages, accounted for close to half (45 percent) of all urban protests. Incidents of collective action by "urban residents" – which I defined as individuals residing in urban areas whose protests were not work-related and who were not identified as members of a particular occupational group – accounted for 16 percent of the all urban incidents or about 11 percent of all documented mass incidents. Among urban mass incidents, protests over wages and working conditions accounted for 47 percent of all incidents, conflicts with police and officials 9 percent, ethnic conflicts 7 percent, nationalist demonstrations (mostly aimed at Japan) 6 percent, and protests over pensions by retirees 5 percent. Quality of life related protests, which include NIMBY-type protests, made up just 5.5 percent of all urban mass incidents (see Table 10.1). Among protests by urban residents, protests sparked by confrontations with police accounted for over a third of all protests, protests over quality of life issues and pollution 30 percent, and against house demolitions 22 percent (see Table 10.2). Protests against nuisance facilities and pollution accounted for over just over half of all quality of life protests by urban residents (see Table 10.3).

Table 10.1 Focus of Urban Protests, 1990–2012

Issue	*Number*	*Percent*
Wages and working conditions	1,393	47.03
Police or official misconduct	274	9.25
Demolitions	201	6.79
Ethnic	195	6.58
Nationalism	173	5.84
Quality of life	163	5.50

Issue	*Number*	*Percent*
Pensions	153	5.17
Redress of injustice	94	3.17
Other	316	10.67
Total	2,962	

Table 10.2 Focus of Protests by Urban Residents, 1990–2012

Issue	*Number of incidents*	*Percent incidents*
Police (official corruption)	163	34.24
Quality of life (pollution)	145	30.46
Demolitions	106	22.27
Land	16	3.36
Medical malpractice	14	2.94
Redress	11	2.31
Scam	8	1.68
Election (local dispute)	4	0.84
Housing prices	3	0.63
Political	2	0.42
Campus conditions	1	0.21
Ethnic conflict	1	0.21
Religion	1	0.21
Rent increases	1	0.21
Total	476	

Table 10.3 Quality of Life Related Protests by Urban Residents, 1990–2012

Issue	*Rural*	*Urban*	*Total*	*Percent Rural*	*Percent Urban*	*Percent Total*
Nuisance facility	42	54	96	43.75	36.24	39.18
Pollution	48	22	70	50.00	14.77	28.57
Living conditions	4	46	50	4.17	30.87	20.41
Discrimination	0	15	15	0.00	10.07	6.12
Food safety or consumer rights	0	4	4	0.00	2.68	1.63
Total	96	149	245	100.00	100.00	100.00

Although NIMBY protests are generally associated with urban residents, quality of life-related protests by villagers and rural residents were almost exclusively related to either nuisance facilities or pollutions. Such protests, in fact, account for 94 percent of all quality of life-related protests by rural residents. NIMBY-ism, is thus not an exclusively urban or middle-class phenomenon in China but has also taken root in China's villages.

As noted earlier, protests precipitated by some sort of police or official action represented the second largest single category of protests involving urban residents. Although such protests are rarely linked to NIMBY-ism in the literature on middle-class protests in advanced industrial democracies, like NIMBY protests, confrontations between the police and citizens also involve grassroots challenges of authority. As such, they can be thought of as evidence of emerging citizen activism and an increasing willingness to stand up to authority. Among urban residents, protests sparked by confrontations with the *chengguan* (urban management personnel), the police, and officials accounted for over 34 percent of the documented mass incidents. Often triggered by attacks on street venders, hawkers and peddlers, such incidents draw large crowds, mostly of onlookers, and have erupted into attacks on the *chengguan* and police (see Table 10.4). Murders, rapes and accidental deaths, while also a relatively minor source of mass incidents, have in some instances precipitated major rioting, as did what villagers saw as excessively aggressive enforcement of the one child policy.

Table 10.4 Mass Incidents Involving Confrontation with Police

Issue	*Urban*	*Percent Rural*	*Percent Urban*
Police misconduct	126	25.22	45.16
Chengguan misconduct	59	1.74	21.15
Official corruption	29	47.83	10.39
Death, murder or rape	22	0.87	7.89
Official misconduct	12	1.74	4.3
Thug beating and killing	12	7.83	4.3
Traffic accident	7	0	2.51
Security guard misconduct	6	0	2.15
Attacks on doctors	3	0	1.08
Compensation	3	11.3	1.08
One child policy	0	3.48	0
Total	279		

Like protests triggered by confrontations between citizens and authorities, nationalist protests do not fit the NIMBY model. Yet such protests often involve large-scale mobilization of China's growing urban middle class. China has experienced four "waves" of anti-foreign demonstrations. The first in 1999 was precipitated by the American bombing of China's Belgrade embassy during air attacks on Serbia. The other three, which erupted in 2005, 2010 and 2012, were aimed at Japan. Whereas the embassy bombings in 1999 can be linked to a specific accident, the rising tide of anti-Japanese protests, which increased in number from roughly two dozen documented protests in 2005 and 2010 to 107 in 2012, has clearly been fueled by a combustible combination of increasing mass nationalism in China, a rightward tilt by Japanese political leaders, and the two country's dispute over the Diaoyutai/Senkaku islands in the East China Sea. Hostilities have, of course, been stoked by the legacy of the anti-Japanese War (1937–1945) and bitter memories in China of atrocities committed by Japanese forces (Wang, Z 2012).

In sum, although the evidence is indirect, it is clear that China's emerging middle class participates in a variety of collective action protests, including classic NIMBY protests against unwanted facilities in residential communities and that, based on documented cases, there is a clear upward trend in the number of quality of life related protests (see Figure 10.1), including a series of very large protests (see Table 10.5). Most protests by urban residents, including the middle class, are not overtly political, which is in keeping with survey data showing high levels of political efficacy and regime support, particularly among groups that have benefited substantially from the CCP's program of economic reforms (Wright 2010). Most urban protests are rooted in work-related issues and involve the working class, not the middle class. Another major source of urban protest is police misconduct. Once again, it seems likely that most of those involved in confrontations with the police are members of the working or lower middle classes, groups that are arguable more likely to confront abuse by police and officials. Finally, it is not clear whether urban NIMBY protests are purely middle-class affairs. Certainly members of the working class may share common opposition to

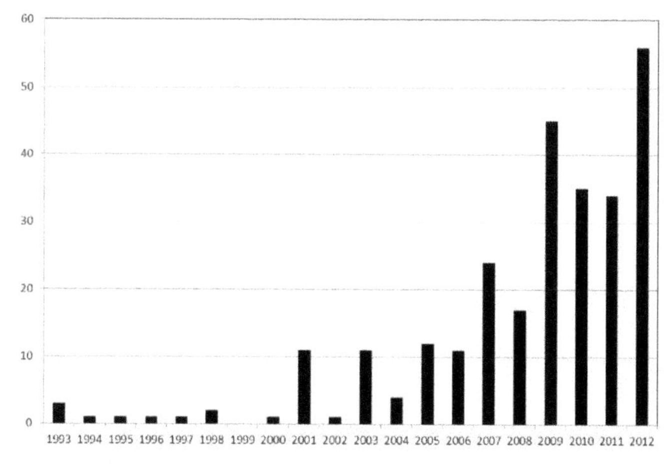

Figure 10.1 Number of Quality of Life Protests

Table 10.5 Major NIMBY Protests, 2009–2013 (Protests Involving 10,000 or More Individuals)

August 2009	Fujian	Xiamen	Protesters clash with police in three days of demonstrations against a chemical factory. The first day was peaceful but the second and third days saw clashes between protestors and baton-wielding police. A dozen protesters injured. Afterwards, protests continued for two days but without clashes.	Washington Post 3/5/2009
September 2010	Zhejiang	Dongyang	Clash between 30,000 farmers and police leaves 1–2 dead and over 120 injured. Farmers overturned 50 police cars when police use clubs and tear gas to break up a demonstration protesting construction of a chemical plant and pollution from other plants.	AFX, 4/11/2005 and SCMP, 4/12/2005.
September 2010	Zhejiang	Xinchang	Farmers attack chemical plant whose pollution had destroyed their crops. Three nights of rioting involving up to 15,000 protesters who clashed with police, over turned police cars and stoned police.	AP, 7/19/2005 and NYT, 7/19/2005
June 2011	Jiangsu	Qidong	Ten thousand students and residents protest against the discharge of waste water by Japanese-owned factory. According to human rights activists, three died in protest and over 100 were arrested.	HKICHRD, 7/25/2012; 7/24/2012; 看中国, 7/24/2012 and 7/31/2012
August 2012	Fujian	Quanzhou	Ten thousand residents demonstrate over the stench from a sewage treatment plan. Ten injured when demonstration turns violent.	AP, September 1, 2009; 看中国, 9/2/2009, 9/1/2009; Global Times, 9/3/2009; HKICHRD, 9/2/2009
September 2012	Zhejiang	Quanzhou	Ten thousand villagers clash with 2,000 riot police in a demonstration over pollution. Protesters pelted police with stones, burned police cars and took an official hostage. Police responded with tear gas and fired shots in the air. At least a dozen villagers reported injured, along with one local official and a policeman.	SCMP, 9/2/2009 and The Guardian, 9/2/2009

nuisance facilities in their communities and may initiate or join in NIMBY protests. The literature on NIMBY-ism suggests, however, that such protests are linked to property ownership and are driven by perceived threats to residents' real assets. The case can thus be made that the upsurge in NIMBY protests in recent years is an outcome of the rise in home ownership by urban residents. Given the costs of urban housing in China's major cities, it follows that many of those joining such protests are likely members of the emerging middle class.

Moreover, NIMBY protests have been successful, even in instances where protesters took on powerful state-owned companies. The first successful NIMBY protest was in June 2009, when 20,000 people took to the streets of Xiamen to protest against a proposed paraxylene (PX) chemical factory and other residents flooded social media with protests messages. Caught off guard, local authorizes postponed approval for the project (Zhao, D 2007). Two years later, authorities in Dalian, agreed to close a PX plant after waves topped a seawall during a storm, triggering panic about a possible chemical spill and protests by some 12,000 residents ("China protest closes toxic chemical plant in Dalian" and Bradsher 2011). In October 2012, students and middle-class residents of Ningbo joined farmers and villagers in a massive protest against the expansion of a petrochemical refinery owned by the politically powerful state-owned Sinopec Corp. Local officials had welcomed the US$8.8 billion project, but ended up retreating after protesters battled riot police with bricks and bottles and over 100 protesters were arrested (Jacobs 2012). More recently, thousands of residents of Kunming repeatedly marched in protest after learning that the state-owned Chinese National Petroleum Corporation planned to build a new oil refinery in a suburban county. Faced with an unexpected uproar, municipal officials said they would stop the project if "most of our citizens say no to it" (Liao 2013; "Poor communications;" Kaimen 2013; "New Protest;" and "Hundreds protest"). That same week, officials in Shanghai announced that the Shanghai Guoxuan New Energy Corporation had cancelled plans to build a lithium battery plant in the Songjiang District after hundreds of middle-class residents protested (Wu 2013; "Shanghai citizens rally;" and "Plans for Shanghai"). In July 2013, the state-owned China National Nuclear Corporation's plans to build a uranium processing plant in Guangdong were thwarted when thousands residents marched through the streets, prompting officials in Heshan city to announce that the city would not seek approval of the project (Chan and He 2013 and "Nuclear fuel project").

Conclusions

To observe that there has been a rise in NIMBY protests does not necessarily suggest a rise in political activism among China's heretofore quiescent middle class. Despite instances of NIMBY protests and participation in other forms of protest by members of China's middle class, polling data suggest that most of the middle class opposed public protests, with only 23 percent in a December 2006-Janaury 2007 poll in Beijing, Chengdu, and Xi'an disagreeing with the statement "in general demonstrations should not be allowed because they frequently become disorderly and disruptive." Middle-class support for collective action was, in fact, nearly 14 percent lower than that among other classes (Chen, J 2010).

The literature on NIMBY protests elsewhere, however, implies that rising NIMBY-ism could have larger political implications and that locally oriented protests can lay the foundations for larger, more political social movements. Successful protests aimed at specific nuisance facilities, at a minimum, show those involved in the protest, and those who hear about it indirectly, that ordinary people can stand up to power and win. Analyses of why citizens participate in social movements, however, suggest that other factors also encourage individuals to join in collective confrontations with authority. Participation in collective action helps foster shared identities that, according to Klandermans, encourage further activism by convincing individuals that others who share common grievances will join in protest Klandermans 2002 and 1984). Researchers have found that people are more likely to join protests if they believe that their actions will generate public sympathy, even if they fail to sway authorities, and if they come to see themselves as activists (Homsey, et al. 2006). Kim and Bearman (1997) argue that there is a "cascade of activism" generated by repeated attempts by grassroots activists that can pull in onlookers and generate an upward spiral in collective actions. Participation in movements is also said to be a function of interpersonal trust and social networks (Mannarini, et al. 2009). As a result, when people join in a protest and see others marching alongside them, they are more apt to assume a sense of community unites them with others and that in future disputes with authority they will not stand alone (Benson and Rochon 2004 and Veenstra and Haslan 2000). In broad terms, therefore, seeing ordinary citizens taking to the streets to challenge authorities and seeing authorities give in to protesters' demands in some cases is assumed to encourage further protests and generate "protest cycles" (Minkoff 1997; Conell and Cohn 1995; Koopsmans, 1993; and Meyer and Whittier 1993).

Viewed in a broadly comparative context, NIMBY protests involving members of China's emerging middle class are perhaps best interpreted as a potential precursor of further protests in the future, particularly if NIMBY protesters continue to "win." This need not, however, mean that NIMBY protests are a precursor of overtly political movements. On the contrary, the finite and focused targets of NIMBY protests and the seemingly selfish, egoistic demands of the protesters can limit the ability of one protest to "spillover" into other communities, unless, that is, residents in other communities see themselves as sharing common concerns and cause. In such circumstances, NIMBY protests in one area may stimulate similar protests in other localities. NIMBY protests linked to fear of environmental degradation and pollution can, moreover, become fused into a largely environmental movement and spawn nongovernmental organizations that can generate the sorts of dense social networks and organizational skills which are associated with the expansion of civil society. Local environmental protests in Taiwan during the 1980s, for example, morphed into a broad environmental movement whose target shifted progressively from local nuisance facilities, to the central government's environmental policies and, ultimately, became a partial springboard for mounting political opposition to the de facto one party dictatorship of the *Guomindang* (Ho 2003; Ho 2011; Hsiao, Milbrath, and Weller 1995; Hsiao 1990; Hsu 2006; Tang and Tang 1997; Tang and Tang 1999; and Tang 2003). Environmental NGOs have, in fact, begun to play an increasingly visible role in China (Xie 2009; Schwartz 2004; Stalley and Yang 2006; and Yang 2005). And heretofore, a number of environmental activists have been detained and some charged with subversion or inciting illegal assemblies.[12] Given the apparent high levels of regime support among China's rising middle class, it would seem unlikely that NIMBY protests currently represent a serious political challenge to the political status quo. If NIMBY protesters are repeatedly rebuffed, harassed, and repressed, however, community opposition to local nuisance facilities could assume greater political undertones.

Whether continued increases in NIMBY protests by relatively affluent urban residents will give rise to a politically conscious middle-class identity is unclear. Although Marx and others assumed that material conditions give rise to collective class consciousness, historical experience in China and elsewhere suggests that individuals' political consciousness are much more complex. Moreover, because the Chinese middle class has only come into existence in the past two decades, it likely remains largely defined in objective terms of relative affluence and property ownership without having spawned a concurrent subjective consciousness based on individuals' sense that they are members a specific class. In many cases, members of the new middle class grew up as members of the working class and only achieved the material attributes of middle-class status as adults. Younger members of the middle class, on the other hand, may have grown up in relative affluence, but they did so in a context in which there is no clear sense of what sort of "class" the newly affluent constitute. What sorts of norms and values should govern China's newly affluent are, in fact, the subject of considerable contestation and even conflict in which some see China's newly affluent at a class without a meaningful consciousness, one for whom the paramount goal is the acquisition of more wealth and the public display of its new wealth. Given NIMBY protests focus on the defense of either individual and narrowly defined community rights it does not seem likely that these protests alone would stimulate the formation of something resembling Marxist class consciousness. Even so, successful NIMBY protests could stimulate a sense of citizen empowerment in the sense that individuals and community come to believe that they can challenge the state on issues of immediate concern. Increasing NIMBY protests by urban residents, in other words, might produce an increase in urban residents' sense of empowerment without necessarily producing a new middle-class consciousness.

Notes

1. Barton, Chen, and Jin's definition of the Chinese middle class is households with disposable income of between US$9,000 and US$34,000. The Chinese middle class is generally defined in terms of relatively high income ($10,000 or more a year), home ownership, ownership of an automobile, the consumption of luxury goods, advanced education, and the holding of a white collar job. As Goodman points out, however, beyond relative affluence, the middle class lacks a strong sense of itself as a class. Moreover, many members of what might be more property called the affluent class continue to work for the state either as officials or as managers of state-owned enterprises and are hence dependent on it rather than forming an independent class as is the case in most advanced economies (Goodman).
2. After the communist take-over in 1949, the middle class was effectively eliminated. Members of the small pre-revolutionary class either fled to Taiwan, Hong Kong, the United States, or elsewhere. If they remained in China, they either either suffered swift downward social mobility and merged into the working class or became members of what might be called the urban-official class. Relative to members of the working class or the peasantry, the urban-official class was more affluent, but that affluence was only relative. For the most part, living conditions for the urban-official class were difficult. Food and consumer goods were in short supply and strictly rationed. Most lived in housing provided by their employer and most had limited property, such as bicycles, sewing machines, and radios.
3. The term "netizen" apparently originates in China and refers to individuals who participate in online discussions and routinely access social media and other websites. In mid 2013, China had close to 600 million Internet users, not all of whom would be considered active or participatory netizens because while they surf the net and may engage in activities such as on-line gaming or shopping on-line, they are not active in sharing their views and opinions.
4. A "stringer" is journalist working either on a short-term contract for a media organization or one who is freelancing.
5. NIMBY-type movements have also been called "not on my street" (NOOS) or "locally unwanted land use" (LULU) protests.
6. The collective action and free rider problems refer to barriers to collective protests created when individual protesters believe they will derived only a small direct benefit from a successful protest action. In such a situation, there will be a strong propensity for individual to eschew participation because they believe that the efforts of others will get the benefit for them or that the costs of participating will out weight the benefits.
7. Mayor Ed Koch of New York went so far as to declare that if NIMBY-ism was left unchecked, "we will find ourselves marching backward toward the imaginary safety of feudal fiefdoms defended by NIMBY walls" (Quoted in Dear 1992): 288–301.
8. In Jinan, Shandong, for example, about a third of urban housing stock was privately owned as late as 1963. By 1976, less than 20 percent of housing stock

remained in private hands, while 61% belonged to work units and 22% was government managed (Zhao and Bourassa 2003): 725.

9. A 2010 study of prices in eight major Chinese housing markets found that in Beijing, real estate prices increased at a compounding rate of 28 percent a year between 2003 and 2009, for a net increase of 330 percent (Wu, Gyourko, and Deng 2010).
10. For purposes of coding, I defined "mass incidents" as incidents involving collective action by at least ten individuals.
11. Urban areas include cities, prefectural and country-level towns, and townships. Within cities, I have tried to differentiate between urban areas and rural counties administrative attached to cities. .
12. An examination of the Congressional Executive Commission on China's "Political Prisoner Database," reveals 17 individuals detained for environmental-related activities. Of the total, seven were detained in 2009. Since then the annual numbers have been two in 2010, two in 2011, and three in 2012. As such, it does not appear that upward trend in NIMBY protests has thus far been matched by an upward trend in detention of activities. Data available at http://www.cecc.gov/resources/political-prisoner-database, accessed September 9, 2013.

Works Cited

"China protest closes toxic chemical plant in Dalian." *BBC News*, 8/11/2011.

"Hundreds protest chemical plant in Kunming." *WantChinaTimes*, 5/4/2013.

"New protest in Chinese city over planned chemical plant." *Reuters*, 5/16/2013.

"Nuclear fuel project pulled in Guangdong after protests." *WantChinaTimes*, 7/13/2013.

"Plans for Shanghai's new lithium battery factory cancelled over protests." *China Daily*, 5/16/2013.

"Poor communication blamed for Kunming chemical protest." *WantChinaTimes*, 5/6/2013.

"Shanghai citizens rally against planned battery plant." *Shanghaiist*, 5/12/2013.

Aldrich, Daniel P. and Kevin Crook. "Strong Civil Society as a Double-Edged Sword: Siting Trailers in Post-Katrina New Orleans." *Political Research Quarterly* 61.3 (September 2008): 379–389.

Barton, Dominic, Yougang Chen, and Amy Jin. "Mapping China's Middle Class: Generational change and the rising prosperity of inland cities will power consumption for years to come." *McKinsey Quarterly*, June 2013, available at http://www.mckinsey.com/ insights/consumer_and_retail/mapping_chinas_middle_class. Web. August 8, 2013.

Benson, Michelle and Thomas R. Rochon. "Interpersonal Trust and the Magnitude of Protest: A Micro and Macro Level Approach." *Comparative Political Studies* 37.4 (2004): 435–57.

Bradsher, Keith. "China Moves Swiftly to Close Chemical Plant After Protests." *New York Times*, 8/14/2011.

Cai, Yungsun. "China's Moderate Middle Class: The Case of Homeowners' Resistance." *Asian Survey* 45.5 (September 2005): 777–799.

Chan, Minnie and He Huifeng. "Jiangmen uranium plant is scrapped after thousands take part in protests." *South China Morning Post*, 7/13/2013.

Chen, An. "Capitalist Development, Entrepreneurial Class, and Democratization in China." *Political Science Quarterly* 117.3 (Autumn 2002): 401–422.

Chen, Jie and Bruce J. Dickson. "Allies of the State: Democratic Support and Regime Support among China's Private Entrepreneurs." *China Quarterly* 196 (December 2008): 780–804.

———. *Allies of the State: China's Private Entrepreneurs and Democratic Change.* Cambridge, MA: Harvard University Press, 2010.

Chen, Jie and Chunlong Lu. "Does China's Middle Class Think and Act Democratically? Attitudinal and Behavioral Orientations toward Urban Self-Government." *Journal of Chinese Political Science* 11.2 (Fall 2006): 1–20.

———. "Democratization and the Middle Class in China: The Middle Class's Attitudes toward Democracy." *Political Research Quarterly* 64.3 September 2011: 705–719.

Chen, Jie. *Popular Political Support in Urban China.* Stanford, CA: Stanford University Press, 2003.

———. "Attitudes toward Democracy and the Political Behavior of China's Middle Class," In Cheng Li, ed., *China's Emerging Middle Class: Beyond Economic Transformation.* Washington, DC: Brookings Institution Press, 2010: 334–358.

———. *A Middle Class Without Democracy: Economic Growth and the Prospects for Democratization in China.* New York: Oxford University Press, 2013.

Conell, Carol, and Samuel Cohn. "Learning from Other People's Actions: Environmental Variation and Diffusion in French Coal Mine Strikes, 1890–1935." *American Journal of Sociology* 101.2 (September 1995): 366–403.

Dear, Michael. "Understanding and overcoming the NIMBY syndrome." *Journal of the American Planning Association* 58.3 (Summer 1992): 288–301.

Dickson, Bruce J. *Red Capitalists in China: The Party, Private Entrepreneurs, and Prospects for Political Change.* New York: Cambridge University Press, 2003.

———. *Wealth into Power: The Communist Party's Embrace of China's Private Sector.* New York: Cambridge University Press, 2008.

———. "China's Cooperative Capitalists: The Business End of the Middle Class." In Cheng Li, ed., *China's Emerging Middle Class: Beyond Economic Transformation.* Washington, DC: Brookings Institution Press, 2010: 291–309.

Fischel, William A. "Why Are There NIMBYs?" *Land Economics* 77.1 (February 2001): 144–152.

Gaulard, Mylene. "Changes in the Chinese Property Market: An indicator of the difficulties faced by local authorities." *China Perspectives* 2013.2 (2013): 3–14.

Goodman, David S.G. *Class in Contemporary China.* Malden, MA: Polity, 2014.

Groothuis, Peter A. and Gail Miller. "Locating Hazardous Waste Facilities: The Influence of NIMBY Beliefs." *American Journal of Economics and Sociology* 53.3 (July 1994): 335–346.

Gu, Edward X. "The State Socialist Welfare System and the Political Economy of Housing Reform in Urban China." *Review of Policy Research* 19.2 (Summer 2002): 181–209.

He, Shenjing. "Two waves of gentrification and emerging rights issue in Guangzhou, China." *Environment and Planning A* 44 (2012): 2817–2833.

Hermansson, Helene. "The Ethics of NIMBY Conflicts." *Ethical Theory and Moral Practice* 10.1 (February 2007): 23–34.

Ho, Ming-Sho. "The Politics of Anti-Nuclear Protest in Taiwan: A Case of Party-Dependent Movement (1980–2000)." *Modern Asian Studies* 37.3 (July 2003): 683–708.

———. "Environmental Movement in Democratizing Taiwan (1980–2004): A Political Opportunity Structure Perspective." In Jeffrey Broadbent and Vicky Brockman, eds., *East Asia Social Movements: Power, Protest, and Change in a Dynamic Region*. New York: Springer, 2011: 283–314.

Hornsey, Matthew J. et al. "Why Do People Engage in Collective Action? Revisiting the Role of Perceived Effectiveness." *Journal of Applied Social Psychology* 36.7 (2006): 1701–1722.

Hsiao, Hsin-Huang Michael, Lester W. Milbrath, and Robert P. Weller. "Antecedents of an Environmental Movement in Taiwan." *Capitalism Nature Socialism* 6.3 (1995): 91–104.

Hsiao, Hsin-Huang Michael. "Environmental Movements in Taiwan." In Yo-shiu F. Lee and Alvin Y. So, eds. *Asia's Environmental Movements: Comparative Perspectives*. Armonk, NY: M.E. Sharpe, 1999: 31–54.

———. "NIMBY opposition and solid waste incinerator siting in Taiwan." *Social Science Journal* 43.3 (2006): 453–9.

Hubbard, Phil. "Accommodating Otherness: Anti-Asylum Centre Protest and the Maintenance of White Privilege." *Transactions of the Institute of British Geographer* 30.1. March 2005: 52–65.

———. "NIMBY by Another Name? A Reply to Wolsink." *Transactions of the Institute of British Geographers* 31.1 (March 2006): 92–94.

Hui, Eddie Chi Man and Francsis Kwn Wah Wong. "Housing Reform in Guangzhou and Shenzhen, China." *Review of Urban & Regional Development Studies* 11.2 (July 1999): 141–53.

Huque, Ahmed Shafiqul. "Shifting Emphasis in the Role of the State: Urban Housing Reform in China." *Asian Journal of Political Science* 13.2 (December 2005): 53–74.

Jacobs, Andrew. "Protests Over Chemical Plan Force Chinese Officials to Back Down." *New York Times*, 10/28/2012.

Kaiman, Jonathan. "Chinese protest at planned chemical plant over pollution fears." *The Guardian*, 5/16/2013.

Karft, Michael E. and Bruce B. Clary. "Citizen Participation and the Nimby Syndrome: Public Response to Radioactive Waste Disposal." *The Western Political Quarterly* 44.2 (June 1991): 299–328.

Kharas, Homi and Geoffrey Gertz. "The New Global Middle Class: A Crossover from West to East." In Cheng Li, ed., *China's Emerging Middle Class: Beyond Economic Transformation*. Washington, DC: Brookings Institution Press, 2010: 32–51.

Kim, Hyojoung and Peter S. Bearman. "The Structure and Dynamics of Movement Participation." *American Sociological Review* 62.1(February 1997): 70–93.

Klandermans, Bert. "Mobilization and Participation: Social-Psychological Expansions of Resource Mobilization Theory." *American Sociological Review* 49.5 (October 1984): 583–600.

———. "How group identifications helps to overcome the dilemma of collective action." *The American Behavioral Scientist* 45.5 (January 2002): 887–900.

Koopmans, Ruud. "The Dynamics of Protest Waves: West Germany, 1965 to 1989." *American Sociological Review* 58.5 (October 1993): 637–658.

Lee, James. "From Welfare Housing to Home Ownership: The Dilemma of China's Housing Reform." *Housing Studies* 15.1 (2000): 61–76.

Li, Chunling. "Characterizing China's Middle Class: Heterogeneous Composition and Multiple Identities." In Cheng Li, ed., *China's Emerging Middle Class: Beyond Economic Transformation*. Washington, DC: Brookings Institution Press, 2010: 135–156.

Li, Xiaorong. "What's Behind the New Chinese Crackdown?" *New York Review of Books*, 7/29/2013.

Li, Zhigang, and Fulong Wu. "Socio-spatial Differentiation and Residential Inequalities in Shanghai: A Case Study of Three Neighborhoods." *Housing Studies* 21.5 (September 2006): 695–717.

Liao, Kuei-ju. "Kunming protesters take to streets again over PX plant." *WantChinaTimes*, 5/17/2013.

Man, Joyce Yanyun. "China's Housing Reform and Emerging Middle Class." In Cheng Li, ed., *China's Emerging Middle Class: Beyond Economic Transformation*. Washington, DC: Brookings Institution Press, 2010: 179–192.

Mannarini, Terri, Michele Roccato, Angela Fedi, and Alberto Rovere. "Six Factors Fostering Protest: Predicting Participation in Locally Unwanted Land Uses Movements." *Political Psychology* 30.6 (December 2009): 895–920.

McKean, Margaret. *Environmental Protest and Citizen Politics in Japan*. Berkeley, CA: University of California Press: 1981.

Meyer, David S. and Nancy Whittier. "Social Movement Spillover." *Social Problems* 41.2 (1993): 277–98.

Ming, Tan, Dwayne Woods, and Jujun Zhao. "The Attitudes of the Chinese Middle Class Towards Democracy," *Journal of Chinese Political Science* 14 (2009): 81–95.

Ming, Tan. "The Political Behavior of the Chinese Middle Class." *Journal of Chinese Political Science* 16.3 (2011): 373–387.

Minkoff, Debra C. "The Sequencing of Social Movements." *American Sociological Review* 62.5. (October 1997): 779–799.

Mithcell, Robert Cameronl and Richard T. Carson. "Association Property Rights, Protest, and the Siting of Hazardous Waste Facilities." *The American Economic Review* 76.2 (May, 1986): 285–290.

Moore, Barrington. *Social Origins of Dictatorship and Democracy: Lord and Peasant in the Making of the Modern World*. Boston: Beacon Press, 1993.

Peterson, Steven A., David A. Kowalewski and Karen L. Porter. "'Dumpbusting:' Symbolic or Situational Politics?" *Polity* 25.4 (Summer, 1993): 617–631.

Rasmussen, Thomas H. "Not in My Backyard: The Politics of Siting Prisons, Landfills, and Incinerators." *State & Local Government Review* 24.3 (Autumn, 1992): 128–134.

Reed, Benjamin L. "Democratizing the Neighborhood? New Private Housing and Home-Owner Self-Organization in Urban China." *China Journal* 49 (January 2003): 31–59.

Shen, Jie and Fulong Wu. "Moving to the suburbs: demand-side driving forces of suburban growth in China." *Environment and Planning A* 45 (2009): 1823–1844.

Takahashi, Lois M. and Michael J. Dear. "The changing dynamics of community opposition to human service facilities." *Journal of the American Planning Association* 63.1 (Winter 1997): 79–94.

Tang, Ching-Ping. "Democratizing Urban Politics and Civic Environmentalism in Taiwan." *China Quarterly* 176 (December 2003): 1029–51.

Tang, Shui-Yan and Ching-Ping Tang. "Democratization and Environmental Politics in Taiwan." *Asian Survey* 37.3 (March 1997): 281–294.

———. "Democratization and the Environment: Entrepreneurial Politics and Interest Representation in Taiwan." *China Quarterly* 158 (June 1999): 350–66.

Tomba, Luigi. "The Housing Effect: The Making of China's Social Distinctions," In Cheng Li, ed., *China's Emerging Middle Class: Beyond Economic Transformation*. Washington, DC: Brookings Institution Press, 2010: 193–216.

Ungur, Jonathan. "China's conservative middle class." *Far Eastern Economic Review* April 2006: 27–31.

Veenstra, Kristine and S Alexander Haslam. "Willingness to participate in industrial protest: Exploring social identification in context." *The British Journal of Social Psychology* 39 (June 2000): 153–72.

Walsh, Edward, Rex Warland, and D. Clayton Smith. "Backyards, NIMBYs, and Incinerator Sitings: Implications for Social Movement Theory." *Social Problems* 40.1 (February 1993): 25–38.

Wang, Donggen Wang and Si-Ming Li. "Housing preference in a transitional housing system: the case of Beijing, China." *Environment and Planning A* 36 (2004): 69–81.

Wang, Zheng. *Never Forget National Humiliation: Historical Memory in Chinese Politics and Foreign Relations*. New York: Columbia University Press, 2012.

Weber, Ian. "Mobile, online and angry; the rise of China's middle-class civil society?" *Critical Arts: South-North Cultural and Media Studies* (March 2011), available online at http://www.tandfonline.com/doi/pdf/10.1080/02560046.2011.552204, accessed 8/8/2013.

Welsh, Ian. "The NIMBY Syndrome: Its Significance in the History of the Nuclear Debate in Britain." *The British Journal for the History of Science* 26.1 (March 1993): 15–32.

Wolsink, Maarten. "Invalid Theory Impedes Our Understanding: A Critique on the Persistence of the Language of NIMBY." *Transactions of the Institute of British Geographers* 31.1 (March 2006): 85–91.

Wright, Teresa. *Accepting Authoritarianism: State-Society Relations in China's Reform Era*. Stanford, CA: Stanford University Press, 2010.

Wu, Changchang. "Micro-blog and the Speech Act of China's Middle Class: The 7:23 Train Accident Case." *Javnost-The Public* 19.2 (2012): 43–62.

Wu, Fulong. "Sociospatial differentiation in urban China: evidence from Shanghai's real estate markets." *Environment and Planning A* 34.9 (2002): 1591–1615.

Wu, Huizhong. "Proposed lithium battery factory in Shanghai cancelled." *Shanghaiist*, 5/16/2013.

Wu, Jing, Joseph Gyourko, and Yongheng Deng, "Evaluating Conditions in Major Chinese Housing Markets," Institute for Real Estate Studies, National University of Singapore, Working Paper 16189 (July 2010) available at http://www.ires.nus.edu.sg/ workingpapers/IRES2010-007.pdf, accessed August 21, 2013.

Zhang, Xing Quan. "Chinese housing policy 1949–1978: the development of a welfare system." *Planning Perspective* 12 (1997): 433–55.

Zhao, Dagong. "The Xiamen Demonstrations and Growing Civil Consciousness." *China Rights Forum* 2007.3: 104–7.

Zhao, Yingshun and Steven C. Bourassa. "China's Urban Housing Reform: Recent Achievements and new Inequalities." *Housing Studies* 18.5 (September 2003): 721–74.

Zhou, Xiaohong and Qin Chen. "Globalization, Social Transformation, and the Construction of China's Middle Class." In Cheng Li, ed., *China's Emerging Middle Class: Beyond Economic Transformation*. Washington, DC: Brookings Institution Press, 2010: 84–103.

List of Contributors

Erin Cavusgil is an Associate Professor of Marketing at the University of Michigan-Flint. She holds a BS in chemical engineering from the University of Michigan, an MS in biomedical engineering from the University of Minnesota, and a Ph.D. in Marketing from Michigan State University. She spent three and a half years working in the pharmaceutical industry as a chemical engineer. Her main research interests include new product development, innovation, marketing strategy and international marketing. Her research has been published in the *Journal of the Academy of Marketing Science*, the *Journal of Product Innovation Management*, the *Journal of Business Ethics*, and the *Journal of Business Research*, among others. Erin teaches Principles of Marketing and International Marketing. Erin is an active member of the American Marketing Association, the Product Development Management Association and the American Academy of Advertising.

Mourad Dakhli is an Associate Professor of International Business at Georgia State University (GSU) and holds a Ph.D. from the Moore School of Business at the University of South Carolina. His research centers on the value-generating processes of human and social capital across different cultural and institutional settings and the implications on learning and innovation. Prior to joining GSU, he served as a faculty member at the American University of Kuwait and taught at various places including the University of South Carolina, Azerbaijan State Oil Academy (Azerbaijan), the Caucasus School of Business (Republic of Georgia), and others. His prior work experience includes developing and marketing industry training programs, managing capacity development projects at a number of academic institutions, and directing the activities of a bi-national chamber of commerce responsible for the promotion and implementation of a wide array of international trade and investment initiatives.

Mohit Gour is Director of International Market research services for Issues & Answers. With over twenty years of experience in various market research capacities, Gour began his career with Issues & Answers as the Manager of Data Processing and then Project Coordinator, prior to his current position as Director of International Field Services. He oversees numerous duties in his current position, including the management of diverse International Projects from survey development to report writing and overseeing multi-country projects involving both qualitative and quantitative methodologies including ethnography and on-site in-depth interviews. He earned his Master's Degree in Business Administration with Market Research as his major. He received Professional Researcher Certification (PRC) from MRA. He is also a member of ESOMAR (European Society of Opinion Market Research).

David A. Grossman holds a doctorate in Business Administration from Southern New Hampshire University. He is an Assistant Professor of International Business and Marketing at Goucher College in Baltimore, Maryland (U.S.A.). His research interests include academic assessment and Faculty Development, International Business Theory and Information Technology, International Marketing, Marketing Services, Global Consumerism, Marketing Research and Market Entry Strategies. His research has appeared in numerous journals, including the *Thunderbird International Business Review*, the *Journal of Business and Industrial Marketing*, the *Journal of World Business*, the proceedings of the Academy of International Business and the Academy of Marketing Sciences.

Emily Hind is an Associate Professor of Spanish at the University of Florida in Gainesville, Florida (U.S.A). Her research interests include Mexican studies (Literature, Film, Culture, Politics, History), Latin American Literature and Film, and 20th- and 21st-Century Critical Approaches within the Interdisciplinary Humanities. Hind has published three books: *La generación XXX: Entrevistas con veinte escritores mexicanos nacidos en los 70. De Abenshushan a Xoconostle* (México: Eón, 2013), *Femmenism and the Mexican Woman Intellectual from Sor Juana to Poniatowska: Boob Lit* (New York: Palgrave Macmillan, 2010), and *Entrevistas con quince autoras mexicanas* (Madrid: Iberoamericana/Frankfurt am Main: Vervuert, 2003). She has written numerous articles on Mexican literature and film, with concentrations on topics such as disability studies, children's literature, pirates and celebrity culture, and the genre of the essay. Hind won the 2005 Feministas Unidas Essay Prize with an article on Rosario Castellanos, published in *Letras Femeninas*. Living writers studied in her recent projects include Vivian Abenshushan, Mario Bellatin, Sabina Berman, Carmen Boullosa, Bernardo Esquinca, Guadalupe Loaeza, and Cristina Rivera Garza. Her current articles contemplate the theory of drugs and the shift toward the value of personality and extroversion.

Rajshekhar (Raj) G. Javalgi is Associate Dean and Professor of Marketing and International Business at the Monte Ahuja College of Business at Cleveland State University. He is also the Director of the Doctor of Business Administration Program. Raj is recognized as a leading scholar in the field of international business and international entrepreneurship. In the area of international business, recently published journals have identified him as one of the top twenty scholars in the in the areas of internationalization of knowledge-based services and internationalization of small and medium-sized enterprises. While performing his duties as Associate Dean and the Director of the Doctor of Business Administration Program, Raj has maintained sustained excellence in research and teaching. He has published over 125 articles in leading, scholarly journals such as the *Journal of the Academy of Marketing Science, the Journal of Consumer Research, the Journal of International Marketing, Industrial Marketing Management, the Journal of Advertising, the Journal of Advertising Research, the Journal of Business Research, Entrepreneurship Theory and Practice, International Marketing Review, the Journal of Business Ethics, Thunderbird International Business Review, the Journal of World Business, and International Business Review*. Several of Raj's articles have received best paper awards and citation excellence awards. He has presented papers in national and international conferences.

Ihsen Ketata is a part-time faculty member at Georgia States University (GSU). She received her Ph.D. in strategic management and her Master's degree in economic analysis, modeling and quantitative analysis from the University of Montpellier I, France. During her doctoral studies, she taught several courses in French both at the University of Montpellier I, France and at the Institut Supérieure d'Administration des Affaires of Sfax (ISAAS), Tunisia. Dr. Ketata has served as a visiting Assistant Professor at the ISAAS, Tunisia and held a temporary appointment for instruction and research in the University of Montpellier I. Prior to joining GSU, she was a post-doctoral fellow at Georgia Tech-CIBER, where she continued her research in the area of multinational company strategies. While teaching at GSU, Ketata served as the director of the GSU-CIBER during the first three years of its existence. Under her leadership, Ketata helped found the Southeast U.S. Higher Education Consortium for International Business. Other notable accomplishments include creating an international business field study course and adding it to the international business certificate. Ketata has also co-chaired numerous conferences such as the "CIMaR 2011" and "Conducting Business in the Middle East."

Hongmei Li (PhD, University of Southern California) is an Associate Professor in the Department of Media, Journalism and Film at Miami University (Oxford, OH, USA). She was the recipient of a George Gerbner Postdoctoral Fellowship at the University of Pennsylvania in 2008–2010. Her research focuses on global communication, advertising and consumer culture, Chinese culture and society, gender and sexuality, national branding and public diplomacy, and new communication technologies. She has published widely in prominent book volumes and leading peer-reviewed journals such as *Communication Theory, International Journal of Communication, Critical Studies in Media Communication, and Public Relations Review*. She is now working on a monograph on Chinese advertising and an edited special issue on nation branding among the BRICS economies (*International Journal of Communication*, with Leslie Marsh).

Leslie L. Marsh is an Associate Professor in the Department of World Languages and Cultures and Director of the Center for Latin American and Latino Studies at Georgia State University (Atlanta, GA, USA). She specializes in Latin American Film and Media Studies, focusing broadly on questions of citizenship. In addition to publications in journals and book volumes, she is the author of *Brazilian Women's Filmmaking: From Dictatorship to Democracy* (University of Illinois Press, 2012). She is currently working on a project that examines contemporary nation branding and Brazil and a special issue on nation branding and the BRICS nations for the *International Journal of Communication* with Hongmei Li.

Altaf Merchant is an Associate Professor of Marketing and the Director of Undergraduate Programs at the Milgard School of Business at the University of Washington, Tacoma (U.S.A.). He joined the Milgard School of Business in 2008 after earning his Ph.D. in marketing from the Old Dominion University. He also holds an MBA from the University of Mumbai. His research interests focus on consumer behavior with an emphasis on nostalgia, charitable giving and family issues. He teaches Introduction to Marketing at the undergraduate and graduate levels. Prior to his academic career he worked for eight years with various marketing organizations (such as Reckitt Benckiser and Glaxo SmithKline) in global brand management and innovations management. His research has appeared in numerous journals including the *Journal of Advertising,* the *Journal of Business Ethics,* the *Journal of Business Research*, the *Journal of Advertising Research*,and the *Academy of Marketing Science Review*. He has received multiple awards, including the Best Paper Award from Journal of Advertising Research (2013), Best Paper Proceedings from the Academy of Management (2013), and the Best Paper Award from the International Journal of Non-profit and Voluntary Sector Marketing (2008).

Manuel (MJR) Montoya, Ph.D. is an Assistant Professor in the Anderson School of Management at the University of New Mexico. He is a professor of global structures, an interdisciplinary scholar of globalization and the factors that produce a global political economy. He is a member of the Council on Foreign Relations and is a Rhodes Scholar. His current research focuses on epistemologies of capital and the construction of global economic identities.

Jennifer Patico received her Ph.D. in sociocultural anthropology from New York University and is an Associate Professor of Anthropology at Georgia State University in Atlanta, Georgia (U.S.A.). She is the author of *Consumption and Social Change in a Post-Soviet Middle Class* (Stanford University Press and Woodrow Wilson Center Press 2008), an ethnography of consumerism, shifting class identities, and moral discourses in post-Soviet St. Petersburg. Additionally, Jennifer has conducted research on international (particularly Russian-U.S.) marriages, questioning assumptions that typically circulate in public debates surrounding online "international marriage brokering." Most recently, she is pursuing field research on parenting practices, children's food and class in urban Atlanta. Her work has been published in journals including *American Ethnologist*, *Ethnos*, *Critique of Anthropology*, *Slavic Review*, and *Gastronomica.*

Ana Raquel Coelho Rocha holds an MBA and a Ph.D. degree in Business Administration from the Pontifical Catholic University of Rio de Janeiro. She is presently developing post-doctoral studies at the Coppead Business School at the Federal University of Rio de Janeiro. She is also an associate researcher at the Center for International Business Research (Núcleo de Pesquisas em Negócios Internacionais) at the Pontifical Catholic University of Rio de Janeiro and a lecturer at Escola Superior de Propaganda e Marketing, in Rio de Janeiro. Before finishing her Ph.D. she worked as an executive for several Brazilian and multinational companies, and as a consultant to retailing companies.

Angela da Rocha is Associate Professor of Marketing and International Business and Coordinator of NUPIN – Center for International Business Research at the IAG Business School, the Pontifical Catholic University of Rio de Janeiro (PUC-Rio). She is a former Professor of Marketing and International Business at the Coppead Graduate School of Business, the Federal University of Rio de Janeiro, where she served twice as Dean. She holds a PhD in Business Administration from the IESE Business School. She is a member of CIMaR – Consortium for International Marketing Research and a senior researcher of the Brazilian National Council for Scientific Research (CNPq). She has published extensively in Brazilian and international journals including *International Business Review, Journal of Business Research, Journal of International Entrepreneurship, International Marketing Review, Entrepreneurship Theory and Practice, Entrepreneurship & Regional Development, International Journal of Retail and Distribution Management, Journal of Product Innovation Management, Journal of International Business Studies, European Journal of Marketing,Latin American Business Review,* and *Brazilian Administration Review.* She has published several books in Brazil and chapters in international and Brazilian books.

Gregory M. Rose is a Professor and Associate Dean in the Milgard School of Business at the University of Washington, Tacoma (U.S.A.). His research interests include consumer socialization, branding, ethics, cross-cultural issues, and consumer money meanings. He has published over thirty journal articles and book chapters, and his research has appeared in the *Journal of Marketing*, *Journal of Business Research*, *Journal of Advertising*, *Journal of Consumer Research*, *Journal of Consumer Psychology*, and the *Journal of the Academy of Marketing Science*.

Xin Wang holds an Ed.D. from Baylor University where he is an Associate Professor of China Studies and Interdisciplinary Studies as well as the

Director of Asian studies. Wang's research interests include contemporary Chinese society and culture and higher education reform in China. His current research project is China's emerging middle class and its social and cultural interests. He has published articles in this area in the *Journal of Contemporary China*, *China: An International Journal*, *Modern China Studies*, and contributed book chapters on the same topic. In addition, he has published articles on Chinese higher education and the book *Higher Education as a Field of Study in China: Defining Knowledge and Curriculum Structure* (Lexington Books, 2010).

Andrew Wedeman received his doctorate in Political Science from UCLA in 1994 and is a Professor of Political Science at Georgia State University. Prior to this appointment, he was a Professor of Political Science at the University of Nebraska-Lincoln, where he also served as the Director of the Asian Studies Program and the Director of the International Studies Program. He has held posts as a visiting Research Professor at Beijing University, a Visiting Associate Professor of Political Science at the Johns Hopkins Nanjing University Center for Sino-American Studies, and a Fulbright research professor at Taiwan National University. His publications include *Double Paradox: Rapid Growth and Rising Corruption in China* (Cornell); *From Mao to Market: Rent Seeking, Local Protectionism, and Marketization in China* (Cambridge); numerous articles in academic journals including *China Quarterly*, *Journal of Contemporary China*; and *China Review*; and chapters in numerous edited volumes.

Yushan Zhao is a Professor of Marketing at the University of Wisconsin, Whitewater. He received his B.S. of engineering from Tianjin University, Tianjin, China and his Ph.D. in Business Administration from Michigan State University, East Lansing, Michigan. He had over thirteen years of business experience before he joined the academic world. He has published over twenty papers in academic journals including the *Journal of the Academy of Marketing Science*, *Journal of Business Research*, *Industrial Marketing Management*, *Journal of Business to Business Marketing*, *Journal of International Marketing*, and *Journal of Business and Industrial Marketing*. His primary research areas are product innovation management, inter-firm relationships management, and sustainability.

Index

For Product Safety Concerns and Information please contact our EU
representative GPSR@taylorandfrancis.com
Taylor & Francis Verlag GmbH, Kaufingerstraße 24, 80331 München, Germany

www.ingramcontent.com/pod-product-compliance
Ingram Content Group UK Ltd.
Pitfield, Milton Keynes, MK11 3LW, UK
UKHW021607240425
457818UK00018B/433

* 9 7 8 0 8 1 5 3 8 6 4 5 2 *